The Annotated Bible

The Holy Scriptures Analysed and Annotated

BY

A. C. GAEBELEIN

Editor of "Our Hope"

The New Testament

Volume I
The Gospels and the Book of Acts

PUBLICATION OFFICE "OUR HOPE"

456 Fourth Avenue, New York

THE GOSPEL OF MATTHEW

CONTENTS

The Gospel of Matthew.

The Key to the Gospel of Matthew.*

The Gospel of Matthew stands first among the Gospels and in the New Testament, because it belongs in the first place and may be rightly termed the Genesis of the New Testament. Genesis, the first book of the Bible, contains in itself the entire Bible. Matthew is the book of the beginnings of a new dispensation. It may be compared to a mighty tree. The roots are deeply sunk in massive rocks while its uncountable branches and twigs extend upward higher and higher in perfect symmetry and beauty. The foundation is the Old Testament with its Messianic and Kingdom promises. Out of this all springs forth in perfect harmony, reaching higher and higher into the new dispensation and to the end of the millennial age.

The instrument chosen by the Holy Spirit to write this Gospel was Matthew. He was a Jew. However, he did not belong to the religious, educated class, to the scribes, but he belonged to the class which was most bitterly hated. He was a publican, that is, a tax gatherer. The Roman government had appointed officials whose duty it was to have the legal tax gathered, and these officials, mostly, if not all Gentiles, appointed the actual collectors, who were generally Jews. Only the most unscrupulous among the Jews would hire themselves out for the sake of gain to the avowed enemy of Jerusalem. Wherever there was still a ray of hope for Messiah's coming, the Jew would naturally shrink from being associated with the Gentiles, who were to be swept away from the land with the coming of the King. For this reason the tax gatherers, being Roman employees, were hated by the Jews even more bitterly than the Gentiles themselves. Such a hated tax

*This Preface should be carefully read before the Gospel is studied.

gatherer was the writer of the first Gospel. How the grace of God is revealed in his call is seen in the record itself. That he was chosen to write this first Gospel is in itself significant, for it speaks of a new order of things about to be introduced, namely, the call of the despised Gentiles.

Internal evidences seem to show that most likely originally Matthew wrote the Gospel in Aramaeic, the Semitic dialect then spoken in Palestine. The Gospel was later translated into Greek. This, however, is certain, that the Gospel of Matthew is pre-eminently the *Jewish* Gospel. There are many passages in it, which in their fundamental meaning can only be correctly understood by one who is quite familiar with Jewish customs and the traditional teachings of the elders. Because it is the Jewish Gospel, it is *dispensational* throughout. It is safe to say that a person, no matter how learned or devoted, who does not hold the clearly revealed dispensational truths concerning the Jews, the Gentiles and the church of God, will fail to understand Matthew. This is, alas, too much the case, and well it would be if it were not more than individual failure to understand; but it is more than that. Confusion, error, false doctrine is the final outcome, when the right key to any part of God's Word is lacking. If the dispensational character of Matthew were understood, no ethical teaching from the so-called Sermon on the Mount at the expense of the Atonement of our Lord Jesus Christ would be possible, nor would there be room for the subtle, modern delusion, so universal now, of a "social Christianity" which aims at lifting up the masses and the conversion of the world. How different matters would be in Christendom if its leading teachers and preachers, commentators and professors, had understood and would understand the meaning of the seven parables in Matthew xiii, with their deep and solemn lessons. When we think how many of the leaders of religious thought reject and even oppose all dispensational teachings, who never knew how to divide the Word of truth rightly, it is not strange that so many of these men dare to stand up and say that the Gospel of Matthew, as well as the other Gospels and the different parts of the New Testament, contain numerous contradictions and errors. Out of this failure to discern dispensational truths has likewise arisen the attempt, by a very well meaning class, to harmonize the Gospel records and to arrange the events in the life of our Lord in a chronological order, and thus produce a life of Jesus Christ, our Lord, as we have a descriptive life of Napoleon or other great men. The Holy Spirit has never undertaken to produce a life of Christ. That is very evident by the fact that the greater part of the life of our Lord is passed over in silence; nor was it in the mind of the Spirit to report all the words and miracles and the movements of our Lord, nor to record all the events which took place during His public ministry, and to arrange it all in a chronological order. What presumption, then, to attempt to do that which the Holy Spirit never attempted! If the Holy Spirit never intended that the recorded events in the life of our Saviour should be strictly chronological, how vain and foolish then, if not more, the attempt to bring out a harmony of the different Gospels! One has correctly said, "The Holy Spirit is not a reporter, but an editor." This is well said. A reporter's business is to report events as they happen. The editor arranges the material in a way to suit himself, and leaves out or makes comment just as he thinks best. This the Holy Spirit has done in giving four Gospels, which are not a mechanical reporting of the doings of a person called Jesus of Nazareth, but the spiritual unfoldings of the blessed person and work of our Saviour and Lord, as King of the Jews, servant in obedience, Son of Man and the only begotten of the Father. We cannot enter more deeply into this now, but in the annotation of the Gospel we shall illustrate this fact.

In the Gospel of Matthew, as the Jewish Gospel, speaking of the King and the kingdom, dispensational throughout, treating of the Jews, the Gentiles and even the church of God in anticipation, as no other Gospel does, everything must be looked upon from the dispensational point of view. All the miracles recorded, the words spoken, the events which are given in their peculiar setting, every parable, every chapter from beginning to end, are first of all to be looked upon as foreshadowing and teaching dispensational truths. This is the right key to the Gospel of Matthew. It is likewise a significant fact that in the condition of the people Israel, with their proud religious leaders rejecting the Lord, their King and the threatened judgment in consequence of it, we may see a true photograph of the end of the present dispensation, and the coming doom of apostate Christendom. The characteristics of the times, when our Lord appeared among His people, who were so religious, self-righteous, being divided into different sects, Ritualists (Pharisees) and Rationalists (Sadducees—Higher Critics), following the teachings of men, occupied with man-made creeds and doctrines, etc., are exactly reproduced in Christendom, with its man-made ordinances, rituals and rationalistic teachings.

There are seven great facts which are prominent in this Gospel and around which everything is grouped. We will briefly review them.

I.—The King. The Old Testament is full of promises which speak of the coming, not alone of a deliverer, a sin-bearer, but of the coming of a King, King Messiah as He is still called by orthodox Jews. This King was eagerly expected, hoped for and prayed for by the pious in Israel. The Gospel of Matthew proves that our Lord Jesus Christ is truly this promised King. In it we see Him as King of the Jews, everything shows that He is in truth the royal person, of whom Seers and Prophets wrote. First it would be necessary to prove that He is legally the King. This is seen in the first chapter, where a genealogy is given which proves His royal descent. The beginning is, "The Book of the generation of Jesus Christ, Son of David, Son of Abraham." It goes back to Abraham and there it stops, while in Luke the genealogy reaches up to Adam. In the Gospel of Matthew He is seen as Son of David, His royal descent, and as Son of Abraham, according to the flesh from the seed of Abraham.

The coming of the wise men is only recorded in Matthew.

They came to worship the new born King of the Jews. His royal birthplace, David's city, is given. The infant is worshipped by the representatives of the Gentiles and they do homage indeed before a true King, though the marks of poverty were around Him. The gold they gave speaks of His Deity. Every true King has a herald, so has the King Messiah. The forerunner appears and in Matthew his message to the nation is that "The Kingdom of heaven has drawn nigh"; the royal person so long foretold is about to appear and to preach that Kingdom likewise. When the King who was rejected comes again to set up the Kingdom, He will be preceded once more by a herald who will declare His coming among His people Israel, even Elijah the prophet. In the fourth chapter we see the King tested and proven that He is the King. He is tested thrice, once as Son of Man, as Son of God and as the King Messiah. After the testing, out of which He comes forth a complete victor, He begins His ministry. The Sermon on the Mount is given in Matthew in full. Mark and Luke report it only in fragments and John has not a word of it. This should at once determine the status of the three chapters which contain this discourse. It is a teaching concerning the Kingdom, the magna charta of the Kingdom and all its principles. Such a kingdom in the earth, with subjects who have all the characteristics of the royal requirements laid down in this discourse, will yet be. If Israel had accepted the King it would then have come, but the kingdom has been postponed. The Kingdom will at last come with a righteous nation as a center, but the church is not that kingdom. In this wonderful discourse the Lord speaks as the King and as the Lawgiver, who expounds the law which is to rule His Kingdom. From the eighth to the twelfth chapters, we see the royal manifestations of Him who is Jehovah manifested in the flesh. This part especially is interesting and very instructive, because it gives in a series of miracles, the dispensational hints concerning Jew and Gentile, and what comes after the present age is past.

As King He sends out His servants and endues them with

kingdom power, preaching likewise the nearness of the kingdom. After the tenth chapter the rejection begins, followed by His teachings in parables, the revealing of secrets. He is presented to Jerusalem as King, and the Messianic welcome is heard, "Blessed is He who cometh in the name of Jehovah." After that His suffering and His death. In all His Kingly character is brought out, and the Gospel closes abruptly, and has nothing to say of His ascension to heaven; but the Lord is, so to speak, left on the earth with power, all power in heaven and on earth. In this closing it is seen that He is the King. He rules in heaven now and on the earth when He comes again.

II.—The Kingdom. The phrase Kingdom of Heaven occurs *only* in the Gospel of Matthew. We find it thirty-two times. What does it mean? Here is the failure of the interpretation of the Word; all error and the confusion around us springs from the false conception of the Kingdom of Heaven. It is generally taught and understood that the term Kingdom of Heaven means the church, and thus the church is thought to be the true Kingdom of Heaven, established in the earth, and conquering the nations and the world. The Kingdom of Heaven is *not* the church, and the church is *not* the Kingdom of the Heavens. This is a very vital truth. May the annotations of this Gospel be used in making this distinction very clear in the minds of our readers. When our Lord speaks of the Kingdom of Heaven up to the twelfth chapter He does not mean the church, but the Kingdom of Heaven in its Old Testament sense, as it is promised to Israel, to be established in the land, with Jerusalem for a center, and from there to spread over all the nations and the entire earth. What did the pious, believing Jew expect according to the Scriptures? He expected (and still expects) the coming of the King Messiah, who is to occupy the throne of His father David. He was expected to bring judgment for the enemies of Jerusalem, and to bring together the outcasts of Israel. The land would flourish as never before; universal peace would be established; righteousness and peace in the knowledge of the glory of the Lord to cover the earth as the waters cover the deep. All this in the earth with the land, which is Jehovah's land, as fountain head, from which all the blessings, the streams of living waters, flow. A temple, a house of worship, for all nations was expected to stand in Jerusalem, to which the nations would come to worship the Lord. This is the Kingdom of the Heavens as promised to Israel and as expected by them. It is all to be on the earth. The church, however, is something entirely different. The hope of the church, the place of the church, the calling of the church, the destiny of the church, the reigning and ruling of the church is not earthly, but it is heavenly. Now the King long expected had appeared, and He preached the Kingdom of the Heavens having drawn nigh, that is, this promised earthly kingdom for Israel. When John the Baptist preached, Repent ye, for the kingdom of the Heavens has drawn nigh, he meant the same. It is all wrong to preach the Gospel from such a text and state that the sinner is to repent and then the Kingdom will come to him. A very well known English teacher of Spiritual truths gave not long ago in this country a discourse on the mistranslated text, "The Kingdom of God is within you," and dwelt largely on the fact that the Kingdom is within the believer. The context shows that this is erroneous; the true translation is "The Kingdom is *among you;*" that is, in the person of the King.

Now if Israel had accepted the testimony of John, and had repented, and if they had accepted the King, the Kingdom would have come, but now it has been postponed till Jewish disciples will pray again in preaching the coming of the Kingdom, "Thy Kingdom come. Thy will be done in earth as it is done in heaven." That will be after the church has been removed to the heavenly places.

III.—The King and the Kingdom is rejected. This is likewise foretold in the Old Testament, Isaiah liii, Daniel ix:25, Psalm xxii, etc. It is also seen in types, Joseph, David and others. The herald of the King is first rejected and ends in the prison, being murdered. This speaks of the rejection of the King Himself. In no other Gospel is the story of the rejection so completely told as here. It begins in Galilee, in His own city, and ends in Jerusalem. The rejection is not human but it is *Satanic.* All the wickedness and depravity of the heart is uncovered and Satan revealed throughout. All classes are concerned in the rejection. The crowds who had followed Him and were fed by Him, the Pharisees, the Sadducees, the Herodians, the priests, the chief priests, the high priest, the elders. At last it becomes evident that they knew Him who He was, their Lord and their King, and wilfully they delivered Him into the hands of the Gentiles. The story of the cross in Matthew, too, brings out the darkest side of the rejection. Thus prophecy is seen fulfilled in the rejection of the King.

IV.—The Rejection of His Earthly People and their Judgment. This is another theme of the Old Testament which is very prominent in the Gospel of Matthew. They rejected Him and He leaves them, and judgment falls upon them. In the eleventh chapter He reproaches the cities in which most of His works of power had taken place, because they had not repented. At the end of the twelfth chapter He denies His relations and refuses to see His own, while in the beginning of the thirteenth He leaves the house and goes down to the sea, the latter typifies the nations. After His royal presentation to Jerusalem, the next day early in the morning, He curses the fig trees, which foreshadows Israel's national death, and after He uttered His two parables to the chief priests and elders, He declares that the Kingdom of God is to be taken away from them and is to be given to a nation which is to bring the fruit thereof. The whole twenty-third chapter contains the woes upon the Pharisees, and at the end He speaks of Jerusalem and declares that their house is to be left desolate till they shall say, Blessed is He who comes in the name of the Lord.

V.—The Mysteries of the Kingdom of the Heavens. The kingdom has been rejected by the people of the kingdom and the King Himself has left the earth. During His absence the Kingdom of the Heavens is in the hands of men.

There is then the kingdom in the earth in an entirely different form as it was revealed in the Old Testament; the mysteries of the kingdom hidden from the world's foundation are now made known. This we learn in Matthew xiii, and here, too, we have at least a glimpse of the church. Again it is to be understood that both are not identical. But what is the Kingdom in its mystery form? The seven parables teach this. It is seen there is an evil mixed condition. The church, the one body, is not evil, for the church is composed of those who are beloved of God, called saints, but Christendom, including all professors, is properly that Kingdom of the Heavens in the thirteenth chapter. The parables bring out what may be termed the history of Christendom. It is a history of failure, becoming that which the King never meant it to be, the leaven of evil, indeed, leavening the whole lump, and thus it continues till the King comes back, when all the offences will be gathered out of the Kingdom. The parable of the pearl alone speaks of the church.

VI.—The Church. In no other Gospel is anything said of the church except in the Gospel of Matthew. In the sixteenth chapter Peter gives his testimony concerning the Lord, revealed to him from the Father, who is in the heavens. The Lord tells him that on "this rock I will build My assembly—church—and hades' gates shall not prevail against it." It is not I *have built*, but I *will* build My church. Right after this promise He speaks of His suffering and death. The transfiguration which follows the first declaration of His coming death, speaks of the glory which will follow, and is a type of the power and coming of our Lord Jesus Christ (2 Peter i:16). Much that follows the declaration of the Lord concerning the building of the church is to be applied to the church.

VII.—The Mount of Olivet Discourse. Prophetic Teachings Concerning the End of the Age. This discourse was given to the disciples after the Lord had spoken His last word to Jerusalem. It is one of the most remarkable sections of the entire Gospel. We find it in the twenty-fourth and twenty-fifth chapters. In it the Lord teaches concerning the Jews, the Gentiles and Christendom, including the true church. The order is different. The Gentiles stand last. The reason for that is because the church will be removed first from the earth and the professors of Christendom will be left, who are nothing but Gentiles concerned in the judgment of nations as made known by the Lord. The first part of Matthew xxiv is Jewish throughout. From the fourth to the forty-fifth verse we have a most important prophecy, which gives the events which follow after the church is taken from the earth. The Lord takes here many of the Old Testament prophecies and blends them in one great prophecy. Three parables follow in which the saved and unsaved are seen. Waiting and serving is the leading thought. Reward and casting out into outward darkness the twofold outcome. This, then, finds an application in Christendom and the Church. The ending of Matthew xxv is the judgment of nations. This is not the universal judgment, a popular term in Christendom, but it is the judgment of the nations at the time when our Lord as Son of Man sits upon the throne of His glory.

THE SCOPE AND DIVISION OF MATTHEW.

The characteristic keyword of the Gospel of Matthew is the word "Kingdom." As stated before the phrase "Kingdom of heaven" is found thirty-two times in this Gospel. In the third chapter the herald of the King, John the Baptist, announced the Kingdom of heaven at hand. The King in beginning His ministry preached the same message and when He sent forth His disciples He gave them this instruction: "And as ye go, preach, saying, The Kingdom of heaven is at hand" (Chapter x:7). But this preaching suddenly ended. John the Baptist was cast into prison. The Pharisees and Sadducees opposed the King and the Kingdom He preached. After the twelfth chapter we hear no longer the Kingdom announced as being at hand. Instead of the nation-wide proclamation of the Kingdom, the Lord begins to teach the mysteries of the Kingdom, announces His rejection and His death; then goes up to Jerusalem where He was presented as King, suffered, died and was raised from the dead.

The Gospel has therefore two main divisions: The *first* Chapter i–xii and the *second* from Chapter xiii to xxviii.

I. The King and the Offer of the Kingdom. Chapter i–xii.

1. *The King, His Genealogy and His Birth.* Chapter i.
2. *The King Worshipped by Gentiles; Jerusalem in Ignorance of Him; the Child Persecuted.* Chapter ii.
3. *The Herald of the King: the King enters upon His public Ministry.* Chapter iii.
4. *The Testing of the King and His Testimony.* Chapter iv.

5. *The Proclamation of the King.* Chapter v–vii.

6. *The King Manifested by Signs of Divine Power.* Chapters viii–ix.

7. *The Messengers of the King.* Chapter x.

8. *The Forerunner in Prison and the Rejection of the Kingdom.* Chapter xi.

9. *The Rejection Consummated and the Broken Relationship.* Chapter xii.

II. The Rejected Kingdom and the Rejection of the King; His Death and Resurrection. Chapter xiii–xxviii.

1. *The King at the Seashore. The Mysteries of the Kingdom.* Chapter xiii.

2. *John's Martyrdom and the Fourfold Attitude of the Rejected King.* Chapter xiv.

3. *The Corruption of the Scribes and Pharisees. The Canaanitish Woman. Multitudes Healed.* Chapter xv.

4. *The Predictions of the Rejected King Concerning Himself.* Chapter xvi.

5. *The Coming Glory. The Helpless Disciples and the Power of the King.* Chapter xvii.

6. *Instructions to His Disciples. Concerning Forgiveness.* Chapter xviii.

7. *Departure from Galilee. Concerning Divorce. The Little Children Blessed. The Rich Young Man.* Chapter xix.

8. *The Parable of the Laborers in the Vineyard. The Healing of the Two Blind Men.* Chapter xx.

9. *The King's Entry into Jerusalem. The Parables of the Two Sons and the Householders.* Chapter xxi.

10. *The Parable of the Marriage Feast. Questions Answered. The Unanswered Question.* Chapter xxii.
11. *The Woes of the King and the Lamentation over Jerusalem.* Chapter xxiii.
12. *The Olivet Discourse.* Chapter xxiv–xxv.
13. *The Passion of the King.* Chapter xxvi–xxvii.
14. *The Resurrection and the Great Commission.* Chapter xxviii.

Analysis and Annotations

1. The King and the Offer of the Kingdom.

Chapter i–xii.

1. *The King; His Genealogy and His Birth.*

CHAPTER I.

1. Jesus Christ, the Son of David, the Son of Abraham. 1.
2. From Abraham to David. 2–6.
3. From David to the Captivity. 6–11.
4. From the Captivity to the Birth of Christ. 12–17.
5. The Birth of Jesus Christ. 18–25.

The first two words in the Greek (*Biblos geneseos*) "the book of generation" corresponds to the same term in the Book of Genesis (Gen. ii:4, etc.). The question of a genealogy is an important one with the Jew. The legal right to the throne of David must be first of all proven so that no doubt can be attached to His claim of being the promised King. Because it is the question of Kingship, "Son of David" precedes "Son of Abraham." An uninspired writer would have put "Son of Abraham" in the first place. As He is the promised King who comes to the nation Israel, the fact that He is the Son of David is put into the foreground. But He is also the Son of Abraham through whom the promises of blessing to the Gentiles are to be fulfilled.

The genealogy of our Lord in Matthew differs from the one in Luke. The one in the Gospel of Luke (chapter iv) proves that Mary, the mother of Jesus, is of David through the house of *Nathan*. The genealogy of Matthew shows Joseph, who was supposed to be the father of Jesus (Luke iii:23), is a descendant of David through the line of *Solomon*. The descendants of Solomon have the legal right to the throne. But the last King of Judah, Jeconias, a son of Solomon, was so wicked that a curse was pronounced upon him and he was to be childless, "no man of his seed shall prosper, sitting upon the throne of David" (Jer. xxii:30). However, this curse did not affect the *legal* claim to the throne. But Jesus was not the son of David through Joseph, but through Mary the virgin, who came of David through the line of Nathan. No curse rested upon that line. As the supposed son of Joseph He inherited the legal title to the throne through Joseph, but being the son of David through Mary, the curse which rested upon Jeconias was not upon Him. The genealogy in Matthew shows, therefore, that Joseph, the supposed father of Jesus, is in point of law entitled to the throne, therefore Jesus is legally heir to the throne of David. If Mary, the mother of our Lord, had not been legally the wife of Joseph, a son of David, the Jews could have rejected the claims of Jesus to the throne. We see, then, that legally He was the son of Joseph with the full crown rights upon Him; in His true humanity, He is of Mary the virgin, also of David; then at the close of the chapter we read that He is the Son of God.

The genealogy tells the story of decadence. Corruption, ruin and hopelessness is written therein. As generation after generation is given, we follow the shameful history of Israel, a history of unbelief and judgment. At last all is dark and hopeless. Like Sarah's womb (the type of the nation) the nation is dead. But God can bring life from the dead. "When the fulness of time was come, God sent forth His Son, come of woman, come under the law" (Gal. iv:4). The genealogy has three divisions, each division has fourteen generations. David alone has the title, the King (verse 6). Solomon's name is not given as King, to show the promises made to David concerning a son to come from his loins (2 Sam. vii:8–16) were not fulfilled in Solomon.

Notice the four Gentile women in the genealogy of the King. *Tamar* (telling out the ravages of sin); *Rahab* (she was saved by faith); *Ruth* (under the curse of the law, but brought into relation with Israel); then the one of *Uriah,* that is Bath-Sheba (David's sin brought into remembrance). These four women tell out beforehand the story of the Gospel and how the promised King would also be the Saviour of the Gentiles.

The story of His birth concludes this chapter. The virgin birth is here fully revealed and this birth is given as the fulfilment of Isaiah vii:14. The two Gospels, which mention His birth, Matthew and Luke, show in the most perfect way that the Son of God, the eternal Word, became man, born of the virgin, a true human being, yet "that holy thing," absolutely without sin. His human nature proceeded directly from the Spirit of God. The early Jews never attacked the accounts of the birth of our Lord. Many, many years later wicked hands wrote a vulgar and blasphemous account of the birth of our Lord. Apostate Christendom has sided with the wicked denials of Jewish and Gentile infidels of the past. Can there be anything more blasphemous, more wicked, more immoral, than the teaching, so widespread to-day, that our Lord as to His human nature was not "conceived by the Holy Spirit?"

2. The King Worshipped by Gentiles; Jerusalem in Ignorance of Him; the Child Persecuted.

CHAPTER II.

1. The Visit of the Wise Men. 1–12.
2. The Flight into Egypt. 13–18.
3. The Return from Egypt. 19–25.

The authenticity of the story of the visit of the wise men seeking the new-born King of the Jews has been doubted, because no other Evangelist reports this incident. It belongs properly into the Gospel, in which our Lord is portrayed as the King. This is the reason of its being reported only in Matthew's Gospel. The wise men were not three persons, nor were they Kings. It must have been a larger company, for it troubled Herod and all Jerusalem with him. Nor did the visit take place immediately after the birth of our Lord. The correct rendering of the first verse is, "But Jesus having been born," that is, some time after and not immediately after. The pictures which portray the wise men worshipping the child in a stable are unscriptural, for it says they found the young child in a house. It was most likely a year after His birth, that the wise men from the East appeared. Luke ii:41 shows that His parents went to Jerusalem every year; they must then also have visited Bethlehem again.

The promised King is unknown in His own city, Jerusalem. His own people are ignorant of Him. Gentiles come first to do Him homage. The ecclesiastical authorities are indifferent to His claims, the civil ruler, Herod, the King, hates Him, and as Satan's instrument seeks His life. The history of the King and His Kingdom is outlined in this story. His own are not going to receive Him. The indifference of the chief priests and scribes points to their coming antagonism. But Gentiles seek Him first. Simeon's prophetic song is seen here in its coming fulfilment, "A light to lighten the Gentiles," but in the end also, after God's purpose in this age is accomplished, "the glory of thy people Israel" (Luke ii:32). They bring gold, typical of divinity; frankincense, indicating the fragrance of His life and worship; and myrrh, that which is used in burial, a hint as to His death. Note that this is not a fulfilment of Isaiah lx:6. That passage refers to the time when the Kingdom is set up on earth. Myrrh in Isaiah is not mentioned.

Throughout the chapter the child always occupies the first and prominent place. It is never "Mary and the child," or "the mother and the child," but "the little child and His mother"—The child is above the mother. What a rebuke to the Romish church, which in idolatry puts the mother above the child.

See Hosea xi:1 on the flight to Egypt and the return. All indicates what is to be done to Him, who is the King.

3. *The Herald of the King; the Entrance upon His Public Ministry.*

CHAPTER III.

1. The Herald of the King. 1–6.
2. His Message and His Baptism. 7–12.
3. The King in Jordan's Waters. 13–17.

John the Baptist, the Herald of the King, is now introduced. See Luke i:15–17 for the angelic announcement of his birth and mission. He is predicted in the Old Testament. Isaiah xl:3–5, Mal. ii:1. He appeared like Elijah the Prophet (2 Kings i:8). But He was not Elijah. See also Matthew xvii:12. And before the King comes the second time there will be once more a forerunner. Mal. iv:5–6 will then be fulfilled. John knew his mission (John i:23). His testimony as reported by Matthew concerns the nation. In the Gospel of John we find the record of another testimony given by the forerunner. He knew the King also as the Lamb of God.

He calls the nation to repentance, because the Kingdom of heaven is at hand. The phrase "Kingdom of heaven" (literally "of the heavens") occurs here for the first time. It does not mean the offer of salvation, nor does it mean the church, nor the social betterment of the people, but it signifies the Messianic Kingdom as promised by the Prophets of God, a Kingdom which is to be set up on earth and over which the Son of David is to be King. This the forerunner announced. This Kingdom the Lord Jesus and His disciples preached, till it became evident that Israel would not have this Kingdom. Then the preaching ceased.

In verses 11 and 12 there is a blending together of the first and second coming of Christ. As a result of the first coming of Christ the baptism with the Holy Spirit took place. The fire baptism refers to judgment. The twelfth verse describes the fire baptism of judgment when the King comes again.

The baptism of John has nothing to do with Christian baptism. It was baptism unto repentance only. By being baptized in Jordan (the type of death) they confessed that they had deserved death.

Then the King entered upon His public ministry. He too entered the waters of Jordan and was baptized; not that He needed it, but to signify He came to be the substitute of sinners and to take the sinners' place in death. In the baptismal scene we have His whole blessed work foreshadowed. He is the holy One, who needed no baptism for He had no sin. His *death* is foreshadowed when He went into Jordan; His *resurrection*, when He came out of the water; His *ascension*, when heaven was opened unto Him. The gift of the *Holy Spirit* is seen next and this is followed by the declaration of *Sonship*. Into this the believer enters. We are dead and risen with Him; Heaven too is opened unto us and we have received the Spirit of Sonship.

4. *The Testing of the King and His Testimony.*

CHAPTER IV.

1. The Testing by the Devil. 1–11.
2. His Testimony and His Disciples. 12–22.
3. The Powers of the Kingdom. 23–25.

Then He was led (literally: carried) by the Spirit into the wilderness to be tempted of the devil. "And immediately the Spirit drives Him out into the wilderness" (Mark i:12). And He was there with the wild beasts (Mark i:13). After He had fasted for forty days, the tempter came to Him. What a contrast with the first man, Adam, in the garden of Eden!

The devil is a person and not an evil influence. The "new theology" invented by the father of lies has no use for a personal devil. The Lord's temptations, according to that theology, were only imaginations. The denial of the personality of the devil is a serious thing.

In studying this chapter it must be remembered that the Lord Jesus was absolutely holy. Therefore He could not fall nor be tempted by sin. If He could have fallen into sin He would have needed a Saviour and could not have been our Saviour. He was tempted in all things as we are "apart from sin." A better word for tempting is "testing." The devil came to test Him. He was tested as to His ability to do that for which He came. The test proves that He is pure gold, the Holy and Spotless One, Who is fit to put away sin by the sacrifice of Himself. Satan makes three tests. Each test is met by the Lord Jesus with the Word of God, with a "It is written." And He quotes the Word exclusively from Deuteronomy, the book of obedience. The devil with his three temptations tried to keep Him back from doing the will of God. He wanted Christ to act independently from His Father. If He had acted thus for Himself He would have proven His unfitness to suffer and to die. If He had been disobedient in the smallest matter, He could not have been obedient unto death. The two first temptations were a challenge to prove Himself the Son of God. The last was the presumptuous offer of the usurping prince of this world to give to Christ the Kingdoms of the world, if He would fall down before him. He knew that eventually, by the way of the Cross, the Son of God would obtain the Kingdoms, that they would become His and he, the proud usurper, would be spoiled of all, stripped of his power and cast into the lake of fire. He wanted Christ to be disobedient to the Word as he led the first man to disobedience. He tried to keep Him from going to the Cross. The Lord defeated him completely and he left Him for a season.*

The report reached Him that John, the forerunner, had been cast into prison. He then departed into Galilee. It is His Galilean ministry which Matthew reports; the events of the Judean ministry are not given by him. These we find in the Gospel of John. He preached in Nazareth and dwelt in Capernaum. What happened in Nazareth is more fully reported by Luke (Chapter iv:14–32). His own townspeople were filled with wrath and thrust Him out of the city, trying to cast Him down a hill. The first murderous attempt was made in Nazareth.

He preached the message of the Kingdom throughout that region. Peter, Andrew and the two sons of Zebedee, James and John, are called by Him into service. They left all, the nets, the ship and even the father to follow Him and became fishers of men.

---

*For a complete exegesis of the temptation see our larger Commentary on Matthew, Vol. I, pages 79–96.

For the first time in Matthew we read of the signs which were linked with the preaching of the Gospel of the Kingdom. The healing of the sick and the demon-possessed were truly signs that the King is Jehovah manifested in the flesh and that the Kingdom had drawn nigh.

5. *The Proclamation of the King Concerning His Kingdom.*

CHAPTER V.

1. The Characteristics of the heirs of the Kingdom. 1–16.
2. The Confirmation of the Law and its Expansion. 17–48.

In chapters v–vii we have the full report of the so-called Sermon on the Mount. Mark and Luke give fragments of this discourse, but the complete discourse is found only in Matthew. The Sermon on the Mount is the proclamation of the King concerning His Kingdom, and may well be called the "Magna Charta of the Kingdom of heaven." This discourse does not expound the Gospel of Grace, the way of salvation, the privileges and blessings of true Christianity. The teachers who say that the Sermon on the Mount is the Gospel are ignorant of what the Gospel is. We mention three wrong applications which are being made of this discourse.

1. The application to the unsaved, as if in this discourse the way to righteousness is shown, which man by his own effort is to attain. The discourse in the beginning speaks of saved persons, of disciples. The Lord does not address sinners. He taught His disciples. As the great unfolding of the salvation of God as revealed in the Epistle to the Romans is abandoned in Christendom, the false application of this discourse in increasingly followed. There is little preaching of the lost and helpless condition of man, the necessity of the new birth and the reception of eternal life. What is put in the place of the true Gospel is ethical teaching; and this has culminated in a Christian-socialistic attempt to save society. The Sermon on the Mount is taken as the program for this. But it condemns this spurious Gospel of works and evolution.

2. The second wrong application is the one which makes this discourse exclusively Christian and applies it to the Church. The magna charta of the Church is in the Epistles of Paul, to whom the full revelation of the Church was given. Christian position is not revealed in the Sermon on the Mount. The Sermon on the Mount is not given as the standard of Christian experience and walk.

3. The third false application is the one which makes this discourse exclusively Jewish. Some Christians refuse to consider these chapters as having any message or instruction for them at all. This is the other extreme and equally wrong. We repeat, the Sermon on the Mount is the proclamation of the King concerning His Kingdom. That Kingdom is not the church, nor is it a state of righteousness of the earth brought about through the agency of the church. It is the Kingdom as it will be set up by the King with the coming age. While in the Old Testament we have the outward manifestations of that earthly Kingdom revealed, we have here from the lips of the King the inner principles of that Kingdom. When the Lord Jesus Christ comes again the Old Testament predictions concerning the Kingdom will be literally fulfilled and the Kingdom itself will be a Kingdom of righteousness according to this proclamation. However, this does not exclude application to us, the heirs of the Kingdom.

The beatitudes give the character of the heirs who enter the Kingdom. They do not speak of what a person should be, or strive to be, but what *they are.* Only the Grace of God can produce such a character. The blessings are in possession of those, who have believed on the Son of God. And the Lord Jesus manifested all these characteristics in His humiliation. But these beatitudes have also a significance in connection with the future believing remnant of Israel, waiting amidst the great tribulations and under the severest persecutions at the end of the age for the return of the King. See Zephaniah iii:12 and Isaiah lxvi:2; Micah vii:1–7.

The Law is then taken up by the King in this proclamation. He is the Lawgiver and therefore He confirms, expands and supplements the Law. Here we are on Jewish ground. Believers in Christ have nothing to do with the law. We are dead to the law (Rom. vii:4; Gal. iii:24–25.) The better righteousness needed to enter the Kingdom is not man's own righteousness, but that which is by faith in Jesus Christ.

As He speaks with authority He uncovers the heart of man and shows the depths of corruption and the hopelessness that the natural man could ever attain such a righteousness. The words of the King condemn every man and prove him lost. The condemnation of the natural man is written there.

CHAPTER VI.

1. The Better Righteousness. 1–18.
2. Kept in the World; Single-eyed; Trusting God. 19–34.

He makes now known the motive of the true righteousness, which the heirs of the Kingdom are not only to possess, but also to practice. The motive is to act in the presence of the Father. The word Father is found ten times in the beginning of this chapter. The Father sees, the Father knows. Here a relationship is acknowledged and made prominent, which is unknown in the Old Testament. How the heirs of the Kingdom are brought into this relationship is not taught in Matthew. The Gospel of John reveals this.

In verse 1–4 we see the motive of true righteousness in relation to man; in verses 5–15 in relation to God and in verses 16–18 in relation to self.

In verses 9–13 the King gives to His disciples a model prayer. It has been called "the Lord's prayer." A better name would be "the disciples' prayer." The Lord had no need to use it Himself. The ritualistic use of this form of prayer, its repetition at many occasions, as if it were a meritorious act, must be condemned. It was given to His Jewish disciples. In connection with the announcement of His departure and the coming of the Holy Spirit, our Lord did not teach His disciples the continued use of this form of prayer, but He said, "Hitherto ye have asked nothing in my name; ask and ye shall receive, that your joy may be full" (John xvi-24). We do not find this prayer used in the Acts of the Apostles; nor do we find in the Epistle an exhortation that it should be used by the church. It had a special meaning to the disciples, as it will have again for the remnant of Israel at the close of the age. Yet the prayer is perfect, beautiful and embodies heavenly wisdom. The Christian believer finds under the guidance of the Spirit the deeper meaning and can enter into all the petitions.

In the second half of this chapter the heirs of the Kingdom are seen as in the world, subject to its cares and temptations. Our Lord tells us how to behave in the midst of the world and what are our privileges and comforts. The natural man lives for the earthly things; his delight is in treasures which are here below. It is to be different with the true disciple (verses 19–21). In connection with His exhortation, "lay not up for yourselves treasures, which are on earth," read the following passages: Col. iii:2–3; 2 Cor. iv:18; 1 Tim. vi:9–11, vi:17–18; Heb. xiii:5. May we heed these words in a day when professing Christians heap together treasures in the last days (Jas. v:1–3). And how great is the comfort that we have a Father, who careth! "Be not careful"—oh, how blessed it sounds, how full and rich it comes to the heart of the believer! And it is the Son of God who exhorts us to trust the Father, who gives us the assurance if we seek first the Kingdom of God and His righteousness, that all these things shall be added unto us.

CHAPTER VII.

1. The Judgment of Righteousness. 1–14.
2. Warning against False Prophets. 15–20.
3. Warning against False Professors. 21–29.

The first few verses are warning against judging. The attention is called to the conduct of a disciple toward another disciple. The Lord does not forbid here the righteous judgment and condemnation of what is evil. We are told elsewhere to do this (1 Cor. v:12, 13). The judgment of motives is forbidden. These are known to God alone. Verse 6 must be compared with 2 Pet. ii:22. The dogs and the swine represent mere outward profession, who were never born again.*

The great proclamation of the King closes with warnings against false prophets and false, religious professors. The warning of verse 15 is for our age as well and has a special significance in the end of the age. False teachers and false spirits are on all sides, and false prophets increase. See Acts xx:29, 30; Col. ii:8; 1 Tim. iv:1; vi:20; 2 Pet. ii:1; 1 John iv:1–3; 2 Cor. ii:17, xi:13–15. How different these divine warnings are in comparison with the optimistic vision of Christendom of an age which increases in righteousness. When the King comes again "in that day" the false prophets and false professors will be discovered. The false prophets, though they used His Name (like "Christian Science" and the "Russell Cult"), will be disowned by Him. The house built upon the sand of a mere profession and not the rock of ages will be swept away by the judgment.

6. *The King Manifested by Signs of Divine Power. Chapters viii–ix.*

CHAPTER VIII.

1. The Healing of the Leper. 1–4.
2. The Healing of the Centurion's Servant. 5–13.
3. The Healing of Peter's Wife's Mother. 14–15.
4. The Healing of All. 16–17.
5. The Self-seeking Scribe and the Test of True Discipleship. 18–22.
6. His Power over Nature. 23–27.
7. His Power over the Demons. 28–34.

The King who had uttered this great proclamation now manifests more fully His divine power by signs and miracles.

---

*Christendom has in fact done shamelessly what the Lord here forbids, and has proved the truth of His words in consequence. Baptism and the Lord's Supper, perverted from their original meaning and application, have been used above all to give the grossest evils toler-

These signs showed Israel that the Kingdom was at hand. In Isaiah xxxv we find a prophetic description of the Kingdom powers; and the King shows that He has come to make good these promises. The arrangement in Matthew shows that these miracles are taken out of their chronological order. They are found in Mark and Luke in a different setting. This is not a discrepancy as so often claimed by the deniers of inspiration. The Holy Spirit has grouped them together in such way to show first of all that the King proved Himself as the promised Messiah-King. In the second place the Spirit of God put them in the order, in which they appear in these two chapters to teach thereby certain dispensational purposes of God.

The first four miracles show His dispensational dealings with the Jews and the Gentiles in a most striking manner. The leper is a type of the sinner and also a type of the nation Israel (Isa. i:5–6). Jehovah alone can heal this awful disease (Num. xii:13; 2 Kings v:1–15). The attitude and faith of this leper should have been Israel's. He had come to heal the nation. The leper was healed and is sent by the King to the priest. The priest, however, does not proclaim the good news that Jehovah had appeared in the midst of His people. Thus Israel's failure to recognize and receive the Messiah and be healed is seen in the first miracle. The Centurion was a Gentile. The Lord found there greater faith than among His own people. He healed the servant not by touch, but He was absent from the place where he was. This miracle stands for the fact that Gentiles would believe on Him during this age, while He is absent.

---

ance in the house of God, and to make Babylon the great "a cage of every unclean and hateful bird." They have thus been trampled under foot by the profane, and Christianity been rent and mangled fearfully, as all the centuries bear witness. The "judgment of charity" is continually invoked to take darkness to be light, and credit the most barren profession with what it dares not even claim for itself. But the false judgment of laxity has here its woe upon it, as much as the false judgment of censoriousness: upon that which puts good for evil, and that which puts evil for good alike.—*Num. Bible.*

Then He healed Peter's wife's mother by going to the house and touching her. After this present dispensation is passed He will restore His relationship with His people Israel and heal and restore her to service. Then follows the healing of all. Verses 16–17 show the Kingdom blessings for the world after His second coming. And the King manifests power as the Lord of Creation, by rebuking the winds and the sea. He has power over demons, who acknowledge Him as Son of God and tremble in His presence.

CHAPTER IX.

1. A Man Sick of the Palsy Healed. 1–8.
2. The Call of Matthew. 9.
3. With the Publicans and the Sinners. 10–13.
4. The Question of John's Disciples. 14–17.
5. The Ruler's Request. 18–19.
6. The Woman Healed of an Issue of Blood. 20–22.
7. The Maid Raised from the Dead. 23–26.
8. The Two Blind Men Healed. 27–31.
9. The Dumb Man with a Demon Healed. 32–33.
10. The Blaspheming Pharisees and the Compassionate Shepherd of Israel. 34–38.

The King next manifests His power to forgive sins and when that power is questioned by the scribes and He is accused of blasphemy He healed the paralytic so that he arose. By this miracle full proof was given that the Son of Man has power on earth to forgive sins. Well did the scribes and Pharisees say, "Who is able to forgive sins but God alone?" (Luke v:21). By healing the paralytic they received the conclusive evidence that He who had spoken "thy sins are forgiven" is God manifested in the flesh. The miracle foreshadows His gracious work for every sinner who believes on Him. Our bodies, too, are redeemed, but we still wait for that redemption (Rom. viii:21). The miracle foreshadows likewise the healing of Israel. The day will come when the remnant of His earthly people will have forgiveness of their sins and be healed (Isa. xxxiii:24). It will be when He comes again (Isa. lix:20; Rom. xi:26–27). Thus will they witness in reality to the truth expressed in Ps. ciii:1–5.

The call of Matthew follows next. He left his office as taxgatherer and yielded ready obedience. And then the King eats and drinks with the publicans and the sinners, showing that He came to call sinners to repentance. A change of dispensation is indicated by Him in verses 16–17. The old garment and the old bottles (literal: wine-skins) stand for the law with its ordinances. The piece of the new cloth and the new wine stand for the better righteousness, the Gospel. The old wine-skins and the new wine do not go together; neither does law and grace.

The daughter which had died is the type of the daughter of Zion, spiritually and nationally dead. The Lord is on the way to raise her up. The woman, who touches Him and is healed represents Gentiles, who touch Him in faith. This miracle is a parenthetical event, just as the present age with its era of salvation to the Gentiles is a great parenthesis. And as He raised the daughter of the ruler, so will He in the future raise up Israel. For the first time in this Gospel we find here the awful blasphemy of the religious leader of the people. They accused the Lord from heaven of using satanic power in casting out demons. But the King continued in His ministry of preaching the Kingdom and healing the sick. Then He beheld His poor scattered sheep in their deplorable condition. His loving heart was moved with compassion (see Ezek. xxxiv:7–31).

7. *The Messengers of the Kingdom.*

CHAPTER X.

1. The Twelve Disciples. 1–4.
2. Their Commission. 5–15.
3. Persecutions Promised. 16–23.
4. Words of Encouragement. 24–33.
5. Not Peace but the Sword. 34–36.
6. True Discipleship and Rewards. 37–42.

The King now calls His disciples to go forth as the messengers of the Kingdom. The commission He gives them was temporary and ended with the complete rejection of the Kingdom by Israel. He told them not to carry the Kingdom message to the Gentiles, not even to the Samaritans. It was a message for the lost sheep of the house of Israel. They were to preach the good news of the Kingdom and the King conferred upon them His own Messianic power to heal the sick, cleanse the lepers and to raise the dead. Freely they had received it and freely they were to give. All this has nothing whatever to do with the preaching of the Gospel of Grace among all the nations. We have here not the commission of the church, but the ministry of a transition period. Christian Science and other cults claim that they are obedient to this commission and that they practise the healing of the sick. They, however, know nothing of raising the dead. Neither are they obedient to the command "freely ye have received, freely give." Their cults are for filthy lucre sake and are the cults of deception.

Persecutions and severe sufferings are predicted by the King. His messengers were to suffer, to be delivered to councils, to be scourged and put to death. Part of the fulfilment of all this is recorded in the book of Acts, where in the beginning the Gospel of the Kingdom is still preached.

Verse 23 tells us of an unfinished testimony. "For verily I say unto you, Ye shall not have gone over the cities of Israel, till the Son of Man be come." The Coming of the Son of Man is His second Coming. Before He comes again the Gospel of the Kingdom will be preached once more both in Israel's land and also among all nations (see Matt. xxiv: 14). The heralds in the future will again be a company of believing Jewish disciples. The predictions concerning persecution and tribulation will then all be finally fulfilled in that period of time, which is called in the Word of God "the great tribulation" (chap. xxiv:21). The true church will then be no longer on earth. Before that time of trouble comes, preceding the second visible Coming of Christ, the church will be gathered home to be with Christ (1 Thess. iv:13–18).

Verse 34 describes the present age. There is no peace on earth while the King and His Kingdom is rejected. When He comes again He will establish the promised peace (Ps. xlvi:9; Zech. ix:10).

8. *The Forerunner in Prison. The Kingdom Preaching Rejected.*

CHAPTER XI.

1. John Imprisoned Sends his Disciples. 1–6.
2. The King's Testimony Concerning John. 7–19.
3. The King Announces Judgment. 20–24.
4. The Greater Invitation. 25–28.

Once more the King takes up the work of teaching and preaching in the cities of Galilee. It is now becoming increasingly evident that Israel is not going to repent and accept the offered Kingdom. The present chapter is the beginning of the crisis, the rejection is consummated in the chapter which follows.

John the Baptist imprisoned is assailed with doubt; he was but human. He did not send to the Lord for the sake of His disciples, but wanted comfort and assurance for himself. Beautiful it is to see how the Lord speaks of him.

Verse 12 needs some comment. "And from the days of John the Baptist until now the Kingdom of heaven suffereth violence, and the violent take it by force." The wrong interpretation is that which makes the violent, who seize the Kingdom of heaven, unsaved sinners. According to this the sinner must exert his own strength and by force lay hold on the Kingdom of heaven. It means, however, the opposite. The Pharisees and scribes, who listened to the words of the Lord, are the violent who used force in connection with the Kingdom of heaven.* They rejected the Kingdom. In this sense the Kingdom of heaven suffered violence. No sooner did John the Baptist preach "the King-

*The student must remember that the Kingdom of heaven does not mean the Gospel at all, but is still the literal Kingdom promised to Israel.

dom of heaven is at hand," than the leaders of the nation raised their opposition. It increased till it culminated in the rejection and crucifixion of the King.

Then the King pronounced His woe upon the unbelieving cities. But more than that, upon the evident rejection of the Kingdom message, the King lifts His eyes to heaven and addresses the Father. For the first time He announces the greater invitation of the Gospel of His Grace. It is now "Come unto me *all*"; the message of the Kingdom will cease and the message of His Love will be sent forth into all the world. That message comes from the Cross.

9. *The Rejection Consummated and the Broken Relationship.*

CHAPTER XII.

1. The Hungry Disciples and the Accusing Pharisees. 1–9.
2. The Man with the Withered Hand Healed. 10–13.
3. The Hatred of the Pharisees. 14.
4. The King in Rejection. 15–21.
5. The Demon Possessed Man Healed. 22–23.
6. The Blasphemy of the Pharisees and the King's Answer. 24–37.
7. The Sign of Jonas and his Warning Prediction. 38–45.
8. The Broken Relationship. 46–50.

This chapter is the great turning point in this Gospel. It brings before us the full rejection of the Kingdom. After this chapter we hear no longer the Kingdom preached to Israel.

The King manifests Himself as the Lord of the Sabbath and answered the charge of the accusing Pharisees. That the disciples, the messengers of the Kingdom, were hungry shows that the people had no sympathy for the messengers and for the message. To pluck ears of corn on the Sabbath is nowhere forbidden. The tradition of the elders had added the commandment on account of which the Pharisees brought their accusation. He silences them with David's action, who, though he was God's anointed, yet rejected, entered the house of the Lord and did what was not lawful for him to do (1 Sam. xxi).

Their first attempt to accuse Him and His disciples failed. They tried again by the man with the withered hand. He silenced them again and healed the man, who obeyed His Word. He, too, is a picture of Israel in their spiritual and national withered condition. Then they held a council to plan the destruction of the King. And after He healed the man who was possessed with a demon, who had robbed him of his sight and his speech, the Pharisees charged the Lord with driving out the demons by Beelzebub, the prince of demons. This was the crowning sin of the unbelieving Pharisees. It is the blasphemy against the Holy Spirit. This is the sin against the Holy Spirit for which there is no forgiveness in this age nor in that to come.

Interesting are His words in verses 43–45. The nation Israel is here again in view. The unclean spirit which left Israel was the spirit of idolatry. But that unclean spirit will return with seven others and take possession again of that house, and the last condition, the end, becomes worse than the beginning. This condition will yet be reached among the apostate Jews during the time of the Antichrist.

In the end of this chapter the King refuses to see His own. This action was symbolical. He declared through it that the relationship with His own nation, to whom He came as the promised King, was now broken off. He announces a new relationship (verses 49–50). As stated already after this event He announces no longer the Kingdom at hand. The message of the Kingdom had been given and had been rejected. The first part of the Gospel of Matthew ends here.

II. The Rejected Kingdom and the Rejected King.

Chapters xiii–xxviii.

1. *The King at the Seaside. The Mysteries of the Kingdom.*

CHAPTER XIII.

1. The King at the Seaside. 1–2.
2. The Parable of the Sower. 3–9.
3. The Question of the Disciples and His Answer. 10–17.
4. The Parable of the Sower Explained. 18–23.
5. The Parable of the Good Seed and the Tares. 24–30.
6. The Parable of the Mustard Seed. 31–32.
7. The Parable of the Leaven. 33–35.
8. The Parable of the Good Seed and of the Tares Explained. 36–42.
9. The Parable of the Treasure in the Field. 44.
10. The Parable of the Pearl of Great Price. 45–46.
11. The Parable of the Drag-net. 47–52.
12. Rejected in His Own Country. 53–58.

This is an important and most interesting chapter. It is perhaps the most misinterpreted chapter in the entire Gospel. Precisely that which our Lord did not teach has been read into it. If the parables were correctly understood the consequences would be the most far-reaching. The King having declared the relationship with His people broken left the house (symbolical of this fact) and sat by the seaside. Then He began to teach in parables. These parables, repeated in full only in Matthew, concern the mysteries of the Kingdom of heaven. He makes known things hidden from the foundation of the world (verses 11, 34–35). The Kingdom of heaven is now no longer that Old Testament Kingdom promised to Israel, for that Kingdom was not an unrevealed secret. The parables of the mysteries of the Kingdom of heaven give a description of what is to be on the earth religiously after Israel's rejection of the Kingdom.

The parables contain a wonderful revelation of the present age, beginning with the sowing of the good seed by the Son of Man and ending with the harvest, the end of the age, when He comes the second time. To say that our Lord speaks of the church in these parables would be incorrect. He speaks of what we term to-day "Christendom," the sphere of Christian profession.

The first four parables were spoken by Him before the multitudes. After He sent the people away (verse 36) the Lord spoke the last three to His disciples. The first two parables our Lord explained to the disciples and gives the key to the entire seven. The field mentioned in different parables means "the world." The Man (sower—; the man who buys the field; the merchantman) is the Lord Himself. Birds (picking up the seed; flocking into the mustard-tree) are unclean beings. Wheat (sown by Him; the wheat in the three measures) stands for the doctrine of Christ and what it produces, the children of the Kingdom.

The first two parables go together. They refer to the beginning of the present age and reveal the conditions which continue to the time of the harvest, the end of the age.* The good seed, the Gospel, is now to be scattered in the field, that is, the world. It is a different work from the work of the vineyard (Israel is the vineyard, Isa. v:1–7). But only the fourth part of the sown seed springs up. The devil, the flesh and the world are the three things which make the universal success of the Gospel impossible in this present age. World-conversion is not to be expected in the age when the King is absent. The second parable shows the mixed conditions. Wheat and tares grow together till the harvest comes. Then the wheat will be gathered and the tares burned up. The parables of the mustard seed and of the woman who hid leaven in the three measures of meal foretell the external development and the internal corruption of the Kingdom of heaven in its form during this pres-

*The word "world" in verses 39, 40 and 49 is "age." The same is true of Chapter xxiv:3.

ent age. The mustard seed shows an unnatural, an abnormal growth and the birds lodging there bring defilement. Such is Christendom with its worldly ambitions and its unsaved masses.

The parable of the woman with the leaven is the most misunderstood. The woman does not mean the church, nor does the leaven stand for the Gospel and the doctrine of Christ. Leaven is *always* in the Word of God the type of evil (Matt. xvi:11–12; Mark viii:15; 1 Cor. v:6; Gal. v:9). If our Lord taught here (as almost universally claimed) that leaven is something good and that the "Gospel-leaven" is leavening the whole lump of unconverted humanity, etc., then would He contradict Himself, for the first two parables teach the opposite. Leaven stands for a corrupting process of evil, which is introduced by woman under the control of satanic influence, to corrupt the doctrine of Christ. Here is, no doubt, a prophecy, which has been abundantly fulfilled. The woman "Jezebel" in Rev. ii:20 is the same as the "Mother of Harlots" in Rev. xvii; it is the Romish apostasy. Rome speaks of "Mother church" and *she* is the corrupteress of true Christianity. We may well think here of other wicked corruptions of the doctrine of Christ. Christian Science (Mrs. Eddy); Seventh day Adventism (Mrs. White); Spiritism (Fox sisters); Theosophy (Mrs. Blavatsky) and other systems, which originated with women (1 Tim. ii:14). This process of corruption in this present age is also witnessed to by the Holy Spirit in 1 Tim. iv:1–3; 2 Tim. ii:17–18, iii:1–5, iv:3–4; 2 Pet. ii:1–3; Jude. The fire of judgment will arrest it all, as the fire arrests the working of the natural leaven.

The parable of the treasure and of the pearl also go together. The Man in both is not the sinner who seeks a treasure and a pearl, who gives up all in order to get all. The Man is our Lord, who buys the field. He gave all He had to have the treasure (Israel) hid in the field, who sold all to have the one pearl of great price (the church). The parable of the drag-net brings us to the end of the age. The net is cast into the sea (nations) and in that net (Christendom) the good and the bad, the true and false are gathered. They remain there till the end of the age, when they will be separated.*

2. John's Martyrdom. The Fourfold Attitude of the Rejected King.

CHAPTER XIV.

1. John's Martyrdom. 1–11.
2. The Disciples of John with the Lord Jesus. **12.**
3. Feeding the Five Thousand. 13–21.
4. Praying on the Mountain-top. 22–23.
5. Walking on the Sea; Coming to His Disciples. 24–36.

The details of the martyrdom of John are given first. It is the story of lust, crime and bloodshed. Such is the entire age in which the King is absent. We see Him in a fourfold attitude, an attitude which teaches us much. First the disciples of John seek Him for comfort—"they came and told Jesus." Then He fed miraculously the multitudes, who had followed Him into the desert place. He used His own. They put the little they possessed in His hands. Next we behold Him praying on the mountain (typical of His presence with the Father in glory) and the final scene in this chapter is the storm on the sea, the wind contrary (a perfect picture of this age), the disciples in danger and He coming across the stormy seas to bring salvation and peace. Then follows a still greater manifestation of His Kingly power. We can come to Him for comfort and help; He will feed those who follow Him; He prays and intercedes for His own and at last comes again. With that blessed event the time of peace and blessing for this world will come.

*We hope all students will procure our complete exposition of these parables. "The Kingdom Parables" by A. C. G. Price 10 cents postpaid.

3. *The Corruption of the Scribes and Pharisees; the Canaanitish Woman and Her Faith; the Multitudes Healed.*

CHAPTER XV.

1. The Question of the Scribes and Pharisees. 1–2.
2. His Answer. 3–9.
3. The Multitude Called. 10–11.
4. The Disciples Instructed. 12–20.
5. The Canaanitish Woman. 21–28.
6. The Multitudes Healed. 29–31.

The events which follow the rejection of the offered Kingdom by Israel, revealing their enmity, are now brought more fully in view. The scribes, the Pharisees and the Sadducees take a leading part. They test Him and bring their questions, but He silences them all. His wisdom is gloriously manifested. A delegation came from Jerusalem. The question concerned a mere traditional law of the elders. Nothing is said whatever in the Old Testament about washing the hands before eating.* He uncovers their hypocrisies and shows their corruption.

The Canaanitish woman addressed Him as "Son of David." She had no claim on Him as Son of David. But when she took the place He gave to her and appealed to Him as "Lord" He healed her daughter. Thus the rejected King ministered to a Gentile. The first part of this chapter reveals the desperate condition of Israel. The second part, the healing of the daughter of the Canaanitish woman, shows typically the call of the Gentiles and the salvation in store for them, if they believe. The last part, the healing of the multitude, reveals the dispensation to come, the Kingdom age.

---

*Several years ago we read in a Jewish volume printed in Poland, that evil spirits alight over night on the hands and if hands are not washed as prescribed by the traditional law those evil spirits find their way into the mouth and the stomach of the transgressor and defile him. This foolish superstition is founded upon a Talmudical statement of great antiquity. It will throw light on the above passage.

4. *The Great Announcements of the Rejected King Concerning Himself.*

CHAPTER XVI.

1. Pharisees and Sadducees Asking a Sign. 1—4.
2. Instructions Concerning the Leaven. 5–12.
3. Peter's Confession. 13–16.
4. The Future Building of the Church Announced. 17–20.
5. The Announcement of His Death and Resurrection. 21.
6. Peter's Rebuke and the Lord's Answer. 22–23.
7. The Path of the Disciple. 24–26.
8. His Second Coming Announced. 27–28.

Seven things are seen in this chapter, the center being the predictions of the King concerning Himself: 1. The Rejection of the Lord. Pharisees and Sadducees making common cause to tempt Him. 2. The Confession of Him as the Christ the Son of the living God. 3. The Building of His church. 4. His Death. 5. His Resurrection. 6. The Path of the Disciple. 7. His Return.

Of greatest interest is the fact that we find the word "church" mentioned in this chapter for the first time in the Bible. The King had not said a word about a church, an outcalled company (this is the meaning of the Greek word), when He preached "the Kingdom of heaven is at hand." No prophet ever mentioned the church. When the Lord mentioned the church, that body was not yet in existence, for He said, "I *will* build my church." The church therefore did not exist in the Old Testament; at the time the Lord spoke these words the church was still future. The rock upon which this church is to be built is Christ the Son of God (not the Son of David, the promised King). Christ raised from the dead is the great rock foundation. Peter is not the rock. Peter means in the Greek "petros," a stone; the word rock in Greek is "*petra.*" This word is used in Matt. vii:24, 25. Therefore Christ is *the* rock and Peter a part of the rock. This brings out the blessed truth that every true believer in possession of eternal life is one with Christ. The testimony of Peter in 1 Pet. ii:4–6 must be read in connection with this first announcement of the church.

The keys of the Kingdom of heaven do not mean that Peter (and his alleged successors) have a supremacy in the church. The Kingdom of heaven is not the church, but it is the professing sphere of Christendom. Peter used the authority conferred upon him on the day of Pentecost, when preaching to the Jews and again in the house of Cornelius, preaching to the Gentiles. See what Peter said of himself (1 Pet. i:1, v:1). The power to bind and to loose has nothing whatever to do with salvation. It refers only to discipline on earth. The same power was conferred upon all the other disciples (Matt. xviii:18; John xx:23). And they represent the church which was to come into existence.

For the first time the rejected King announces His coming suffering, His death, His resurrection and His second Coming in Glory. The break in the chapter at verse 28 is unfortunate. The transfiguration which follows solves the difficulty of the last verse of this chapter.

5. *The Coming Glory; the Helpless Disciples and the Power of the King. The Tribute Money.*

CHAPTER XVII.

1. The Transfiguration. 1–13.
2. The Helpless Disciples and the Power of the King. 14–21.
3. The Second Announcement of His Death and Resurrection. 22–23.
4. The Tribute Money. 24–27.

At the close of the previous chapter the Lord announced His Coming in Glory. This means His personal and glorious Return. Some, He predicted, who were standing there would not taste death till they would see the Son of Man coming in His Kingdom. The transfiguration, which took place a week later, witnessed to the yet future coming of the Son of Man in the glory of the Father to receive the Kingdom. Three of His disciples saw this startling occurrence. The transfiguration scene is typical of the second, visible and glorious coming of our Lord (2 Pet. i:16–21). The Man of humiliation is transfigured and thus a glimpse of His coming glory is given. Moses glorified represents the Saints of God who died; Elijah represents the Saints caught up to meet the Lord in the air (1 Thess. iv:16–18). The Saints come with Him in Glory (Col. iii:4; 1 Thess. iv:14). The three disciples seeing the transfiguration represent here the Jewish remnant awaiting the coming Kingdom. The desperate condition the Lord finds coming down is a little picture of the condition of the world under Satan's power. He will bring deliverance with His return. The tribute money brings out His glory. He is the omniscient One, who knows all and the omnipotent One, who commands the fish to take up a coin in the bottom of the sea and brings that fish to Peter's hook. He provided what was needed. "For me and thee" shows the most blessed identification of the Lord and the disciples. All is His and into the riches of Himself He brings His own.

6. *Instructions to His Disciples. Concerning Forgiveness.*

CHAPTER XVIII.

1. Concerning the Little Ones and Offences. 1–10.
2. The Son of Man to Save What is Lost. 11–14.
3. The Church Anticipated and Instructions Concerning it. 15–20.
4. Concerning Forgiveness.

The question of the disciples may have been occasioned by the words of the Lord to Peter in chapter xvi. When He had announced twice His coming passion and set His face like a flint to go up to Jerusalem, they were reasoning among themselves who should be the greatest (Luke ix:46). With what patience and tenderness He instructs them! The object lesson is a little child. He gives them the characteristics of those who have entered the Kingdom in reality and the principles which are to govern them. The Kingdom must be entered in. It is the same truth, which Nicodemus heard from His lips. A new life is given; the believing sinner is born again and enters the Kingdom as a little child, as the child enters the world by the natural birth. The characteristics of the child are lowliness and dependence. Such must be the leading characteristic of the heir of the Kingdom. And the Lord teaches His identification with every one, who is born again, who has become a little child. Honor done to one of these little ones is done unto Him; and injury done to one of them is done unto Him.

Then He gives additional instructions concerning the church. It relates to discipline and gives the true way how offences are to be dealt with in the new relationship about to come into existence (verses 13–19). But it must be remembered that the true meaning of the church as the body of Christ, etc., is not revealed here at all. Nor was it fully made known on the day of Pentecost when the church began on earth. Through the Apostle Paul the full revelation of the church was given. But verse 20 gives us the center around which the church is gathered. "Where two or three are gathered unto my name (not *in* my name) there am I in the midst of them." Not the name of a man, but unto the name of the Lord Jesus Christ, who is the Head of the body, the church. Connected with this is the blessed assurance of prayer to be heard and answered.

7. *Departure from Galilee. Concerning Divorce. Little Children Blessed and the Rich Young Man.*

CHAPTER XIX.

1. The Departure from Galilee. 1–2.
2. Concerning Divorce. 3–12.
3. The Blessing of Little Children. 13–15.
4. The Rich Young Man. 16–26.
5. The Rewards in the Kingdom. 27–30.

The Pharisees appear to tempt the Lord, this time concerning divorcing a wife. It is again a question which had it to do with their traditional laws and sayings of the elders. The Ritualists in Christendom like the legal, ritualistic Pharisees, are also much more occupied with their man-made rules than with the Word of God. Perhaps their question was the result of the Lord's teaching in chapter v:31–32. This statement of our Lord in the Sermon on the Mount dealt a severe blow to the rabbinical traditions held by the Pharisees concerning divorce. They were divided among themselves. Some had adopted the views of Hillel, that a wife may be put away for almost any cause. Others again held with the teaching of Shammai, another rabbinical authority, that divorce was only permissible in case of adultery. He answers them in His divine wisdom. He calls their attention to the beginning. Marriage as instituted by the Creator is an argument against polygamy and divorce. In the new creation this relationship has a still deeper meaning (Eph. v:21–33). The answer of the Pharisees reveals their ignorance (verse 7). Moses did not command divorce; he allowed it because of the hardness of their hearts (Deut. xxiv:1). The scandalous thing Moses mentioned is explained by our Lord to be fornication. This is the only ground for divorce. Professing Christendom pays no heed to this instruction. The increase of unlawful divorces is alarming and a sign of the last days.

The relation of little children is next seen in this chapter. They belong to the Kingdom of heaven, are subjects of it and therefore He blessed them. The young man who asks the Lord "what good thing shall I do that I may have eternal life?" pictures the condition of thousands in the professing Christendom. He was a religious and moral young man. But all his morality and religiousness had not given him the assurance of eternal life. He wanted to do something in order to get eternal life. Eternal life is the gift of God through Jesus Christ our Lord. The Lord did not promise him eternal life if he were to sell all he had and give it to the poor. He wanted to convince him that his profession of loving his neighbor as himself was spurious. That law demanded that he should sell all and give it to the poor. He did not understand the lesson and went away sorrowful from the Lord.

Verse 28 is often misunderstood. It must be read in the following way: "Verily I say unto you, that ye who have followed Me—In the regeneration, when the Son of Man shall sit upon the throne of His Glory," etc. The word regeneration (*paliggenesia*) means here the re-creation promised in the Word of God, when all things will be made new and groaning creation put back in its right place, where it was before the fall of man. This regeneration comes when the Son of Man comes the second time. Then the rewards are given.

8. *The Parable of the Laborers in the Vineyard. The Healing of the Two Blind Men.*

CHAPTER XX.

1. The Parable of the Laborers in the Vineyard. 1–16.
2. The Third Prediction of His Death and Resurrection. 17–19.
3. The Ambitiousness of the Disciples. 20–28.
4. The Healing of the Two Blind Men. 29–34.

Notice verse 30 of the preceding chapter and the same statement contained therein repeated in verse 16: "*So* the last shall be first and the first last." The parable which comes in between these two verses illustrates this fact, that many who are first shall be last; and the last shall be first. The parable speaks of rewards. The great principle of the parable is, that God will distribute rewards as He chooses in fullest accord with justice. While God owns every service and loss for the sake of Christ, yet He manitains His sovereignty to do as He will. The Lord wants us to leave the rewards with Him and not to think anything of our service. The parable appears to correct Peter's self-occupation (Chapter xix:27). Jew and Gentile are also in view here in a dispensational way. Then after the third prediction of His death and resurrection, and the ambitiousness of the sons of Zebedee, He healed the two blind men.

Here we have again a dispensational foreshadowing, the importance of which should not be overlooked. These two blind men sitting at the wayside, groping in the dark, crying to the Son of David for deliverance, are types of the poor and feeble remnant of Israel in the end of this age, after the testimony of the church for Christ the Son of God by resurrection from the dead, has been finished and the church is no longer upon this scene. The remnant of Israel will cry to Him as Son of David and call upon Him for deliverance. The entrance into Jerusalem, which follows in the next chapter, foreshadows also that coming of the Son of David to Jerusalem, when He comes as King crowned with honor and glory. And as the two blind ones called upon Him when He was on the way to Jerusalem, and He heard and delivered them, so will that remnant of His earthly people seek Him, and in that darkness which precedes His return to Jerusalem cry to the Son of David, without seeing Hin in person, though they believe on Him, that He is the promised One. And as the cry of the blind men was the work of the Holy Spirit, so will the seeking, the longing, the prayer of that future remnant be produced by the Spirit of God.

9. *The King Enters into Jerusalem. The Parables of the Two Sons and the Householder and His Vineyard.*

CHAPTER XXI.

1. The King Enters Jerusalem. 1–11.
2. The Second Cleansing of the Temple. 12–17.
3. The Figtree Cursed. 18–22.
4. His Authority Impeached and His Question. 23–27.
5. The Parable of the Two Sons. 28–32.
6. The Parable of the Householder. 33–39.
7. The Lord's Question and the King's Sentence. 40–46.

The King with His disciples draws near to Jerusalem to hold His royal entrance into His city.

Criticism has given a strange motive for the Lord's entrance into Jerusalem. It has been said that He was carried away by enthusiasm and expected that the people would now surely receive Him as the Messiah-King; while other critics explained His entry to the city as a kind of a concession to the messianic expectations of His disciples. How dishonoring to Him are all such foolish speculations. The simple fact is that He is the King and as such He had to come to Jerusalem and fulfil that which had been predicted by Zechariah, the prophet (Zech. ix:9).

What a sight it must have been the thousands coming to meet Him with Palm branches in their hands, waving them over their heads, while the multitudes which followed did the same. And then they broke out in the glad shouts, quoting partly from the cxviii Psalm "Hosanna to the Son of David! Blessed is He that cometh in the name of the Lord; Hosanna in the Highest." Hosanna means "save now."

What a triumph it was! The King entering Jerusalem. And in all He is undisturbed. Others might have been swept away by this enthusiasm; but He is calm in all His kingly majesty. Luke's Gospel tells us that He wept. "And when He was come near, He beheld the city, and wept over it." And what kind of weeping was this? He wept at the grave of Lazarus and that was a still, a silent weeping. But before Jerusalem He broke out in loud and deep lamentations. This is clearly proven by the different words used in the original.

The King knew what was soon to be, and on yonder hill He saw looming up the cross. True, they were crying, "Son of David, save now!" But the question, "Who is this?" is answered in the terms of rejection. Instead of "the King, Jehovah-Jesus, the Messiah," the multitude answers "Jesus, the Prophet of Nazareth of Galilee."

Then He cleansed the temple. This is the second time that the Lord acted in cleansing the temple. The first is recorded in the Gospel of John (ii:13–17), and it took place at the beginning of His ministry. There it is the zeal for God's house, but here He acts in all His Kingly authority.

But a more refreshing scene follows. The temple is cleansed. The noise and confusion is at an end. Nothing is said of the return of these evil occupants. But instead of them, there came the blind and the lame to Him in the temple and He healed them. The vacancy was filled by the crowd of poor, stricken suffering ones, who were delivered of their pains and diseases. Blessed and glorious foreshadowing of what will be when He comes again and when by His life-giving, healing touch, He will cure "all diseases" and make perfectly whole.

Then followed the cursing of the fig tree. The King was hungry. He who was rich, had indeed become poor. There by the wayside is a fig tree bearing many leaves; there He looked for some of the old fruit, or perhaps some of the unripe figs. He finds nothing and a curse follows, which withers the tree. It is well known that the fig tree is the type of Israel. The cursing of the fig tree stands for the national rejection of the people.

The mountain mentioned in verse 21 is a type of Israel in unbelief. The nation was a mountain and by its disobedience and rejection of the Lord, the nation was an obstacle in the path of the Gospel. But on account of faith this mountain was indeed cast into the sea, the type of the nations. Precious to faith has ever been and ever will be the word, the author and finisher of the faith speaks here. "And all things whatsoever ye shall ask in prayer, believing, ye shall receive."

The two parables need no comment. Even the chief priests and the Pharisees understood that He spoke of them (verse 45). Their hatred rose high. Verse 44 is of a deeper meaning. The Jews at this first coming fell on this stone (He is the stone) and were nationally broken. At His second Coming, He, the stone, will fall on the Gentiles, deal with them and their dominion in judgment (see Dan. ii:37–45).

10. *The Parable of the Marriage Feast. The King's Answers and His Question.*

CHAPTER XXII.

1. The Parable of the Marriage Feast. 1–14.
2. The Herodians Answered. 15–22.
3. The Sadducees Answered. 23–33.
4. The Pharisees Answered. 34–40.
5. The Unanswered Question. 41–46.

A significant parable follows. The same parable appears in the Gospel of Luke. A comparison will show that in Matthew the dispensational features stand out more prominently. The third verse speaks of the offer of the Kingdom as made to Israel by the King and His disciples. It was refused. In verses 4–6 there is a repeated offer and how this second offer was treated. This took place after the cross ("all things are ready"; the cross of Christ has done that). The beginning of the Book of Acts reveals that offer made exclusively to Jerusalem. Those who had rejected Christ and crucified Him had a chance to repent. They did exactly with the message and the messengers what our Lord predicts in this parable. Verse 7 is a prediction of what should befall Jerusalem. This was fulfilled in the year 70. The city, which had become a city of murderers (Isa. i:21) was burned. Then the King predicts the world-wide offer made to the Gentiles (verses 8–10).

The wedding garment corresponds to "the best robe" in the parable of the prodigal. The Lord Jesus Christ Himself is the wedding garment and all who are mere professors of Christ, without having put on the Lord Jesus Christ, will share the fate of which the Lord speaks in the parable.

Then He answered the questions of the Herodians (politicians), the Pharisees (ritualists) and the Sadducees (rationalists). They all tried to entangle Him, but failed miserably. The Herodians had to marvel and the Sadducees were astonished. Then He asked the Pharisees a question, which they failed to answer.

It is from the cx Psalm the Lord draws His question. This Psalm is one of the great messianic prophecies in the Old Testament. It is very prominent in the Epistle to the Hebrews, where it is quoted a number of times as being fulfilled in Him, who is now the man of glory, seated at the right hand of the majesty on high, waiting till His enemies are made His footstool. This will be done when He comes again. In sending Him, the First begotten, into the world, God will put down all His enemies. It is almost impossible to believe that, with the evidences from Scripture, such as the word of our Lord and the testimony of the Holy Spirit in the Epistle to the Hebrews, certain men who call themselves "scholars" and assume the place of "critics" can deny the cx Psalm was composed by David and that the Psalm has any messianic reference at all. This surely is wicked unbelief, as pronounced, perhaps more so, than the unbelief of the Pharisees.

Well, the Pharisees here answer that Messiah is to be the Son of David. They were professed teachers of Israel and still they did not understand the Scriptures. The question the Lord now puts to them, David calling Him who is to be a son of his, Lord, that is Jehovah, they could not, perhaps would not, answer. The passage teaches clearly who Messiah is. He is Jehovah incarnate, the Son of David and David's Lord. And the interrogator is He. His Davidic descent could not be denied; that He has a legal title to the throne of David is clearly proven by the genealogy. In His ministry throughout these years, He had manifested Himself in His mighty works as Jehovah. They could give Him no answer. Solemn moment it was. No answer! No repentance! They are silenced, and when they open their lips again it is to cry "Crucify Him!" The end is now coming on rapidly. In the next chapter He speaks as Judge pronouncing His judgment upon the leaders of the nation.

11. *The Woes of the King and His Lamentation over Jerusalem.*

CHAPTER XXIII.

1. The Hypocrisy of the Pharisees. 1–12.
2. The Woes of the King upon Them. 13–36.
3. The Lamentation over Jerusalem. 37–39.

The chapter which is before us contains the "Woes" of the King upon the Pharisees. It is one of the most solemn ones in Matthew. Pharisaism is still on the earth; Ritualism, Traditionalism and with it the rejection of the authority of the Lord and His written Word, is Pharisaism, that evil leaven against which the Lord warns. This Christian Pharisaism is far worse than the old Jewish system. And where in Christendom is a little of that leaven lacking? Only the Grace of God, an unbroken fellowship with the Father and

His Son in the power of the Holy Spirit, can keep the individual believer from manifesting a Pharisaical spirit.

And now the Lord takes up His "Woes." It is a fearful uncovering of the hearts of the Pharisees and their corruption. And thus He lays bare the hidden things. He will do so again. There are eight woes given in this chapter, though it has been claimed that the fourteenth verse does not belong to this chapter. It is, however, found in both the Gospels of Mark and Luke, so that it is evident the Lord also uttered these words.

He now pronounces judgment upon them and uncovers all they are. Pharisaism keeps the outside clean, while inside there is corruption and death. There is a self-righteous religious boasting of being more advanced than the fathers and more tolerant than they were. But the omniscient One reads their hearts and declares that they fill up the measure of the fathers. They were unsaved men, not the offspring of God, but of vipers; their father, the devil; and they were facing judgment of Gehenna.

And then His lamentation, how He must leave the house desolate and turn away from His beloved city. The King is the King of love and His heart yearns over Jerusalem.

But the discourse which has nothing but Woes ends with a "Blessed," and here comes in the bright ray of hope for Israel. "Ye shall in no wise see me henceforth until ye say, Blessed be He that comes in the name of the Lord." This is the promise of His second Coming, and when He comes He will find a believing remnant of that very people, welcoming Him with the messianic greeting of the cxviii Psalm. Then the Shekinah-Glory will spread over Jerusalem and Israel's land, and He that scattered Israel will gather them from the four corners of the earth. It is a strange and evil doctrine which maintains that inasmuch as the woes were spoken upon these Pharisees, that they are also to see Him again. It is claimed that these wicked Pharisees, the offspring of vipers, who could not escape the judgment of hell, are all to be raised from the dead when Christ comes again and have "a second chance" to see Him, and that then they will receive Him. Such Jewish universalism has no Scripture foundation whatever. It is a remnant which will behold the King coming out of the opened heavens in the day of His manifestation.

12. *The Olivet Discourse; the King Reveals the Future of the Kingdom. Chapters xxiv–xxv.*

CHAPTER XXIV.

1. The Destruction of the Temple Foretold. 1–2.
2. The Questions of the Disciples. 3.
3. The End of the Age; Events Preceding His Coming. 4–14.
4. The Great Tribulation and what will Happen. 15–26.
5. The Visible and Glorious Return of the King. 27–31.
6. The Exhortations of the King. 32–44.
7. The Parable of the Faithful and Evil Servant. 45–51.

The Olivet discourse is the last great utterance of the King. It was delivered to the disciples and concerns the future. It is divided into three parts: First, He answers the three questions of His disciples (verses 4–44); then He speaks three parables (45–xxv:30); the last part contains a great judgment prophecy (chap. xxv:31–46). The first part concerns the end of the age, and in it the King describes what will take place on earth immediately before His visible Return. The second part reveals the conditions in the Kingdom of heaven (Christendom) and how He as King and Judge will deal with those conditions. The third part is a prophecy concerning the judgment of the nations the King finds on His return to this earth.*

The first part has nothing to do with the destruction of the temple and Jerusalem. Jerusalem and the temple are not even mentioned by Him. The interpretation that all His predictions in verses 4–44 found their fulfillment during the siege of Jerusalem in the year 70 is totally wrong. The destruction of the temple is foretold by Him in verse 2

*It is impossible to give satisfactory annotations of this great and important discourse in a small pamphlet. The readers will find the complete exposition in our Commentary on Matthew.

before the disciples asked the questions, which resulted in His discourse. Luke reports the destruction of Jerusalem and the scattering of the nation (Luke xxi:20–24). But in Matthew the Holy Spirit records the regathering of His elect, earthly people (verse 31). Nor does the answer of the Lord to His disciples have anything to do with this Christian age. The church is not mentioned by Him at all. The disciples had asked about the end of the age.* They only knew their Jewish age and were ignorant of this Christian age. The Jewish age did not fully terminate with the rejection of the Messiah and the worldwide dispersion of the nation. It was only interrupted in its course. The interruption is this present Christian age during which the church is gathered out. When that purpose is accomplished, the true church will be removed from the earth to be joined to the Head in glory. Then the dealings of God with His ancient people Israel will be resumed. The end of their age of unbelief ends. It will last seven years, the last week of the great prophecy of Daniel (Chapter ix, see our commentary on Daniel).

It is this end, these seven years still future which our Lord describes in the first part of His discourse. True it is that throughout the age in which we live all these things He mentions, wars, earthquakes, famines, pestilences, persecutions of the godly have taken place. All these will occur in a more intensified form during the end of the age, when the true church is no longer on earth. Then the remnant of Jews who believe, like the disciples of the King when He appeared the first time, will preach the Gospel of the Kingdom among all nations. In Revelation vii we find this remnant sealed and in the second half the result of the preached testimony, a multitude which comes out of the great tribulation.

When these seven years are ended the King appears in

*Again we remind the students of this Gospel that the word "world" is incorrect. The end of the world cannot come for a long time. Before the end of the world can come this earth must first be put in order and delivered from the curse.

all His Glory in the clouds of heaven. For the church and His Saints there is another Coming (1 Thess. iv:13–18). The Saints come with Him in that day (Zech. xiv:1–5).

Verse 34 has been a difficulty with many. The word generation does not mean the people who were then living; it has the meaning of "this race."* The Jewish race cannot pass away till these things be fulfilled.

With verse 45 the second part begins. It concerns Christendom. While the seven parables of the Kingdom (chapter xiii) teach the beginning, the development and end of Christendom, the three parables of the Olivet discourse show the moral aspect of those who profess Christianity. The true and the false, the faithful and the unfaithful are uncovered and dealt with.

CHAPTER XXV.

1. The Parable of the Ten Virgins. 1–13.
2. The Parable of the Servants and the Talents. 14–30.
3. The Judgment of Nations. 31–46.

The parable of the ten virgins describes Christendom and what will take place some day. In the beginning of this age the entire Christian profession expected the promised return. He delayed and they all slumbered and slept. They gave up the Hope which energized them in the beginning. The midnight cry aroused entire Christendom again. This is now an accomplished fact. Many years ago during the first half of the nineteenth century the Spirit of God revived the blessed Hope. And still the cry is heard and will be heard till He comes. The next is He comes. His true people who have the oil enter in with Him. Those who possess not the oil (the Holy Spirit), because they have never believed on Him, face a shut door and hear the awful word "I know ye not."† Then an account must be

---

*Same as 1 Pet. ii:9, "a chosen generation," *i.e.*, class of peoples.

†Some teach on this an invention. They say the foolish virgins represent worldly minded believers, who will pass through the great tribulation. The Lord will never say to any one who trusts in Him, "I know ye not."

given how His gifts were used. The man with one talent unused represents an unsaved soul.

The third section is a prophecy. The King returned will occupy the throne of His Glory. The judgment is not a judgment of the entire human race. None of the dead are here. The dead Saints are raised when He comes in the air to receive His own and the dead martyrs of the tribulation period will also have been raised at the close of that period. The rest of the dead does not live till the thousand years of the Kingdom are ended (Rev. xx:5). Here the living nations are seen judged. The standard is the treatment they accorded to the last messengers of the King, these are "the brethren" of the King, of the Jewish race. If these nations believed that testimony they treated the messengers with kindness; if they rejected this final message they refused help to the messengers. The righteous nations who believed will remain on the earth for the Kingdom. The unrighteous will go into everlasting punishment.

13. *The Passion of the King. Chapter xxvi–xxvii.*

CHAPTER XXVI.

1. His Death Planned. 1–5.
2. Mary of Bethany Anointing the King. 6–13.
3. The Betrayal. 14–16.
4. The Last Passover. 17–25.
5. The Lord's Supper Instituted. 26–29.
6. Peter's Denial Announced and the Scattered Sheep. 30–35.
7. In Gethsemane. 36–46.
8. Judas and His Deed. The Arrest of the King. 47–56.
9. Before Caiaphas and the Sanhedrin. 57–68.
10. Peter's Denial. 69–75.

The great last discourse of the King being ended there remains now nothing else to record than the story of His passion, His suffering, death and resurrection. This is the record of the remaining three chapters of the first Gospel. Two of these are the longest in the whole book. He had foretold in His great prophecy in the Olivet discourse the future of the Jews, the Christian profession and the future of the nations. Now He is to go and fulfill all the predictions concerning His sufferings and death, as written in Moses, the Prophets and the Psalms. The twenty-sixth chapter is one of contrasts. Here we behold Him in all His wonderful perfection again. With what calmness and dignity He enters upon that great work, which the Father gave Him to do. On the other hand we see wickedness and Satanic powers revealed which now cast themselves in all their fury upon the holy One. What a wonderful story it is which we have followed in this first Gospel. How marvelous the events and how perfect and divine the entire arrangement! Man could never have written such an account.

Notice the last prediction of His death. This is the fourth time He predicts His death in this Gospel. He not only predicts the manner of His death, but now also the time; He is to be crucified at the time of the Passover. All this manifests His Deity. He knew all beforehand. Let none think that all that which was before Him dawned upon Him gradually; He knew every one of the sufferings and all that which was now to come upon His holy head. But what calmness breathes in these words, in which He predicted His coming crucifixion! There is no anxiety, no concern about anything, but to do the will of Him that sent Him and to give Himself as the true passover Lamb.

How beautiful the scene in Simon's house! Mary was fully devoted to her Lord. We first see her at His feet listening to His words. "One thing is needful, and Mary hath chosen that good part." She acknowledged Him in His office as Prophet. In John xi we see her again at His feet. There she is weeping on account of the death of Lazarus; a little while later He weeps with her. She knew Him as the sympathizing One, as He is now our Priest. And here she anoints Him, and does it for His burying. In faith she realizes the near approach of that death, of which He had spoken. She believed He, the Lamb of God, would soon die; she understood more of that death than all the other disciples. Perhaps when she sat at His feet He had spoken to her about His coming death and burial and resurrection. But some readers of the Bible have a difficulty. Here in our Gospel she anoints His head, but in the Gospel of John she is at His feet and anoints them, wiping His feet with her hair. Critics and infidels who deny the inspiration of the Bible have pointed this out as one of the glaring contradictions, while others have thought of two different occasions when the anointing took place. There is, however, no difficulty here at all. She anointed both His feet and His head. The Holy Spirit reports the anointing of the head of the Lord in Matthew, because this is in harmony with the object of the Gospel. He is the King, and while He is the rejected King, her faith no doubt looked beyond death and burial. In John the Holy Spirit gives the anointing of the feet and leaves out the anointing of the head, because the King is the Son of God; as such He is described in the Gospel of John, and that attitude of Mary before His feet anointing them is in fullest harmony with the fourth Gospel.

And after the Passover and the institution of that blessed and most precious memorial feast which we call "the Lord's Supper" we see Him in the garden. Who can fathom the deep anguish of His soul, who can understand the agony of those midnight hours? Worship is demanded here. He looked on toward the Cross, where He who knew no sin was now to be made sin. From this His holy soul shrank. But it had to be. He knew all the depths into which He had to plunge.

Then after His willing arrest we see Him first before Caiaphas and the elders. Before that council He had to appear first. But all their schemes failed. They found nothing in Him. The question of the High priest concerning His Sonship is answered by the King. The blessed One could not be condemned by false witnesses. His own confession of who He is could alone bring about His unjust condemnation. The King is condemned.

"What think ye?" And they answering said, "He is liable of the penalty of death?" (verse 66). What a justice! Satanic, fiendish injustice rather. But there He stands, the silent Lamb of God. What a picture! Oh, that we might behold Him once more as He stood before this company of His enemies. What calmness! "Majestic in His silence, majestic in His speech; unmoved by threats to speak, unmoved by threats when He had spoken."

And how affecting the scene which follows. His confession set the powers of darkness loose and the undefending Christ, the Son of God, is tasting a little of the cup He had to drink. Oh, to think of it! They spit in His face! That face, which in loving tenderness had gazed with compassion upon the multitudes, yea, that face, the image of the invisible God, was covered with the vile spittle of men. How He must have suffered! They buffeted Him, struck Him with the palms of their hands, mocked Him. And not a word, not a murmur came from His blessed lips. "When reviled, He reviled not again, when suffering, He threatened not." And reader! it was all for such vile sinners as we are! He loved us and gave Himself for us. What a Saviour!

CHAPTER XXVII.

1. Delivered unto Pilate. 1–2.
2. The Suicide of Judas. 3–10.
3. Before Pilate. 11–14.
4. The Awful Choice. 15–26.
5. Crowned with Thorns and Crucified. 27–44.
6. The Death of the King. 45–50.
7. The Rent Veil and the Earthquake. 51–56.
8. The Burial. 57–66.

In this chapter we follow Him to the cross. What a journey it was! He, who had lived that wonderful life, preached the Kingdom, had healed the sick, cast out the demons, raised the dead, He, who is announced in the beginning of this Gospel to be Immanuel, God manifested in flesh, the Beloved of the Father is in the hands of men, led away to the cross. What sufferings were His! Who is able to follow the depths of that shame, which He despised, the cross which He endured!

Judas filled with remorse ends his life by hanging himself.

What is written in Acts i:18 is not a discrepancy. The rope must have broken and the terrible thing described in Acts must have happened. Judas was a disciple, yet not born again. He never called the King "Lord."

The silver pieces he cast into the temple and the priests, as covetous as Judas, stoop down to pick them up. That which follows is only reported in this Gospel, in the other Gospel records no mention is made of the fate of Judas. It is put only in the Gospel of Matthew on account of its dispensational bearing. The priests judge very religiously that it is not lawful to put the money into the *Corban*, the treasury of the temple. They decide to buy with the pieces of silver, the field of the potter for a burying ground for strangers. This was in partial fulfillment of what was spoken by Jeremias. The full prophecy is found in Zechariah, but the Spirit calls here attention to what is also spoken by Jeremias. We read in that book (chapters xvii and xix) of a potter's field, which was situated on the side of the valley of Hinnom. That valley is also called "Tophet," a fearful type with its awful memories of Gehenna.

And then we see the Lord in fulfilment of His own words, delivered into the hands of the Gentiles. Then the people have their choice between Him, their King and Barabbas (son of the father), the child of the devil.

And now he puts the important question: "Which of the two will ye that I release unto you?" It does not take long to bring forth the answer. Barabbas is the people's choice. Barabbas! Barabbas! Not a voice was heard for the Lord. Where were now the multitudes who had followed Him? Where they who had cried "Hosanna"? But Pilate convinced of the awful choice, which had been made, against the authority which he had, makes another attempt: "What then shall I do with Jesus, who is called Christ?" What a solemn question it was; and it is so still. The question was answered there and it must also be answered by every person to whom the Lord Jesus Christ is offered. He must either be accepted as Saviour and Lord or rejected. The choice decides the eternal destiny; those who accept Him and own Him as their Saviour are saved and all who reject Him as Son of God and Saviour are lost. Pilate's second question is answered by a great cry, that fearful cry: "Let Him be crucified." Again Pilate asks: "What evil then has He done?" But his voice is drowned in a greater demand: "Let Him be crucified." Pilate was fully convinced of the innocence of the silent victim before him, but miserable coward he was, he would not act. When he saw he availed nothing and a great tumult was rising, he took water, washed his hands before the crowd and said: "I am guiltless of the blood of this righteous one, see ye to it." And what did they answer to the governor's action and "see ye to it" his word to them? And all the people answering said, "His blood be on us and our children. Then he released unto them Barabbas; but Jesus, having scourged Him, he delivered up that He might be crucified."

Terrible answer it was. Barabbas is the nation's choice and the blood of the Holy One is wished by them upon their heads and the heads of their children. Has that awful wish been granted? Let the history of the Jews answer down to the present day, how His blood came upon them and their children; the end is not yet. Barabbas has been their choice and there is still that false Christ to come, who comes in his own name and whom they will receive. Crowned with thorns, mocked, spit upon and dishonored the King is led away to Golgotha. And they crucified Him.

It may be well to group together the different events of the cross. 1. They brought Him to Golgotha (Matt. xxvii:33; Mark xv:22; Luke xxiii:33; John xix:17). 2. The refusal of the vinegar and the gall (Matt. xxvii:34; Mark xv:23). 3. Crucified between the two thieves (Matt. xxvii:35–38; Mark xv:24–28; Luke xxiii:33–38; John xix:18–24). 4. The first word from the cross, "Father, forgive," (Luke xxiii:24). 5. The soldiers part His garments (Matt. xxvii:35; Mark xv:24; Luke xxiii:34; John xix:23). 6. The Jews mock their King (Matt. xxvii:39–44; Mark xv:29–32; Luke xxiii:35–38). 7. The thieves rail on Him, but one repents and believes (Matt. xxvii:44; Mark xv:32; Luke xxiii:39–43). 8. The second word from the cross, "Today shalt thou be with me," etc. (Luke xxiii:43). 9. The third word "Woman, behold thy son" (John xix:26, 27). 10. The darkness (Matt. xxvii:45; Mark xv:33; Luke xxiii:44). 11. The fourth word "My God, my God, why hast Thou forsaken me?" (Matt. xxvii:46, 47; Mark xv:34–36). 12. The fifth word "I thirst" (John xix:28). 13. The sixth word, "It is finished." 14. The seventh word "Father into Thy hands I commend my Spirit" and the dismissal of His Spirit (Matt. xxvii:50; Mark xv:37; Luke xxiii:46; John xix:30). The rent veil was the first testimony from God's side that the work of the sinbearer is done, that the great work is finished and the new and living way into the Holiest is made by the blood of the Lamb of God (Heb. x:19–20). His resurrection is the second testimony. But the resurrection mentioned in verse 52 did not take place immediately upon His death on the cross, but those graves were opened "after His resurrection" (verse 53).

And He was buried. Isaiah liii:9 was fulfilled. The literal translation reads: "And men appointed His grave with the wicked, but He was with the rich in His death." The enemy, who could not frustrate His death, is at work to make all secure, but instead he makes his own defeat a perfect defeat. They remembered His promise of resurrection. The disciples had forgotten that promise completely. The stone is sealed, the guard is placed there to make fraud and illusion impossible. Little did they realize that they were even then working to make the glorious resurrection of the Son of God a fact, which is secure beyond all controversy.

14. *His Resurrection and the Great Commission.*

CHAPTER XXVIII.

1. His Resurrection. 1–10.
2. The Lying Report of the Jews. 11–15.
3. The Great Commission. 16–20.

We have reached the last portion of our Gospel. The end is brief and very abrupt. The account of the resurrection of the Lord as given by Matthew is the briefest of all the Gospels. Only a few of the facts are mentioned. Then the characteristic feature of this last chapter is that no mention is made of the ascension of the Lord. However, the fact of His ascension is implied in numerous places in this Gospel. In the Gospel of Mark we find the statement that He was taken up into heaven and sat at the right hand of God. In Luke we read that He was "carried into heaven," but in Matthew no such statement is made. The Gospel ends as if He were still on the earth, all power in heaven and on earth in His hands and with His own to the end of the age. All this is in perfect harmony with the scope of this Gospel.

The resurrection account needs no further comment. In our annotations on the Gospel of Luke the reader will find a brief review of the resurrection as reported by the synoptics.

Three classes are seen in connection with the resurrection of the Lord in Matthew. The soldiers represent unbelieving Gentiles, the women, believers and then the Jews. The soldiers are terror-stricken. They were lying around on the ground as if they were dead. It is the effect upon the natural man of God's power made known. On what greater scale this will be repeated when He comes again in resurrection Glory, as King of kings and Lord of lords.

Then the resurrection of Him who was dead, that glorious and unassailable fact, was officially reported to the chief priests. The Sanhedrim is once more assembled. Lying, fraud of the most ridiculous nature is resorted to, to deny what had taken place.

The whole story they invented is, of course, incredible. It is far easier to believe He arose from the dead than to believe what the Jews invented about His resurrection. If His disciples could have stolen the body, if it had been possible, they surely would not have done it. But if they had a desire to steal the body, they could not have done so, for with the guard placed at the tomb, it was an impossibility. The disciples had forgotten all about the resurrection promise; they were a scattered, poor and timid lot of people. But even if they had been anxious to steal the body, how could they have done it? Here was the company of armed men. They were experienced guards and careful watchers, trained in that profession. Then there was the sealed, heavy stone. How could they have rolled away the stone and carried away the body without being detected? Impossible. But the utterly ridiculous side of the whole lie came out with the report which these soldiers were to circulate, being well paid for it by the Sanhedrim. The disciples came and stole the body, while they were sleeping! In the first place, it is incredible that all these men had fallen asleep at the same time. All were fast asleep, so fast asleep that the commotion of rolling away the stone and the carrying away of a dead one did not disturb them. Furthermore, sleeping at a post meant death for the Roman soldier. One might have nodded and thus risked his life, but that all slept is an impossibility. But the report is foolish; they were asleep, and while they were asleep they witnessed how the disciples stole the body of Jesus. How ridiculous! The whole proceedings were out and out fraud and falsehood. And this was indeed the only statement they could possibly bring against the resurrection of the Lord Jesus Christ.

Then follows the great commission.

This is the *Kingdom* commission. In Luke xxiv we have the proper Christian commission. A time is coming when this great commission here will be carried out by a remnant of Jewish disciples, who are represented by the eleven. It is the same remnant as in Matthew xxiv.

All power is His; all power in heaven and on earth. Soon

the day will come when indeed He will have all things put under His feet. And the last word, "And behold, I am with you all the days until the completion of the age." Precious promise of faith! He will never leave nor forsake, and He who is with us is the "I am," the mighty Jehovah, the Immanuel, having all power in heaven and on earth.

The Gospel of Matthew begins with Immanuel, "God with us," it ends with Immanuel. With Him, our Saviour and Lord, we shall be in all eternity. Forever with the Lord. With all our hearts we praise God for such a Saviour, for such a Lord, for such a Gospel and for such a future with HIMSELF, the King of kings and Lord of lords.

THE GOSPEL OF MARK

The Gospel of Mark.

The Gospel of Mark is the briefest of the four Gospels. The traditional view, which holds that the Apostle Peter dictated this record into the pen of Mark, so that he was only an amanuensis, has been proven erroneous. Equally incorrect are other theories, that the Gospel of Mark was written first and served Matthew and Luke in giving their account, copying from it and making additions, or, the hypothesis that there was an original record, a common source, which the Evangelists used. All these opinions are mostly the inventions of men who disbelieve the inspiration of the chosen instruments of God in giving a fourfold picture of His blessed Son on earth. An unswerving faith in the inspiration of the four Evangelists solves all the supposed difficulties and discrepancies of which we hear so much in our days. Inspiration makes error impossible.

Mark was not an Apostle. Two Apostles were chosen to write Gospel records, Matthew and John. The other two, Mark and Luke, did not belong to the twelve. Mark's and John's Gospels give us the chronological account, while Matthew and Luke were led under the guidance of the Holy Spirit not to pen the events chronologically, but to arrange them in such a way as to bring out the distinctive features of their respective Gospels.

While Matthew describes the Lord Jesus Christ as the King, Luke as the Son of Man in His perfection, John as the true God and the eternal life, Mark was chosen to write the account of our Lord as the obedient Servant. It was announced by the Prophets that He would appear as a servant. Isaiah beheld Him as the Servant of God. Through Zechariah the Spirit of God announced, "Behold, I will bring forth my Servant, the

Branch" (Zech. iii:8). And after He had been on earth in the form of a servant, the Holy Spirit in the Epistle to the Philippians tells us again that He who ever existed in the form of God "made Himself of no reputation, and took upon Him the form of a servant, and was made in the likeness of men" (Phil. ii:7). Mark, himself a servant, was graciously called to give a pen picture of this blessed Servant and to record His toil, His service of love and patience, as well as His mighty works. All which does not stand in definite relation to our Lord, as the Servant is carefully omitted, and many other things omitted by the other Evangelists are added, to describe the manner and perfection of the Servant's work.

The purpose of the Gospel of Mark must never be lost sight of in studying it. Well may we call it the neglected Gospel, for it is the least studied. God gave it that we His redeemed people might as His servants have a pattern in our service. One thing, however, is absolutely necessary in the intelligent and spiritual study of Mark and that is a constant comparison with the Gospel of Matthew. Such a comparison will bring out the beauties of the record given by Mark and shows the divine power which guided infallibly these men of God.

We have therefore given in the analysis the parallel passages from the Gospel of Matthew and from the Gospel of Luke. The analysis contains many hints and annotations, which will help in a closer study. At the close of the analyzed Gospel the reader will find several articles on the personality of Mark, the characteristic features of this Gospel and other information, which, we hope, will prove of help to all students of this part of God's Holy Word.

THE ANALYSIS OF THE GOSPEL OF MARK.

"For even the Son of Man came not to be ministered unto, but to minister, and to give His life a ransom for many." Chapter X:45.

Part I. The Servant; who He is and how He came. Chapter I:1-13.

Part II. The Servant's work; not to be ministered unto, but to minister. Chapter I.14—X:52.

Part III. The Servant in Jerusalem. Presented as King and rejected. Chapter XI-XIII.

Part IV. Giving His Life a ransom for many. Chapter XIV—XV:47.

Part V. The Servant Highly exalted. Risen and Ascended; His commission to His servants and working with them. Chapter XVI.

PART I. THE SERVANT; WHO HE IS AND HOW HE CAME.

Chapter I:1-13.

1. The Servant, the Son of God. Verse 1.

2. His coming promised and announced. Verses 2-8. Matthew III:1-11; Luke III:1-18; John I:19-30.

3. The Servant comes forth. Verses 9-11. Matthew III:13-17; Luke III:21-22; John I:31-34.

4. The Servant in the wilderness. Verses 12-13.... Matthew IV: 1-11; Luke IV:1-13.

1. The Servant, the Son of God. Verse 1. No other gospel begins in this way. The Deity of our Lord is first of all emphasized. Nothing is said about the virgin birth, nor is a genealogy given. The miraculous birth is most fully brought out in Luke's Gospel, the Gospel of our Lord's humanity. No genealogy appears in Mark; a servant does not need such. Nor do we find Bethlehem mentioned, or the event, which is characteristic to the Gospel of Matthew, the visit of the wise men, seeking the newborn King of the Jews. All these and other matters are omitted because they do not fall within the scope and purpose of the Gospel of Mark. The Servant is the Son of God. This great truth is fully attested by His obedience in always doing the will of Him that sent Him and by His mighty miracles which accompanied His loving service. If He were not the Son of God He could not have rendered the perfect service. Sonship and Service always go together. Only a Son of God can be a servant of God. Grace makes us, if we believe on the Lord Jesus Christ, sons of God. True service for God is the result of the enjoyment of our sonplace in Christ Jesus. A deeper realization and enjoyment of our sonship will be followed by a more obedient and constant service. The Gospel of John gives the fullest witness that Jesus is the Christ, the Son of God (John xx:31). The Gospel of Mark shows that He is the Son of God by His wonderful character as the Servant.

2. **His Coming promised and announced. Verses 2-8.** Prophets promised His Coming (Malachi iii:1). The passage proves Him to be Jehovah. In Malachi we read that Jehovah says "he shall prepare the way before Me." The Spirit of God changes the "Me" to "Thy Face." The servant is none other than Jehovah, who spoke to the Prophets. Isaiah xl:3 is likewise quoted. Here too we find the same testimony that Jesus the Servant is Jehovah. "Prepare ye the way of Jehovah."

The account of the ministry of John the Baptist is the briefest in the Gospel of Mark. A few sentences only describe his testimony in the wilderness and his person. All the land of Judea and they of Jerusalem went out to him. The baptism of John in the river of Jordan was the outward sign of repentance. They confessed their sins. A comparison with the record of the Baptist's ministry in Matthew, Luke and John is very instructive. In Mark all the preaching of John concerning the state of the nation is omitted, for the Holy Spirit describes in Mark John's ministry only as a necessary preliminary to introduce the Servant and His ministry. Of the baptism which Christ is to bring Mark mentions "the Holy Spirit;" "and with fire" is left out. The fire baptism is His judgment work stated in Matthew and Luke. Christ as the humble Servant does not execute judgment, but the coming King (Matthew) and the Son of Man coming again (Luke) will judge and burn the chaff with unquenchable fire.

3. **The Servant comes forth. Verses 9-11.** The Servant appears to begin His service. From Nazareth of Galilee He came forth. There too during the hidden years He had served. The Servant was absolutely sinless and yet He was baptized in

Jordan. He showed His perfect willingness to take, in obedience to the Father's will, the sinner's place in death. In verse 19 the word "straightway" is found for the first in Mark. It is the characteristic word of this Gospel describing the promptness of His service. The anointing by the reception of the Spirit follows. In Matthew we read "heaven was opened unto Him." In Luke, "heaven was opened." In Mark "He saw the heavens opened." Encouraging sight for Him, who had taken the lowest place! All God's servants need the vision of the opened heavens. The Father's voice proclaimed Him then as His beloved Son.

4. The Servant in the Wilderness. Verses 12-13. Upon this He was driven immediately into the wilderness to be tempted of Satan. His fitness to be the Servant to minister and give His life for a ransom was fully proven in His victorious conflict. The different temptations are not reported by Mark; they belong to the Gospels of Matthew and Luke, where we find them. But here we have a statement which is peculiar to Mark. "And was with the wild beasts." It tells of his deep humiliation. Moses and Elijah were in the wilderness being prepared for service. David also had been alone in the solitary places. None, however, was in the place which He took, whose eternal abode was the Father's bosom. The wilderness and the wild beasts are the witnesses of a marred creation; the mighty Creator had come in the form of the creature to meet and overcome under such conditions the fallen being, Satan. Some have taught that He was in danger of being attacked by the wild beasts. This was impossible (Psalm xci:9-13).

PART II. THE SERVANT'S WORK; NOT TO BE MINISTERED UNTO, BUT TO MINISTER.

Chapter 1:14—X:52.

Chapter I:14-45.

The Ministry in Gallilee after John's Imprisonment.

1. The Servant in Galilee preaching the Gospel of the Kingdom. Verses 14-15. Matthew IV:12-17; Luke IV:14-15.
2. The Calling of fellow servants. Verses 16-20. Matthew IV: 18-22; Luke V:1-11.
3. The Servant in Capernaum. Verses 21-28; Luke IV: 31-37.
4. Peter's Mother-in-law raised up. Verses 29-31. Matthew VIII:14-15; Luke IV:38-39.
5. The Servant heals many and casts out demons. Verses 32-34. Luke IV:31-37; Matthew VIII:16-18; Luke IV:40-41.
6. The Servant in prayer. Verse 35.
7. The Interruption and the renewed service. Verses 36-39. Luke IV:42-44.
8. The Leper healed. Verses 40-45. Matthew VIII:1-4; Luke V:12-16.

1. The Servant in Galilee preaching the Gospel of the Kingdom. Verses 14-15. The Servant begins His blessed service in Galilee immediately after John had been put into prison. And now the Lord takes up the hushed testimony of the forerunner. The heralding of the Kingdom at hand through the presence of Him who came to His own is less prominent in Mark. In the first twelve chapters of the Gospel of Matthew it is one of the leading features. The time, indeed, was fulfilled. While Matthew and Luke report the preaching of the Gospel of the Kingdom with the demand to repent, here in Mark the words are added "and believe the Gospel." This gospel is of course not the Gospel of our salvation. That was not preached till after He had finished the work the Father gave Him to do.

2. The Calling of fellow servants. Verses 16-20. It is a blessed scene which we have before us. The Servant of God calls fellow servants, weak and sinful men, to become fishers of men. These are Simon and Andrew, James and John. They knew Him and had believed in Him. They were his disciples.

But now He calls them into service. "Come ye after Me." The Grace which called them gave them power to forsake earthly things and to come after Him. Boats and nets, their trade as fishermen and even their father, Zebedee, were left behind. Oh! blessed place to serve the Lord Christ and yield obedience to His call. We must own Him as Lord and follow Him in His own path of faith, obedience and humility. To seek others and bring them to Himself is the service to which He still calls. Note the word "straightway" in verses 17 and 20.

3. The Servant in Capernaum. Verses 21-28. The Servant and His fellow servants went to Capernaum. Straightway he entered the synagogue on the Sabbath to teach. His first preaching in Nazareth (Luke iv:16-30) is not reported by Mark. It is after they thrust Him out of the city where He had been brought up, that He went to Capernaum. The blessed Servant knew no discouragement nor self pity. They laid their wicked hands on Him in Nazareth, then He went on to Capernaum and straightway taught there. His doctrine uttered with authority and power astonished all, yet He ever was the meek and lowly One. But the Word had another effect. A man with an unclean spirit interrupted Him in the synagogue. Satan's power was present and the demons were forced to confess "Jesus of Nazareth" as "the Holy One of God." Then the Servant's power is manifested. He rebuked him and commanded the demon to come out of him. The Servant's fame spread abroad throughout all that region.

4. Peter's Mother-in-law raised up. Verses 29-31. This miracle is found in the Gospel of Matthew in a different setting. For the dispensational setting see "The Gospel of Matthew," chapter viii. The place given to this miracle here is equally significant. The first healing of disease in the Gospel of Mark follows the casting out of the demon, the defeat of Satan's power. This order will be followed when He comes again, not as the lowly Servant, but as the mighty King. Then Satan will be bound first and the greatest spiritual and physical blessings will come to this poor world at last. Concerning the healing of Peter's wife's mother, Matthew tells us "He touched her hand;" Luke "He stood over her and rebuked the fever." Mark's testimony by the Holy Spirit is "He took her by the hand and lifted her up." How beautiful! It reveals the tenderness, the loving sympathy of the blessed One. With what gentleness He must have lifted her up so as to avoid another pang of pain in her feverish body; but immediately she was healed. And He is still the same.

5. The Servant heals many and casts out demons. Verses 32-34. Deliverance from demons and divers diseases came to many on that memorable day "when the sun did set." We must view these deliverances and healings in Mark's Gospel not so much as the evidences of His power as the manifestations of the great love and goodness of the Servant. Then He suffered the demons not to speak, because they knew Him. He loved to be unknown and did not want the applause of men nor the witness of the unclean spirits. Of His unostentatiousness we shall find further evidences.

6. The Servant in Prayer. Verse 35. And after such a day of uninterrupted toil, preaching, healing diseases, driving out demons, occupied from early morning till the sun did set, we find Him, rising a great while before day, in a solitary place, praying. He is alone in the presence of the Father. Thus it was fulfilled, "He wakeneth morning by morning, He wakeneth mine ear as the instructed" (Isaiah 1:4). Only Mark gives us this precious information. It tells us that the Servant, though the Son of God, walked in complete dependence on God His Father. Prayer is the expression of such dependence. He had been anointed with the Spirit for His work, heard the Father's loving approval, defeated Satan, cast out demons, healed divers diseases, yet He is still the dependent One. Independence in service for God is a snare, the very spirit of Satan. The perfect Servant had His times for quietness, retirement and prayer, in which He cast Himself anew upon Him, whom to glorify He had come to earth. "And if He thus retired to be with God, Himself the Lord God, before He entered upon the work of the day, can we wonder that we fail so much in outward labor, who fail yet more in this inward intimacy with our Father? Be assured, the secret of holy strength and endurance in service is found there alone."* What child of God does not feel the deep necessity of this and deplores the neglect of this blessed privilege?

7. The Interruption and the renewed service. Verses 36-39. But He is followed by his disciples and is interrupted even in prayer. No rebuke comes from His lips. Willing He responds to the new demands. For that He came "not to be ministered unto, but to minister."

8. The Leper healed. Verses 40-45. Leprosy, that vile and loathsome disease, is a type of sin. Like sin it is incurable and only Jehovah could cure leprosy. When Jehovah had healed the disease the priest had to pronounce the leper

*W. Kelly. "Gospel of Mark."

clean. This leper recognized in the humble Servant the mighty Jehovah. He kneeled in His presence and expressed his faith in His power and implored Him to make him clean. Here again Mark tells us something of our blessed Lord, which we find neither in Matthew or Luke's account. He was moved with compassion. Thus the Spirit of God in some brief additions portrays the Servant in His loving service. The leper is healed. The Servant is Jehovah and both His love and His power are revealed. He charged him to say nothing to any man. In this the Servant once more manifests His humility, that He served in an unostentatious way. He did not want honor from man. His Father knew all His service; that was enough for Him. Yet the enemy through the cleansed leper attempted the popularity of the Servant. He sought the desert places once more to hide Himself. May we serve after this great pattern Servant.

Chapter II.

1. The Servant again in Capernaum. The healing of the Paralytic. Verses 1-12. Matthew IX:1-8; Luke V:17-26.

2. Levi called. With the Publicans and Sinners. Verses 13-17. Matthew IX:9-13; Luke V:27-32.

3. The Question concerning Fasting. Verses 18-22. Matthew IX:14-15; Luke V:33-39.

4. The Question concerning the Sabbath. Verses 23-28. Matthew XII:1-8; Luke VI:1-5.

1. The Servant again in Capernaum. The healing of the Paralytic. Verses 1-12. His second visit to Capernaum brought out a large multitude. We see Him occupied with preaching the Word. He always preached the Word first, to make known the Truth; for this He had come (i:38). Then in the next place He confirmed His Word by His mighty works. The paralytic tells of man's impotence; leprosy is the type of sin as a defiling, incurable disease, paralysis shows man's helpless condition. The paralytic is likewise the picture of Israel. The helpless paralytic is brought into the presence of the Lord. Mark alone tells us that four carried him and describes fully the obstacles in the way. They had faith in His love and in His power. How it must have refreshed His heart! As His servants we can still bring sinners into His presence and honor Him by our confidence. "Son, thy sins be forgiven thee." With this blessed Word He touches the root of all evil. To deal with it He had come. The proof that He is Jehovah and has power to forgive sins is the healing of the paralytic. Love and Power are here blessedly manifested. Love in forgiveness, power in healing and restoration. It is ever repeated in the case of every believing sinner. The two great elements of the Gospel are here. In some future day converted Israel will know this (Ps. ciii:1-3).

2. Levi called. With the Publicans and Sinners. Verses 13-17. Levi, the son of Alphaeus, is Matthew, the writer of the first Gospel. He was a tax gatherer. As such he was despised by the nation Israel. Not alone were they considered thieves, but they were the miserable hirelings of the Romans and as such hated as Apostates. What Grace to call such an one to the office of an Apostle! And the feast which followed reveals both the loving condescension of the Servant-Son and His Grace to seek that which is lost. The Servant had taken a low place by associating with the tax-gatherers. In the eyes of the self-righteous Pharisees it was an abomination. God in the person of His Son had come in Love and Grace seeking man.

3. The Question concerning Fasting. Verses 18-22. The disciples of John approach Him next with a question. The Servant's ear was always ready to listen to the perplexities, difficulties and sorrows of others. He was always approachable. Under the Law they fasted. The Grace of God had now appeared and Grace was soon to take the place of the Law. He Himself is the Bridegroom. No need of fasting and mourning while He was with them. His rejection would come and with it their fasting. A significant parable follows. The old garment and the old wineskins are symbolic of Judaism with its laws and ceremonies. The new piece and the new wine stand for the Gospel. Law and Grace must not be mixed. If the Gospel of Grace, the new wine, is put into the old wineskins, Judaism with its laws, the wineskins go to pieces and the new wine is spilled. Much in Christendom to-day is neither Law nor Grace. The Servant announced a change of dispensations.

4. The Question concerning the Sabbath. Verses 23-28. The question concerning the Sabbath is closely connected with the preceding parable. The Sabbath, not a seventh day, but the seventh day, was the day on which God rested in Creation. It was also the sign of His covenant with His people Israel. Plucking ears of corn on the Sabbath to eat them is nowhere forbidden in the Law. It was one of the hard and burdensome man-made traditional injunctions. The Lord cites David's case. Mark adds that David was not alone hungry, but "he had need." David, though anointed King, was despised and in need. His greater Son and His disciples were in the same condition. What is greater with God, the maintenance of an ordinance or the need of Man? Surely the latter. He, the humble Servant, was none other than the Lord of the Sabbath. He had rested in His Creation work and instituted the Sabbath for His people. He had become the Son of Man for the need of Man. As the Lord of the Sabbath He speaks, "The Sabbath was made for man and not man for the Sabbath." On the ground of Grace the Sabbath no longer exists. We have the Lord day, the first day of the week to enjoy communion with our risen and glorified Lord, resting from our daily occupation. Blessed privilege to adore Him on that day and to follow His own example of doing good.

Chapter III.

1. In the synagogue. The man with the withered hand healed. Verses 1-6. Matthew XII:9-14) Luke VI:6-11.

2. The Withdrawal of the Servant. Many healed. Verses 7-12. Matthew XII:15-21: Luke VI:17-19.

3. On the Mountain calling the Twelve. Verses 13-19. Matthew X:1-4: Luke VI:12-16.

4. The interrupted meal. Verse 20.

5. The Servant charged with madness. Verse 21.

6. The Blasphemy of the Scribes; His Warning. Verses 22-30. Matthew XII:22-32; Luke XI:14-23.

7. Old relationship disowned and a new relationship announced. Verses 31-35. Matthew XIII:46-50; Luke VIII:19-21.

1. In the Synagogue. The Man with the withered hand healed. Verses 1-6. This incident stands in closest relation to the preceding chapter. In their blindness they watched Him, if He would heal on the Sabbath. "Is it lawful to do good on the Sabbath day, or to do evil; to save life or to kill?" He answered the question by healing the sufferer. Note the addition by Mark, which is not found elsewhere. "When He had looked round about them with anger, being grieved for the hardness of their hearts." It was a righteous wrath when

He saw them in their wicked and wilful hardness. His service was rendered in the deepest emotions of His holy soul. He did good, but Pharisees and Herodians were ready to destroy Him.

2. The withdrawal of the Servant. Many healed. Verses 7-12. The sudden departure of the Lord is not without meaning. Not alone did He withdraw Himself from the hatred of the Pharisees and Herodians to continue His ministry of love and power elsewhere, but His withdrawal indicates that the nation Israel was to be set aside dispensationally. He withdrew Himself to the sea. The sea is symbolical of the Gentile nations. Again they crowd about Him—a great multitude from the border land of the Gentiles (Tyre and Sidon). Satan's power was likewise manifested. Unclean spirits, when they saw Him, fell down before Him. These were demon possessed persons. They had to own and confess the Glory of the Servant. But He did not want their witness and forbade them to make Him known.

3. On the Mountain calling the Twelve. Verses 13-15. In Matthew we find all these events and actions of our Lord in a different setting. In vain do we look in our Gospel for the Sermon on the Mount. It is not reported and only given in full in the Gospel of Matthew. The Sermon on the Mount is the proclamation of the King concerning His Kingdom. Mark, describing Him as the ministering One, had to omit the utterances of the King. If we look for a place in Mark where the Sermon on the Mount belongs chronologically, it is at this point. For the peculiar arrangement of the events in the Gospel of Matthew see "Exposition of Matthew." He ordained the twelve to be with Him and endowed with supernatural power to be sent forth by Him. In Luke we read He prayed all night. The calling of the Twelve was for the extension of His loving ministry. Notice also the giving of names. "Boanerges" for the sons of Zebedee is only found here.

4. The interrupted Meal. Verse 20. This is likewise mentioned by Mark exclusively (see chapter vi:31). It shows that the Servant was ever ready to minister, forgetting his own physical need.

5. The Servant charged with madness. Verse 21. This is also a characteristic statement in Mark's Gospel. It shows that His own relations were ashamed of Him. They looked upon Him as being out of His mind. Thus His perfect service of love, the untiring labor, never ceasing toil, was judged by them.

6. The Blasphemy of the Scribes. His Warning. Verses 23-30. Still worse, the Jerusalem Scribes attributed His Divine power to Satan. What an awful accusation! They could not deny the power, but refused to believe that it was the power of God. Under Satanic impulses they called the Holy Spirit a demon power. But the perfect wisdom of the Lord silenced their blasphemy. The power He manifested was a power in the most blessed mercy to man, the prey of Satan and his demons. If it were Satan's power then his kingdom is divided. This is the unpardonable sin. No forgiveness for this sin. The words "is in danger of eternal damnation" are better rendered by "is guilty of an eternal sin" (see 1911 Bible).

7. The Old Relationship disowned and a new Relationship announced. Verses 31-35. He refused to see His relations. This refusal indicates the broken relationship with Israel. He no longer recognizes His own, and speaks of a new relationship, founded upon obedience to the will of His Father. It was spoken in anticipation of the present dispensation.

Chapter IV.

1. Teaching by the Seaside. The Parable of the Sower. Verses 1-20. Matthew XIII:1-23; Luke VIII:4-15.

2. The Word to shine forth in testimony. Verses 21-25. Luke VIII:16-18.

3. The Parable of the Growth of the Seed and the Harvest. Verses 26-29.

4. The Parable of the Mustard Seed. Verses 30-34. Matthew XIII:31-35; Luke XIII:18-19.

5. The Storm on the sea and the wind rebuked. Verses 35-41. Matthew VIII:23-27; Luke VIII:22-25.

1. Teaching by the Seaside. The Parable of the Sower. Verses 1-20. In the Gospel of Matthew the scene which closes the preceding chapter is followed by the seven parables (Matthew xiii). In the seven parable discourse the Lord teaches the mystery of the Kingdom of Heaven in its present form. These parables belong into the first Gospel because it is the Gospel of the King. First He proclaimed the principles of the Kingdom (Matt. v-vii); then after His rejection He taught in parables the Kingdom in mystery. Only two of these parables are reported by Mark, the parable of the Sower and of the

Mustard Seed. Both relate to His work of ministry. Another parable, however, is added, which is found nowhere else in the Gospels.

The parable of the Sower is explained by Himself (verses 13-20). He Himself is the great Sower and His fellow servants sow after Him. That which is sown is the Word, even as He came to preach the Word. The devil, the flesh and the world are the hindering forces.

The Parable of the Sower is very simple. It is also noteworthy that Mark adds a sentence, which is not found elsewhere. "Know ye not this parable? And how then will ye be acqainted with all parables?" It is a fundamental parable and a key to other parables. He graciously explains it. What patience He had with His dull fellow servants! He is the Sower. That which is sown is the Word; for this He came. Man cannot bring any fruit. That which He sows can produce fruit. The devil, the flesh and the world are antagonistic to the Word and the causes of failure and unfruitfulness. Those who hear the Word and receive it (believe) yield fruit. But the devil, the flesh and the world are even then active and influence fruitbearing.

2. The Word to shine forth in testimony. Verses 21-25. The Word received in faith gives life and yields fruit. It must also shine forth in testimony. This testimony may be obscured by "the bushel and the bed." The bushel stands for the cares and material things of this present age; the bed for ease and comfort. The cure for occupation with earthly things and for an ease-loving life, the hindrances of a bright shining testimony, is to remember the coming day of manifestation (verse 22). How bright and perfect the example of the Servant. He did not know the bushel nor the bed.

3. The Parable of the Growth of the seed and the Harvest. Verses 26-29. This parable is not recorded by any of the other evangelists. It is closely linked with the words which precede. The day of manifestation is the day of the harvest. The seed sown grows in secret. None knows how. Life is in the Word. The blade, the ear and the full corn, after that the harvest. This is the comforting assurance of the Servant. He sowed the seed and then "slept and rose"—He died and rose from the dead. In view of it He could rejoice in the knowledge that the seed would spring up, increase and bring a harvest. And the sower will put in the sickle. The harvest (the end of the age) is more fully revealed in Matthew xiii. What was His comfort is the comfort of all His true servants who sow the word.

4. The Parable of the Mustard Seed. Verses 30-34. The unexpected growth of the Kingdom during the absence of the Sower is taught in this parable. In Matthew it is linked with the parable of the leaven. The external growth (mustard seed) and the internal corruption (leaven) of Christianity are foretold by Him. Christendom has developed into a powerful world institution and become the lodging place of the fowls of the air. These typify unclean beings (iv:4, 15). The humble Servant never meant the Word to produce such an abnormal growth.

5. The Storm on the Lake and the Wind rebuked. Verses 35-41. The close of the chapter fits in beautifully with the whole. The Servant is seen in chapter iv as the rejected One. He is sowing the seed. He leaves the earth while the seed groweth unto the harvest. The storm on the lake gives the picture of the trials and dangers of His own during this age; but He is in the ship. Note a statement peculiar to Mark. "They took Him even as He was in the ship." The Servant, though Lord of all, had a real human body. Here we have a little picture of His weariness as Servant. Yet what a scene! He had perfect rest in the midst of the storm while His disciples were unbelieving. And then He manifested His power in rebuking the wind.

"Reader, do you think that the power of the Son of God and God's counsels could have failed because of an unexpected storm? Impossible! The disciples were in the same boat with Jesus. Here is a lesson for us. In all the difficulties and dangers of the Christian life, during the whole journey upon the waves, often agitated by the tempestuous sea of life, we are always in the same boat with Jesus, if we are doing His will. It may seem to us that He is sleeping; nevertheless, if He allows the tempest to rise in order to prove our faith, we shall not perish since we are *with Him* in the storm; evidently neither He or we can perish. His security is our own."

Chapter V.

1. The Servant's Power over Satan's work. Verses 1-20. Matthew VIII:28-34; Luke VIII:26-39.

2. The Servant's Power over disease and death. Verses 21-43. Matthew IX:18-26; Luke VIII:40-58.

1. The Servant's Power over Satan's work. Verses 1-20. The Storm on the Lake was the work of Satan, but here the power of the enemy is more prominent. The description of the demoniac differs from Matthew's and Luke's account. His condition is described in fullest detail. He dwelt in the place of the dead. No one could chain him; Satan's dominion and power cannot be conquered by the effort of man. Then there is self-torture and delusion in thinking of Christ as a tormentor. The complete identification of the legion of demons with this poor victim is seen in verse 9. The power of the Lord delivers the man. This miserable world is still in the thraldom of Satan and his legion of demons. Demon possessions have not ceased. And the Lord Jesus Christ is still the same. The demons enter the swine by their own request and when granted the herd of swine rushed to destruction. This is an evidence of the character of the devil. He is the murderer from the beginning. But oh! the blessed change which had come for the demoniac. Delivered completely, in the attitude of rest, no longer rushing to and fro in torment, his nakedness covered and in his right mind. These are still the results of salvation. He would remain in constant fellowship with His deliverer. But the Servant demands service—and He announces directly what the Lord had done for Him. This is still the blessed privilege of all who have been delivered. They asked the Servant, with His loving Power to save to the uttermost, to leave their coast. "When the presence of God is felt, it is more terrible than that of Satan. Man would wish to free himself from the latter, but cannot; but the presence of God is insupportable when it makes itself felt, and indeed man has driven God (in the person of Christ) out of this world." It shows once more the rejection of the Servant.

2. The Servant's Power over disease and death. Verses 21-43. And now He manifests Power over disease and death. The daughter of Jairus was sick unto death. The willing Servant responds at once to the request of her father. While on the way the poor, suffering woman touches the hem of His garment. Verse 26 is found only in Mark. The Lord knows the touch of faith and healing power goes forth from Him. She is healed. The sick daughter had died, but the Lord raised her up. All has its blessed spiritual and dispensational lessons. Man is dead in trespasses and sins but One has power to give life and raise the dead. Faith is beautifully illustrated in the woman who touched Him. Jairus' daughter represents Israel. The Lord will come again into this earthly scene and then will call the remnant of Israel to spiritual and national life. The woman, so hopeless, so helpless, suffering and getting worse, is typical of the Gentiles. The hand of faith can touch Him still. In verse 43 we see once more how the Servant loved secrecy and despised ostentatiousness.

Chapter VI.

1. The Servant rejected in Nazareth. Verses 1-6. Matthew XIII:54-58; Luke IV:16-30.

2. The Servant sends forth the Twelve. Verses 7-13. Matthew X:5-15; Luke IX:1-6.

3. King Herod troubled. Verses 14-16. Matthew XIV:1-2; Luke IX:7-9.

4. The Martyrdom of John. Verses 17-29. Matthew XIV:3-12.

5. The Servant's withdrawal for Rest. Verses 30-31. Luke IX:10-11.

6. The feeding of the Five Thousand. Verses 32-44. Matthew XIV:13-21; Luke IX:12-17; John VI:1-13.

7. The Servant alone and His Return walking on the waters. Verses 45-52. Matthew XIV:22-32; John VI:15-21.

8. New Manifestations of His love and Power. Verses 53-56. Matthew XIV:34-36.

1. The Servant rejected at Nazareth. Verses 1-6. Once more we find Him in Nazareth. The first thing is teaching, and though they were astonished at His wisdom and power, they did not own Him as the Lord, but called Him the Carpenter and were offended in Him. Such is the heart of man. Unbelief tied His hands, yet in Love He healed a few and marvelled because of their unbelief. But did He abandon them? Oh! the infinite patience and seeking Grace of this perfect Servant! "He went round about the villages teaching," if perchance faith might yet respond to His willingness and power to heal.

2. The Servant sends forth the Twelve. Verses 7-13. Now He sends His Apostles forth and endows them with power.

They are to depend in their ministry upon Himself. Thus they were to be His followers for He was ever dependent on God. Blessed principles are here which still hold good, though the sending forth had a special meaning for Israel (see Matthew x:5-15).

3. King Herod troubled. Verses 14-16. It is the story of a troubled conscience and fear produces the thought that it is John the Baptist risen from the dead.

4. The Martyrdom of John. Verses 17-29. The faithful herald of the Servant suffered martyrdom. In the whole sickening scene of lust and bloodshed the prince of this world, the god of this age is manifested in this awful rule and power. It is a picture of the present age in opposition to God. The lust of the flesh, the lust of the eyes and the pride of life hold sway. And this evil age is not gradually improved and getting better. It is not abandoning its lusts and pride, its hatred of God and His Christ. As long as Satan is the ruler the age must be evil. In such a scene the Holy One came to minister and to give His life.

5. The Servant's withdrawal for Rest. Verses 30-31. We have noticed different withdrawals of the Lord. He withdrew for prayer and to the sea and now when the Apostles gathered unto Him, the One to whom the fellow servants must ever gather, to give a report of what they had done and taught, He withdrew with them into a desert place. The Lord does not say anything about their success (verse 14). There was danger of the self-exaltation of the messengers. The silence of the Lord puts a check upon it. It was His own power, which in goodness and mercy had done all this. Instead we hear Him say, "Come ye yourselves apart into a desert place and rest awhile." This again is found nowhere but in Mark. How needful for all servants it is to heed this loving word. How easily in constant service a servant can be lifted up and attribute something to himself. True service only is possible by being occupied with the Lord. And therefore we must ever learn to seek the presence of God. He remembered the need of His messengers and the time of rest with Him gave them new strength.

6. The Feeding of the Five Thousand. Verses 32-44. Here we have the compassion of the Servant in remembering the physical need of the people. But before He supplied that need, "He began to teach them many things." The Word stands always first. He came to serve. The giving of the Word followed by the works of goodness and power is the order maintained in His service. Note the contrast between Him and the request of the disciples. How untiring, loving, gracious He was in all His service for man. May we learn of Him. A comparison of the account of this miracle in the four Gospels will teach us many lessons. He feeds the poor with bread (Ps. cxxxii:15) as the true Shepherd of His people. He is the miraculous giver, but He uses His disciples in dispensing His blessing. His power for the good of others is at the believer's disposal. And the little put into His hands was not only sufficient for all but more was left over than they had given to Him. And still He delights to take the little things and manifest through them His power, if we but trust Him.

7. The Servant alone and His Return walking on the Waters. Verses 45-52. All is full of blessed meaning. He is once more alone in the mountain to pray. His disciples are alone on the stormy sea. He is absent now and has sent the people (Israel) away. He is in the presence of God as our intercessor. The stormy sea with the contrary wind is a type of this present age. Trouble and perplexity is the lot of His disciples during His absence. About the fourth watch of the night He came unto them walking upon the sea. Mark does not mention Peter going forth to meet Him. They see Him coming, but do not recognize Him, believing Him a spirit. His loving voice soon assures them, "Be of good cheer; it is I, be not afraid." Thus He will return across the stormy sea to meet and deliver His own. Blessed are we if we ever behold Him as the mighty One, who is above all circumstances and if we hear His words of comfort. How He cares for us. And when He comes the wind will cease.

8. New Manifestations of His Love and Power. Verses 53-56. What a scene of toil! What ministry in doing good! Dispensationally it stands for the blessed time, yet in store for this world, when He comes again. Then He who was the Son of Man in humiliation will, as Son of Man, with power and glory, be known to all. Then the earth will be blessed as Gennesaret was.

Chapter VII.

1. The Opposition of the Pharisees. Verses 1-23. Matthew XV:1-20.

2. Grace shown to the Syrophenician Woman. Verses 24-30. Matthew XV:21-28.

3. The healing of the deaf man. Verses 31-37. Matthew XV:29-31.

1. The Opposition of the Pharisees. Verses 1-23. This paragraph is of much importance. The scope of the analysis forbids a full annotation, but we refer the reader to the exposition of Matthew, chapter xv:1-20, the parallel passage. The Servant in His divine wisdom uncovers the hypocrisy which lies underneath the traditions of the elders. He shows that the Pharisees had rejected the commandment of God for the sake of men-made inventions and traditions. Their ritualistic service founded upon tradition was dishonoring to God and His Word. Such ritualism springing from tradition must always be. He condemns religiousness, which knows nothing of heart obedience and holiness of life. And this outward, human, man-made religion, which boasts of being something and doing something, He condemns. Then He shows that man's defilement does not consist in what enters into him, but the things which come out of him. He shows what man is within (verses 21-23). No, mere religiousness cannot take away this defilement. Thus He uncovers the hypocrisy of an outward religion and the true state of the heart of man. The product of the natural heart of man, though it may delight in religious observances, is nothing but vileness.

2. Grace shown to the Syrophenician Woman. Verses 24-30. While the omniscient Lord in the form of the Servant showed what the heart of man is, He now also uncovers His own heart in showing Grace to one, who belonged to the Gentiles. In the borders of Tyre and Sidon the blessed Servant sought quietness and entered a house; but He could not be hid. Note again that Mark mentions this exclusively, because it brings out His character as Servant. He also informs us that she was a Gentile, a Syrophenician, belonging to the enemies of God's people, Israel. But Mark leaves out Matthew's statement, that she appealed to Him as "Son of David." Matthew's Gospel is the proper place for that. What evidences all along we find of the inspiration of these records. She had no claim on His Mercy and Power, for she was under the curse. Her daughter had a demon. And though she had no claim on His power and no promise, she believed in His love. She takes the place He gave to her and the daughter was restored. What a manifestation of Grace! And how it must have cheered the Servant's heart! In that moment His omniscient eye must have beheld the multitudes of Gentiles, who, after His death on the Cross, as lost sinners with no promise, aliens from the commonwealth of Israel, would believe in His love.

3. The healing of the deaf man. Verses 31-37. A comparison with Matthew shows that the account here is peculiar to Mark's Gospel. In Matthew xv:29-31 we find the dumb man mentioned among others whom He healed. He represents Israel. Altogether deaf, unable to hear God's voice, which spoke through the One who had come and an impediment in speech. They attempted to speak of God and praise God. And such is man's natural state. And such He came to heal. Israel might have had the ear opened by Him, the Servant, whose ear was always open, and Israel might have the tongue loosed, to praise His Name. He heals the afflicted one. And how the Servant looked to heaven and groaned. What must He have felt!

Chapter VIII.

1. The feeding of the Four Thousand. Verses 1-9. Matthew XV:32-39.

2. The Pharisees ask a sign. Verses 10-13. Matthew XVI: 1-4.

3. The Warning against the leaven of the Pharisees. Verses 14-21. Matthew XVI:5-12.

4. The healing of the blind man. Verses 22-26.

5. Peter's Confession. Verses 27-30. Matthew XVI:12-16; Luke IX:18-20.

6. The first announcement of His coming, rejection and death. Verses 31-33. Matthew XVI:21-23; Luke IX:22.

7. His Disciples to follow in His path. The Coming Glory. Verses 34-38. Matthew XVI:24-28; Luke IX:23-27.

1. The Feeding of the Four Thousand. Verses 1-9. The compassion and loving care of Him who came to minister is once more seen. Again He meets the need of the multitude in a miraculous way. But here we have seven loaves and seven baskets are left over. It points clearly to the manifestation of Divine power, for the number seven occurs twice. He in

His great goodness and great power is sufficient to meet all human need. The miracle foreshadows the great and perfect blessings of the coming Kingdom age.

2. The Pharisees ask a sign. Verses 10-13. Though the religious leaders had seen so many signs and display of Divine goodness and power they asked a sign from heaven. Unbelief ever looks for something new and is never satisfied. Their request may be looked upon as a temptation. He could have shown a sign from heaven, but with it He would have left the humble path of the Servant. "He sighed deeply," which is another phrase peculiar to Mark's account, showing His deep emotion. He refused the sign. The next sign will be "the sign of the Son of Man in heaven" at the time of His glorious return. Then a believing remnant of His people will welcome Him.

3. The Warning against the leaven. Verses 14-21. He warns against the leaven of the Pharisees and Herodians. It is the only time the word leaven is found in Mark. It means, as elsewhere in the Word of God, evil. The leaven of the Pharisees is hypocrisy, insincerity of an unbelieving heart in opposition to God. The expression of it is self-righteousness in pride. The leaven of the Herodians is worldliness. He warns His disciples to beware of it for the leaven of the Pharisees was in them too. They did not fully see His Glory, though they believed in Him as the promised Messiah. Their state and the Lord's Power and patience towards them is beautifully brought out in the healing of the blind man.

4. The Healing of the blind man. Verses 22-26. This healing at Bethsaida is only recorded by Mark. It reveals the tender, patient and successful method of the Servant in His ministry. The disciples case is illustrated. They saw "men as if they were trees." Their sight was imperfect. But He did not leave them in that condition. Their clear sight came, when the promise of the Father, the Holy Spirit, was given to them. But many other lessons are found here. See how He led the blind man outside and what pains He took, and though He knew all about the effect of putting His hands upon his eyes, yet He inquired lovingly "if he beheld anything." If we are in His loving hands, separated from Bethsaida ("place of snares," a picture of the world), He will deal with us in the same tenderness and patience. Verse 26 tells us once more how He did not seek honor from man.

5. Peter's Confession. Verses 27-30. How perfectly all is linked together. Though the disciples were imperfect in their sight yet they knew that He was the Christ. That is true faith, which they all possessed, with the exception of Judas, who never addressed Him as Lord. Mark gives the briefest account of Peter's confession. Matthew contains the completest record. The church, as a future thing, is announced in Matthew as well as the Kingdom. The church is not mentioned by Mark. All shows the divine hand which guided the pens of these instruments. What is dispensational is always fully given in the kingly, dispensational Gospel by Matthew and omitted by Mark.

6. The first announcement of His coming rejection and death. Verses 31-33. The Servant now speaks of Himself as the Son of Man, the title both of His rejection and of His exaltation. For the first time He announces His coming death. He knew all from the beginning. He knew it when He went into the dark waters of Jordan. He knew it all along in His ministry of toil. Yet with the vision of His rejection, of His suffering on the cross, constantly before Him, He continued uninterruptedly in His ministry of love. Nothing could swerve Him from it. What perfection and beauty! But He also spoke of His resurrection. He knew the glory that should follow. For the joy set before Him He endured the cross and despised the shame. In our service for God the Cross and the Glory should ever be seen. We, too, must be willing to share His reproach and look forward to the crowning day, the day of His Glory and ours as well. Peter becomes, on account of his blindness, the mouthpiece of Satan, rebuking the Lord. Then "He looked on His disciples," an addition in Mark. What a look it must have been! He rebuked Peter in the words He used when Satan made the same suggestion to avoid the cross.

7. His Disciples to follow in His path. The Coming Glory. Verses 34; IX:1. Well may God's people ponder over these words. Salvation is by Grace. Nothing can save but Grace. Eternal salvation is not dependent on our walk. But the way which leads to Glory is the way of self-denial and suffering. It is His own path. "Is it not true that we naturally like to escape trial, shame and rejection; that we shrink from the suffering which, doing God's will, in such a world as this, must ever entail; that we prefer to have a quiet, respectable path in the earth—in short, the best of both worlds? How easily one may be ensnared into this!" (W. K.) We may not be called upon to lose the life for His sake, but "let him deny himself" we can always do, enabled by His Grace. All the words our ever blessed Lord spoke to His disciples hold good in this dispensation of Grace. He announces His coming Glory. It is His second Coming in the Glory of His Father.

Chapter IX.

1. The Glory to Come foreshadowed in the Transfiguration. Verses 1-13. Matthew XVII:1-13; Luke IX:28-36.

2. The helpless disciples and the secret of failure. Verses 14-29. Matthew XVII:14-20; Luke IX:37-42.

3. The second announcement of His death. Verses 30-32. Matthew XVII:22-23; Luke IX:43-45.

4. The self-seeking disciples. Verses 33-37. Matthew XVIII: 1-5; Luke IX:46-48.

5. The Servant's gentleness and tolerance. Verses 38-41. Luke IX:49-50.

6. The solemn warning. Verses 42-50. Matthew XVIII:6-9.

1. The Glory to Come foreshadowed in the Transfiguration. Verses 1-13. The Lord had the transfiguration in mind when He spoke of some standing there and not tasting death. 2 Peter i:16 gives the meaning of the transfiguration as a type and earnest of His Coming into His Kingdom. On that mountain the three disciples saw the Kingdom of God come with power. The Servant appears in Glory. The Saints are represented by Moses and Elias, those who have died and those changed in the twinkling of an eye. The three disciples represented the Saints on earth, when He comes into His Kingdom; the Shekinah cloud was there. And Peter blundered again when he lowered the dignity of the Lord by putting Him alongside of the two Old Testament Servants of God. The Father's voice is heard once more, vindicating the honor of His Son. What an encouragement the transfiguration must have been for the Servant-Son.

2. The helpless disciples; the secret of their failure. Verses 14-29. The whole scene is of greatest importance. The conditions He finds returning from the mount of transfiguration are typical of the conditions on the earth when He comes again. Here are helpless disciples, triumphant, unbelieving scribes and the manifestation of Satan's power. All this we cannot follow in detail. Notice the additions in Mark's account. They had no power to cast out the demon, because they were "faithless." The Lord told them that lack of prayer and fasting were the causes of their failure. Dependence on God and denial of self are meant. How gracious was the complete deliverance of the afflicted boy. If God's people knew more of real prayer and real denial of self, there would be a greater manifestation of His power through them.

3. The second announcement of His death. Verses 30-32. Passing again through Galilee He announced His death and resurrection the second time. They understood not and were afraid to ask Him. The cross was foreign to them. Other thoughts occupied their hearts.

4. The self-seeking disciples. Verses 33-37. And while He who had made of Himself no reputation, who came to be the Servant of all, was looking towards the goal of His earthly ministry, the cross and its shame, they disputed all the way who should be the greatest. Vain glory filled their hearts in expectation of the earthly kingdom for which they waited. They were unable to enter into His thoughts. They were silent because they realized that their dispute was wrong. Then He taught them. The desire of being first shows only fitness to be last. Such a desire reveals nothing but self. Humility must ever be a leading characteristic of the disciple. Then He illustrates it by the small child He took in His arms. Such in dependence, humbleness in mind and confidence, the disciples must be to enjoy His fellowship. With such He can identify Himself.

5. The Servant's gentleness. Verses 38-41. Another form of self appears among the disciples. John would have the Lord rebuke those who used His name effectually and belonged not to their company. It was a narrow sectarianism. Of all the manifestations of self the religious sectarian self, as expressed in exclusivism, rejecting those who do not fellowship with them—is by far the worst, and in the Epistles by the Spirit of God is designated as a work of the flesh. How very offensive it must have been to God's perfect Servant. Yet what a gentle answer He gives. How we all can learn from Him. The smallest service in doing honor to His name would not be forgotten of God.

6. The Solemn Warning. Verses 42-50. The words are for both saint and sinner. We quote from another on this solemn word. "Nevertheless, as regards themselves, all depends on the faithfulness of Christ; and on this account they need to free themselves from all the things which tend to separate from Christ, which led into sin, and bring on apostasy in the heart as well as outward apostasy. God will keep His own, but He will keep them in making them obedient to His Word. Besides this, God puts all to the proof; the fire of His judgment is applied to all, both to saints and sinners. In the saints it consumes the dross, in order that the pure gold may shine in its true lustre; in the case of sinners it is the fire of eternal judgment that is not quenched.

"'Every sacrifice must be salted with salt' refers to Levit. ii:13. The salt represents the power of the Holy Spirit to keep us from all that is impure and produce holiness in a heart devoted to God, to keep us from all corruption. 'Have salt in yourselves.' He wishes us to exercise diligence in order that our souls, in our walk, may be thus sanctified before God, and then manifest it before the world and that we should walk with others in peace."*

"The burden" where the worm dieth not, and the fire is not quenched, "falls on the conscience stricken like the bell that tolls the felon to his doom. Would that it might kindle our hearts who believe into an unwonted earnestness on behalf of perishing souls!" Many attempts are made to deny the solemn warning in its fearful meaning, but they are eternal truth. The Son of God came from Heaven's Glory, walked on earth as the Servant and tasted death, yea, forsaken of God on the Cross, to save man from the unquenchable fire.

---

* J. N. Darby on "Mark."

Chapter X.

In Judea.

1. **The question concerning Divorce. Verses 1-12. Matthew XIX:1-9.**
2. **Children are blessed by Him. Verses 13-16. Matthew XIX: 13-15; Luke XVIII:15-17.**
3. **The rich young Ruler and Warning against Riches. Verses 17-27. Matthew XIX:16-26; Luke XVIII:18-27.**
4. **Concerning Rewards. Verses 28-31. Matthew XIX:27-30; Luke XVIII:28-30.**
5. **On to Jerusalem. Third announcement of His Death and Resurrection. Verses 32-34. Matthew XX:17-19; Luke XVIII:31-34.**
6. **The Desire of James and John. Verses 35-45. Matthew XX:20-28; Luke XXII:24-27.**
7. **At Jericho. The Healing of Bartimaeus. Verses 46-52. Matthew XX:29-34; Luke XVIII:35-43.**

1. The Question concerning Divorce. Verses 1-12. The Lord restores in teaching the original meaning of marriage and speaks against divorce Moses had permited on account of the hardness of their hearts. Thus He restored the original institution of marriage. His ministry is now almost ended and He is on His way to Jerusalem to go to the cross.

2. Children are blest by Him. Verses 13-16. Again the disciples failed. They showed a kind of self-importance and dignity in rebuking those who brought the little children. He was indignant. They had no right whatever to rebuke and to shut out from His presence. They usurped His place and by their domineering attitude misrepresented Him. And priestcraft has brought this to perfection. But oh! the contrast. He received them and tenderly took them into His arms to bless them. Such is the Kingdom of God. Sin is in them. But the little children present some characteristics of uncorrupted nature. The way into the Kingdom is the new birth; and that must be received as a little child.

3. The rich young ruler and warnings against Riches. Verses 17-27. Here is one, who would inherit eternal life by doing. He "kneeled" (mentioned only by Mark) and showed reverence, and yet he called Him only "Good Master." He was a moral young man but unsaved. The reply of the Lord is significant.

He refuses the address "Good Master." The young man did not believe on Him as Son of God. The logic is perfect. If He is not God, He could not be good, and if He is good, then He is God. Yet "Jesus, beholding him, loved him;" a statement found only in Mark. He did not see the truth that man is not good, but a sinner, and salvation cannot be by works but is by Grace. Note the beautiful answer the Lord gave to His disciples. "Who then can be saved?" And Jesus looking upon them saith, "With men it is impossible, but not with God; for with God all things are possible." Man cannot be saved by what he is or does. Blessed truth. But God has accomplished salvation by the gift of His Son and this salvation is received by faith in Him.

4. Concerning Rewards. Verses 28-31. It was a selfish question, which Peter asked. Somehow he would remind the Lord that while the young man refused to part with his riches, they had left all. And the meek and lowly One answers graciously and gives the promise of reward in this life and in the age to come. But it is reward only if it is done for His sake and the Gospel's. It is a blessed thing to leave the rewards with Him.

5. On to Jerusalem. Third announcement of His death and Resurrection. Verses 32-34. But were they willing to leave all for His sake? As the Servant now at the close of His ministry went up to Jerusalem they were amazed at His calmness and determination to go to the place, where death awaited Him, according to His own predictions. They were afraid of their own lives as they followed Him. The Servant went before them in the lead; the frightened group came behind. The third prediction of His death is the completest.

6. The Desire of James and John. Verses 35-45. Their fear was short-lived. They did not grasp the solemn announcement that the Son of Man would have to die and did not understand that all the promised blessings could only be realized through His death on the cross. They had faith in a coming Kingdom of Glory, faith in the Servant so lowly to be the King and that they were to reign with Him. The request is stated and answered graciously by the Lord. And the two who were afraid when He turned towards Jerusalem now say that they are able to drink the cup with Him and be baptized with the baptism, which awaited Him, the inward and outward sufferings of the cross. But these two forsook Him a few days later and fled. The others were much displeased, no doubt for selfish reasons, and then still other words of instruction came from His lips.

7. At Jericho. The Healing of Bartimaeus. **Verses 46-52.** This healing stands at the beginning of the end of that blessed life lived on the earth. Up to verse 45 He speaks of Himself as "Son of Man." The phrase "Son of David" appears only once in Mark's Gospel. Bartimaeus calls upon Him by that name and is healed. It is the prelude to the great events in Jerusalem, His presentation as King, rejection, suffering and death. The miracle of Jericho holds the same place in the three Gospels. Israel's condition is easily seen in Bartimaeus' blindness. The Son of David had come to give sight to the blind and in Jericho (the place of curse) He shows His gracious Power. Bartimaeus followed Him as the blessed witness of His power.

PART III. THE SERVANT IN JERUSALEM.

PRESENTED AS KING AND REJECTED.

Chapters XI-XIII.

Chapter XI.

1. **The Servant enters into Jerusalem. Verses 1-11. Matthew XXI:1-11; Luke XIX:28-40; John XII:12-16.**
2. **The fig tree cursed. Verses 12-14. Compare with Matthew XXI:19-21.**
3. **The Cleansing of the Temple. Verses 15-18. Matthew XXI:12-19; Luke XIX:45-48.**
4. **The Withered Fig tree. Verses 19-26. Matthew XXI:20-22.**
5. **Again in the City. His Authority Questioned. Verses 27-33. Matthew XXI:27-33; Luke XX:1-8.**

1. The Servant enters Jerusalem. Verses 1-11. He presents Himself as the promised Son of David to the nation as written in the prophecy of Zechariah (ix:9). As King the multitudes welcome Him. Hosanna (save now); Blessed is He that cometh in the Name of the Lord. "Blessed be the Kingdom of our Father David, that cometh in the Name of the Lord: Hosanna in the Highest." They expected the promised Kingdom and they welcomed Him as Son of David with power to save. But He knew what it all meant. He is silent, according to Mark, but enters into the temple and looked around upon all things without uttering a word. There is nothing for Him there. He then left the city and returned to Bethany (meaning: house of affliction). When He comes the second time with Glory, He will be greeted by a remnant of His people and set up the Kingdom of David.

2. The Fig Tree Cursed. Verses 12-14. He was hungry. In all the enthusiasm no one had thought of His need. The rejection of the Servant-Son is evident in this. The fig tree is the emblem of the Jewish nation. He came looking for fruit and found none. "The fig tree was punished not for being without fruit, but for proclaiming by the voice of those leaves that it had fruit; not for being barren, but for being false; and this was the guilt of Israel, so much deeper than the guilt of the nations" (Trench).

3. The Cleansing of the Temple. Verses 15-19. Twice He cleansed the temple, in the beginning of His ministry (John ii:13-16) and at the close. Most likely the desecration of the house was worse at the end than in the beginning. The greed for money is the prominent feature in the defilement of the temple. The actions of the Lord brings out the Satanic hatred of the scribes and chief priests. He was hated as the Servant without a cause and hated unto death. Again He went out of the city.

4. The Withered Fig Tree and Instructions. Verses 20-26. The dried up fig tree is made the occasion to teach the disciples the power of faith in God. The fig tree typifies the religious condition of the people. The mountain, the nation as such, thinking themselves firmly established. But soon that mountain was to be removed and cast into the sea (the sea of nations). Faith was exercised by the Servant and He calls upon His own to have faith in God. Faith can remove every obstacle. For the disciples it meant the obstacle of that mountain, the nation. Verse 24 is precious and has the same meaning to-day as it had when the words were spoken. God ever answers faith. But that faith must be paired with forgiveness.

5. Again in Jerusalem. The Authority of the Servant Questioned and His Answer. Verses 27-33. Visiting the temple again He met His enemies, who questioned Him concerning His authority. His authority was completely established by the mighty works He had done. The omniscient One knew their hatred and asked them a question, which they did not dare to answer. He, the perfect Servant had zeal for God and for His house; they, the religious leaders, had only zeal for their own authority. This is still the mark of all ritualism.

Chapter XII.

1. The Parable of the Vineyard. Verses 1-12. Matthew XXI: 33-46; Luke XX:9-19.

2. The Question concerning the Tribute Money. Verses 13-17. Matthew XXII:15-22; Luke XX:20-26.

3. The Sadducees Questioning concerning Resurrection. Verses 18-27. Matthew XXII:23-33; Luke XX:27-38.

4. The Question of the Scribe. Verses 28-34. Matthew XXII: 34-40.

5. His Question. Verses 35-37. Matthew XXII:41-46; Luke XX:41-44.

6. Beware of the Scribes. Verses 38-40. Matthew XXIII; Luke XX:45-47.

7. The Servant's loving sympathy and praise. Verses 41-44. Luke XXI:1-4.

1. The Parable of the Vineyard. Verses 1-12. The parable is a review of the history of Israel and its culmination in the rejection of the Son. With what calmness the perfect One relates it all. He is ready to have all done unto Him of which He speaks. A comparison with the Gospel of Matthew will show that Mark is brief and passes on rapidly, omitting utterances of the Lord which are not needed in his description of the Servant.

2. The Question concerning the Tribute Money. Verses 13-17. With this paragraph we have the different classes of Jews approaching the Lord to tempt Him. Pharisees and Herodians, Sadducees and a Scribe. The Lord manifests His wisdom and they are defeated. Then He turns questioner and warns against the scribes. His authority they could no longer question and now they tried to catch Him in His words. Pharisees and Herodians, so opposed to each other, could make a common cause in hating God's Servant. If He had answered "yes" the Pharisees would have condemned Him for favoring the Gentile yoke. If He had said "no," the Herodians would have accused Him as an enemy of Cæsar. How wonderful His answer! They even had to marvel and yet it only intensified their hate. Cæsar's image told out the story of their sin.

3. The Sadducees Questioning concerning Resurrection. Verses 18-27. The Sadducees were rationalists and denied the existence of angels and the resurrection. They only believed in the giving of the law and accepted the Pentateuch. It was a fine spun argument. The Lord silences them from the portion of the Scriptures they endorsed.

4. **The Question of the Scribe. Verses 28-34.** A scribe now makes the last attempt. But he was indeed "not far from the Kingdom of God." The one step was the acceptance of Christ, whose wisdom he had owned.

5. **His Question. Verses 35-37.** Then the Lord turned questioner. His wisdom had closed their mouths. In Matthew's Gospel this significant question is more fully given. He refers to Psalm cx. In connection with Matthew four great facts are stated by the Lord. 1. This Psalm was written by David. 2. It was written by inspiration. 3. It is a Messianic Psalm. 4. Christ is David's Lord and David's Son. While it silenced the scribes it also silences the present day Sadducees, the higher critics with their inventions. They claim that Psalm cx was not written by David and Christ is not foretold in it.

6. **Beware of the Scribes. Verses 38-40.** In Matthew the Holy Spirit reports the full discourse against the scribes and Pharisees (chapter xxiii) ending with the solemn statement, "Behold your house is left unto you desolate." In Mark, where the divine design is to give us the picture of the Servant, only a few sentences are given. Yet they contain the chief characteristics of the corrupt leaders of the nation. Love of being seen, love of applause, love of pre-eminence, assumed religiousness and the devouring of the poor are all mentioned. These hireling servants shall have greater damnation.

7. **The Servant's loving sympathy and praise. Verses 41-44.** He had rendered such perfect service free from seeking applause or pre-eminence and now He shows His loving sympathy to one of the poor widows who were being spoiled by the greed of the Pharisees. That poor, yet rich, widow had two mites. It was her all and she gave it. She might have given one mite and retained the other. She cast in all she had. And He saw it and His sympathy was towards her for she reminded Him of His own service in giving all. How it must have refreshed His heart. May we remember that nothing escapes His eye.

Chapter XIII.

1. The Destruction of the Temple Predicted. Verses 1-2. Matthew XXIV:1-2; Luke XXI:5-6.

2. The Questions of the Disciples. Verses 3-4. Matthew XXIV:3; Luke XXI:7.

3. The Olivet Discourse. Verses 5-37. Matthew XXIV:4-42; Luke XXI:8-38.

1. The Destruction of the Temple Predicted. Verses 1-2. He went out of the temple for the last time, when one of His disciples called attention to the temple buildings. They were of the most massive construction, some of them still in process of erection. He predicted a complete destruction, which was fulfilled later in the year 70. The destruction of Jerusalem is more fully foretold in Luke xxi:20-24.

2. **The Questions of the Disciples. Verses 3-4.** Mark gives us their names, which are omitted by Matthew and Luke. What follows is the answer.

3. The Olivet Discourse. Verses 5-37. Mark's report is the briefest, Matthew's the longest. Omitted in Mark are the parables, which have special reference to the Christian profession (Matthew xxv) and the judgment of living nations (chapter xxv:31-46). These belong in Matthew, but would be out of keeping with the purpose of the Gospel of Mark. The Service of our Lord, as we have seen, is in the foreground. The three characteristic discourses in Matthew nowhere else reported in full are: 1. The Sermon on the Mount, which is the Proclamation of the King. 2. The Parable Discourse in Matthew xiii, the mysteries of the Kingdom. 3. The Olivet Discourse, Matthew xxiv-xxv, the future of the Kingdom. But why should there be anything at all in the Gospel of Mark about the future things, such as the end of the age and His Return in Glory, if only the Servant is described? It will be seen that the predictions are in part at least in view of their service. He forewarned them as His servants of what was to come after His departure.

It is not the purpose of this annotated analysis to give an exposition of this discourse. We must ask the reader to turn to our commentary on Matthew. We give here a subdivision of the discourse as contained in Mark: 1. The characteristics of the present age and the end of the age. Verses 5-13. 2. The abomination of desolation or the great tribulation which precedes the Second Coming of Christ. Verses 14-23. 3. The visible manifestation of Christ. He will come again in clouds as Son of Man not as an humble Servant but as the King of Glory. The regathering of the elect Israel then takes place. Verses 24-27. 4. The Signs of His Coming. The budding fig tree is Israel awakening to new national life. Verses 28-33. Note that in verse 32 "neither the Son" is added. This statement of our Lord that even He the Son does not know the hour of His return has been used to deny His Deity. All kinds of theories have been invented to explain it. It is explained by the Lord having taken the place of humiliation as a Servant for "the servant knoweth not what his lord doeth." This is why the statement appears only in Mark. It does not affect the truth of His Person. 5. The solemn exhortation to watch. It behooves the servants to watch during the absence of the Lord.

PART IV. GIVING HIS LIFE A RANSOM FOR MANY.

Chapters XIV—XV.

Chapter XIV.

1. **Seeking by Craft to put Him to Death. Verses 1-2. Matthew XXVI:2-5; Luke XXII:1-2.**
2. **The Anointing. Verses 3-9. Matthew XXVI:6-13; John XII:1-8.**
3. **Judas offers to betray Him. Verses 10-11. Matthew XXVI: 14-16; Luke XXII:3-6.**
4. **The last Paschal feast. Verses 12-21. Matthew XXVI:17-24; Luke XXII:7-18, 21-23.**
5. **The Lord's Supper instituted. Verses 22-25. Matthew XXVI:26-29; Luke XXII:17-20.**
6. **Peter's denial predicted. Verses 26-31. Matthew XXVI: 31-35; Luke XXII:31-34; John XIII:36-38.**
7. **The Suffering in the Garden. Verses 32-42. Matthew XXVI: 36-46; Luke XXII:39-46.**
8. **The Betrayal and Arrest of the Lord Jesus. Verses 43-52. Matthew XXVI:47-56; Luke XXII:47-53.**
9. **Before the High Priest and the Sanhedrim. Verses 53-65. Matthew XXVI:47-68; Luke XXII:47-55; John XVIII:2-24.**
10. **Peter's denial. Verses 66-72. Matthew XXVI:69-75; Luke XXII:56-62; John XVIII:17, 25-27.**

1. Seeking by Craft to put Him to Death. Verses 1, 2. His enemies were plotting, but over all was God and His eternal counsels. They were now ready "to do whatsoever Thy hand and Thy counsel determined before to be done" (Acts iv:28). The Servant is to die as the true passover lamb and He who had ministered in such a perfect way is to give His life a ransom for many. They had resolved it should not be on the feast day. But God's will demanded that it should be on that day; and so it was.

2. The Anointing. Verses 3-9. The woman is not mentioned by Mark. It was Mary of Bethany, who sat at His feet when He had come to her house and who wept at His feet when Lazarus had died. She alone had grasped the meaning of the

Lord's announcement concerning His death and resurrection. She did not go to the grave as others did. She anointed His body for the burial. What love there was in her heart! How it must have delighted His heart when she did this act of faith and love.

3. Judas offers to betray Him. Verses 10-11. The anointing hastened Judas to betray Him (see John xii:5-6).

4. The last Paschal feast. Verses 12-21. First there was the preparation (verses 12-16) and then the feast itself (verses 17-21). What calmness and dignity is seen in all He does! He knew all what awaited Him. During the feast He announced the coming betrayal. Awful are the words coming from such lips, "Good were it for that man if he had never been born." The same is true of every human being who rejects the Lord Jesus Christ and dies in sin.

5. The Lord's Supper instituted. Verses 22-25. It is His own supper, the blessed memorial feast. "Do this in remembrance of Me." They did not know then what it meant. But when the Holy Spirit had come they broke the bread. The passover was the memorial of the deliverance of the people out of Egypt and reminded them of the blood that was sprinkled. A better blood was soon to be shed and a greater deliverance wrought by the Lamb of God. A blessed privilege to carry out His request (1 Cor. xi:23-26).

6. Peter's denial predicted. Verses 26-31. The hymn they sang was composed of Psalms cxv-cxviii. With what emotion of soul He must have sung with His disciples! The shadow of deepest agony and death was upon Him and yet the fullest praise flowed from His lips. He announced the scattering of the sheep and His own smiting by the hand of God. What must it have meant for Him, when He said with His perfect knowledge, "I will smite the shepherd." That smiting, which took place on the cross, is the heart and mystery of the atonement. Peter's denial is then predicted.

7. The Suffering in the Garden. Verses 32-42. In Gethsemane we are face to face with the most solemn event in the life of the Servant-Son, save that hour, when He hung on the cross, forsaken of God. What was His suffering there? No saint can ever fathom its depths. He did not shrink from death, nor was the agony on account of the physical sufferings He knew were to be His lot; nor was Satan, as some foolishly teach, ready to slay Him. All such statements are dishonoring to Him. He was not in danger of death in Gethsemane. What was the cup He dreaded? The Sinless One, who knew no sin, was now soon to be made sin for us. God's face upon which He had ever looked was soon to be hid. And what was it when at last He was made sin for us on the cross? One sentence gives us the answer, "My God, my God, why hast Thou forsaken Me?"

8. The Betrayal and Arrest of the Lord Jesus. Verses 43-52. He surrenders Himself as the willing victim. Peter was ready to fight and cut off the ear of the high priest's servant. Mark omits the healing for he is to picture the Servant in His suffering and all relating to power is now out of place. In John's Gospel the Lord said one word, "I am," and those who came to arrest Him fell backward to the ground. John was guided by the Spirit of God to make a record of it. It could have no place in Mark's Gospel. They all forsook Him and fled. But only Mark tells of a certain young man, who followed and then fled naked. The young man may have been Mark himself.

9. Before the high priest and the Sanhedrim. Verses 53-65. We behold the Servant now delivered into the hands of man and behind man stood Satan. Man's wickedness and Satan's power are there, and in the midst, in solitary grandeur, stands the perfect Servant-Son. Mark tells us exclusively that the witnesses brought against Him did not agree. The Holy Spirit continues to hold Him up as the perfect Servant, in whose character and service not a flaw could be detected. But He witnesses the good confession and upon that blessed Word of Truth as it came from His lips He is condemned. Then they condemned Him to death and man's vile hatred energized by Satan cast itself upon the blessed One.

10. Peter's denial. Verses 66-72. The Lord had given the true testimony and Peter followed with his shameful denial. Mark gives what the other two evangelists omit, the cock crowing twice. The lessons from Peter's fall are simple. He had to pass through this terrible experience to become broken down and learn to know his own weakness. And how we all need to know that we are in ourselves good for nothing; "in my flesh there dwelleth no good thing."

Chapter XV.

1. **Before Pilate. Verses 1-5. Matthew XXVII:1-14; Luke XXIII:1-4; John XVIII:28-38.**

2. **Barabbas released and the Servant condemned. Verses 6-15. Matthew XXVII:15-26; Luke XXIII:16-25; John XVIII:39-40.**

3. **Crowned with thorns and mocked. Verses 16-21. Matthew XXVII:27-32; Luke XXIII:26-43; John XIX:1-16.**

4. **Crucified. Verses 22-32. Matthew XXVII:33-44; Luke XXIII:26-43; John XIX:17-27.**

5. **Obedient unto death, the death of the Cross. Verses 33-41. Matthew XXVII:45-56; Luke XXIII:44-49; John XIX:28-37.**

6. **The Burial. Verses 42-47. Matthew XXVII:57-61; Luke XXIII:50-56; John XIX:38-42.**

1. Before Pilate. Verses 1-5. The council had condemned Him to death and now the whole council delivered Him into the hands of the Gentiles. First the religious power had condemned the blessed Servant and the civil power had to do the same. It will be seen that Mark's account of our Lord's trial before Pilate is the briefest, while Matthew's is the longest. Again the Servant witnesses a good confession. But when accused by the chief priests His blessed lips were sealed. He stood there to witness and not to defend Himself. What a gracious example He gives to all His servants. The hatred of the religious leaders of the people is especially emphasized by Mark. For the complete exposition of this trial before Pilate see "Exposition of Matthew."

2. Barabbas released; the Servant condemned to be crucified. Verses 6-15. The story of Barabbas and his release is full of helpful instruction. "So true it was that, even in this last scene, Jesus delivers others at His own cost and in every sense. He had just before delivered the disciples from being taken; He is now the means of delivering Barabbas, wicked as he was. He never saved Himself. It was the very perfection of the moral Glory of Christ to deliver, bless, save, and in all at the expense of Himself."* Barabbas was released, though guilty and condemned, because the Lord Jesus took his place. Christ was his substitute. Barabbas released might have gone out and looked up to Him, who hung on the cross and said, "He died for me; he paid my penalty." It is a blessed illustration of the atonement. They ask for the murderer Barabbas and

---

*"Gospel of Mark" W. Kelly

demand the horrible death by crucifixion for God's perfect Servant and their King. The chief priests had moved the people to make this fatal choice. See the interesting additions in Matthew's Gospel on account of its Jewish-dispensational character.

3. Crowned with thorns and mocked. Verses 16-21. Oh! the heart piercing scenes of this section of our Gospel! They led Him away to heap the greatest indignities upon the Holy One. That is man's answer to that service of love and power He so unceasingly had rendered. After the cruel scourging they clothed Him with a purple robe in mockery. Matthew reports a scarlet cloak. This is not a discrepancy. "A scarlet military robe was made to represent the imperial purple, hence the designation, a purple robe. And because this is the symbolic import of the robe, there is no discrepancy" (Lange). The scarlet cloak was used to represent in mockery the imperial purple robe. The crown of thorns was made to inflict cruel pain upon His brow. Thorns came on account of man's sin; they are the signs of the curse. He took the curse upon His own head. Mark tells us most definitely who Simon the Cyrenian was, who was compelled to bear His cross, the father of Alexander and Rufus (see Romans xvi:13). God did not forget this service; Simon's sons became believers.

4. Crucified. Verses 22-32. It is interesting to note here that Mark speaks of bringing Him to Golgotha. The word translated "bring" really means "bear" (translated thus in Mark ii:3 and Luke xxiii:26). "And they bear Him unto the place Golgotha." They had to hold Him up. The blessed Servant had spent His strength. What appearance He must have presented after all the scourging and cruel indignities! His face from the awful blows was marred. No wonder that His real human body was weak. But could He succumb? Never. No one could take His life. It could not be touched by man or Satan; death (the result of sin) had no claim on Him. He *gave* His life for a ransom. Mark also reports exclusively that the wine they offered Him was mingled with myrrh. This was considered an anodyne, to relieve and deaden the pain. The Servant who had come to spend all He had and to give Himself did not need it, but refused the concoction. Mark gives the hour of crucifixion as "the third hour." In John's Gospel (xix:14) the sixth hour is mentioned when Pilate said, "Behold your King." The critics triumphantly point to this as a discrepancy. But John gives the Roman way of reckoning the civil day and Mark adheres to the Jewish timekeeping.

The superscription on the cross is the briefest in Mark. He gives the substance of the accusation and not the full wording of it. The perfect Servant who had so fully glorified God and given Himself in all His service, hangs between the two thieves, who had robbed God and man. How true it was (though they knew it not), "He saved others; Himself He cannot save." He did not save Himself for He came to die. He was obedient unto death.

5. Obedient unto death, the death of the Cross. Verses 33-41. What hours those were! What heart can penetrate its deep mysteries or fathom the depths of the sufferings of the Lamb of God, when He was obedient unto death, the death of the Cross! Nature bears witness to it by the supernatural darkness, for the One who created all things suffers for the creature's sin. And what a scene in Heaven, when God's own hand rested upon that One! Worship, praise and adoration is here more in order than an attempt of explanation. He was forsaken of God; and then He paid our penalty and stood in our stead in the presence of a holy God. Never say He was forsaken by His Father. Read John xvi:32. The Servant's cry with a loud voice shows that no one took His life, but that He gave "Himself." And there was the rent veil from top to bottom (rent by God's own hand). Then came the utterance of the Centurion: a Gentile confessing Him as Son of God. And the women are mentioned, who had ministered unto Him. The men had fled, the feeble women were there. All service now after the great victory He won, must be in weakness, depending on Him alone.

6. The Burial. Verses 42-47. Joseph of Arimathea, like Nicodemus, identified himself with Him, who had died on a cross and confessed Him boldly by this action. In Pilate's astonishment that He had died so soon we have additional evidence that the Servant "gave His life." Death by crucifixion, perhaps so often witnessed by the centurion, is a lingering death. They would have given Him the grave of the wicked, but God had predicted it otherwise (Isaiah liii:9 read, "they appointed His grave with the wicked, but with the rich He was when He had died"). The tomb was one in which no other dead had ever been. "The one born of a Virgin-womb could only be fittingly honored in a virgin tomb. He who could not see corruption, could not lie in a tomb which corruption had defiled."

PART V. THE SERVANT HIGHLY EXALTED. RISEN AND ASCENDED; HIS COMMISSION TO HIS SERVANTS AND WORKING WITH THEM.

Chapter XVI.

1. The Resurrection and His Manifestation. Verses 1-13. Matthew XXVIII:1-8; Luke XXIV:1-35; John XX:1-18.

2. The Commission. Verses 9-18. Luke XXIV:36-49; John XX:19-29.

3. The Ascension. Verses 19-20. Luke XXIV:50-53.

1. The Resurrection and His Manifestation. Verses 1-8. Again we notice the brevity of Mark's account of the Resurrection of the Lord. The resurrection of Him who saved and toiled so patiently, who was cast out of His own city and suffered and died on the cross, was the fullest vindication of His person. A still greater vindication lies in the future, when He returns in power and glory. By His resurrection He was declared the Son of God (Romans i:4). Had He not risen in the same body He had taken on in incarnation, His death on the cross would have no more power for redemption than the death of any other human being (1 Cor. xv:12-20). His resurrection is also the completest proof that His work on the cross is accepted by God. The women last mentioned at the cross are the first at the tomb. In the first eight verses the Lord Himself is not mentioned as being seen. The stone rolled away, the empty tomb and the angel's words declare that He is risen indeed. In Mark, Peter is specially mentioned, "but go your way, tell His disciples and Peter." Peter's denial is described by Mark in the fullest way. How fitting that he should record the divinely sent message to Peter. What comfort and peace it must have brought to sorrowing Peter.

Higher criticism declares that the proper ending of the Gospel of Mark is verse 8. They disputed the genuineness of verses 9-20. Another hand, they claim, added later these verses. That spurious translation, which goes under the name of "The Twentieth Century New Testament" (wholly unsatisfactory) also gives this portion as "a late appendix." It is not. Mark wrote it and some of the best scholars have declared that it is genuine. How foolish to assume that the blessed document, which begins with the sublime statement "The Gospel of Jesus Christ, the

Son of God" could end with "they were afraid!" The trouble with these critics is that they approach the Word of God with doubt and reject its inspiration.

2. The Commission. Verses 9-18. To her who came to the tomb very early in the morning He appeared first. Mary Magdalen had been under the control of demons in a most awful way. She is there as a trophy of His Power over Satan; as the mighty victor over Satan He appeared first to her. Knowing Him and His power as well as the risen One, He sends her forth with the glad message. This is fully given in the Gospel of John. The disciples did not believe. Then He appeared to the disciples on the way to Emmaus so fully reported in Luke. Even then they did not believe their testimony. He appeared unto the eleven as they were at meat and at that time He gave them the commission. But before He upbraided them with their unbelief. How it must have humbled them. And such weak, unbelieving, doubting men the perfect Servant sent forth to preach the Gospel to every creature. The commission differs in many ways from that given in the Kingdom Gospel of Matthew. In Mark the Kingdom is not in view, the Servant has served, He has given His life for a ransom and upon that the good news goes forth. The message is to be believed and faith confessed. He that believeth not shall be damned. Signs were to follow them (but not all) that believe and signs did follow. Signs were never universal, not even in the days of the Apostles. The Lord's own sovereign will is over this.

3. The Ascension. Verses 19-20. The Gospel of Matthew makes no record of the ascension. If we had only Matthew we would think the Lord still on the earth even as some day He will be earth's glorious King. The Holy Spirit gives through Mark a brief Word on the Return of the Servant-Son to the Glory from where He had come. The Servant who had stooped so low is lifted so high. There at the right hand of God He has taken His place—the Man in Glory. The work is finished. But the word "work" appears once more in this Gospel. "And they went forth and preached everywhere, the Lord working with them, and confirming the Word with signs following." Nowhere else in the Gospels is the statement given that the risen One works with His servants. How fitting that the Holy Spirit put it at the close of the Gospel of the Servant. He came from God to take the Servant's place; He served on earth; He sacrificed Himself for our sins, and now as His servants go forth to serve in His name He still works with them. What joy it ought to be for all who love and adore Him to be obedient to such a Lord, who was such a Servant on earth and whose delight is still to serve.

Mark the Writer of this Gospel.

Were we to give even the gist of theories on the Gospel of Mark and how it was written, we would have to fill many pages. That is needless and even unprofitable. The chosen instrument to write this Gospel in which the Lord Jesus Christ is so beautifully pictured as the Servant of God on earth, was not an Apostle, but himself a servant. We find his name mentioned for the first time in Acts xii:12-25. His full name was John Mark and his mother's name Mary. In Acts xiii:5, 13 he is called by the first name John, while in xv:39 we read of him as Mark. He accompanied Barnabas and Paul on their first missionary journey as a helper. We read nowhere that he addressed a single gathering. When they reached Perga he left the Apostles and returned to Jerusalem (Acts xiii:13). The reason of this abrupt departure was failure on Mark's side. He did not want to work and had become unprofitable (Acts xv:38, compare with 2 Tim. iv:11). On account of his failure Paul and Barnabas had a falling out and separated from each other. Paul refused him as a companion on the second journey, but Barnabas wanted to take him again (Acts xx:37-40). He went with Barnabas to Cyprus (Acts xv:39). The Holy Spirit has nothing to report of this journey. A period of unprofitableness followed for John Mark till he was restored to service. That such was the case we learn from Col. iv:10; Phil. 24; 2 Tim. iv:11. He had become Paul's fellow laborer. This personal history of John Mark is of blessed encouragement. He who had such an humble place as a servant of the two mighty men of God and who even failed in that, when restored became the divinely chosen and inspired instrument to pen the perfect Servant's path down here. Have we failed as servants? Let us go and tell Him all about it. He will have better service for us.

Tradition linked him with Peter and makes him a Bishop in Alexandria. There is no truth in it. All we know is that he was led to Christ by the Apostle Peter and was with him in Babylon (1 Pet. v:13).

THE CHARACTERISTIC FEATURES OF MARK.*

A careful study of the preceding analysis and comparison with the other Gospel records will bring out the characteristic features of this Gospel. Many events recorded in Matthew, Luke and John are omitted in Mark because they have no bearing upon the Servant's work. We find not a word about a genealogy, nor is there any reference to Bethlehem, David's city. The Lord is called but once the son of David in Mark's Gospel. Nor do we find a word about His childhood spent in Nazareth and the details of His temptations in the wilderness. The sermon on the mount so fully reported in Matthew is altogether omitted, because He spoke it as the king, proclaiming the principles of the kingdom. Many of the parables are omitted by Mark, for instance, five of those which appear in Matthew xiii; also a number of others found in Matthew, notably those of Matthew xxv, and the description of the judgment of the nations, when He comes again. The lengthy woes pronounced upon the religious leaders of the nation (Matth. xxiii) are likewise nearly all absent. All these omissions are the evidences of the verbal inspiration of this Gospel and if closely studied will show

*We can heartily recommend "The Gospel of Mark" by W. Kelly. The excellent notes and hints by the editor of this volume, Mr Whitefield, make the book still more valuable. Also A. Jukes on the four Gospels. We acknowledge our indebtedness to both.

the divine wisdom. The word "Lord" as applying to Him is carefully omitted by Mark. Textual investigation has shown that "Lord" in Mark ix:24 does not belong there. But in the Resurrection chapter He is called "Lord." In a number of passages in the analysis attention has been called to additions, sentences, verses and sections not found in other Gospels. Many have not been mentioned, but the most prominent are pointed out. These additions reveal the quality of His service and give us descriptions of His moral Glory. We ask our readers to look up once more the following passages and compare them with the Gospel of Matthew. Chapters i:13; i:31, compare Luke iv:38; iii:5 comp. Matth. xxii:13; iii:34 comp. Matth. xii:46 and Luke viii:21; iv:33; vi:31 comp. Matth. xiv:15; iv:36; viii:33 comp. Matth. xvi:23; ix:36 comp. Matth. xviii: 2; viii:23; viii:33; ix:27 comp. with Matth. xvii:18; x:16 comp. Matth. xix:13,15; x:21,23 comp. Matth. xix:21-23; xvi:7 comp. Matth. xxviii:7, etc.

The parable in chapter iv:26-27 is found only in Mark. Then there are two miracles which are exclusively reported by Mark. They are characteristic of true ministry. These are the deaf man in vii:32-37 and the blind man at Bethsaida, viii:22-26.

The characteristic word of the Gospel of Mark is the word "straightway." The Greek word "ευθέως" has also been translated "forthwith" and "immediately." It occurs some 40 times in this little Gospel and is the Servant's word.

"But enough. Blessed be God that such service has been seen on earth; that there has been such a hand, such an eye, and such a heart here, among the sons of men. And blessed be God, that by the same Spirit He waits to mould us to His pattern, yea, that He has predestinated us to be conformed to the image of His beloved Son. And if the Head was content to serve thus;—if, while He tarried here, He lived to meet the need of all who sought succour;—if, now risen, He is yet the same, still the loving Worker, interceding within the veil, and working here too for us;—if He shall yet serve us, 'for the less is blessed of the greater,' when in the coming kingdom He shall still lead His flock to living fountains, and wipe away their tears;—shall not we whom He has purchased, in whom He seeks to dwell, who are His witnesses in a world which knows Him not, wait upon Him until His mantle fall on us, and His Spirit, 'the oil which was upon the Head,' run down even to us also; till we catch the mind of heaven, and are made like unto the angels, children of God and children of resurrection, called to stand in the presence of God, and yet to serve, as ministering spirits to them who shall be heirs of salvation? God is serving,—'the Father worketh,'—Oh! what works of love, from the rain and fruitful seasons up to the mighty work of raising man from earth to highest heaven; and Christ has served, and is serving; and the Holy Ghost is serving, taking of the things of Christ, to reveal them to us, and then to work them in us; and angels are serving, and saints are serving, and the Church proclaims her call, that she too because redeemed must be a servant here, and that her rulers are but servants, yea, servants of servants; and heaven is serving earth, and earth the creatures on it. So let us, after our Pattern, being redeemed, go forth to serve also. 'Blessed are those servants whom the Lord when He cometh shall find so doing. Verily, He shall gird Himself, and make them sit down to meat, and He will come forth and serve them.' O Lord, Thou canst perform it; perform it to Thy praise; Oh! shew us the glory of Thy service, full of grace and truth, that in its presence we may be changed; and as we have borne the image of the earthy, may even here bear to Thy glory the image of the heavenly. Amen."*

---

*A. Jukes

THE GOSPEL OF LUKE

The Gospel of Luke.

The Gospel of Luke is the third of the so-called synoptics. The word synoptic means "seeing the whole together or at a glance." Matthew, Mark, and Luke are called the synoptic Gospels, because they present a common narrative, relate the same incidents of our Lord, with much the same words, though characteristic differences, omissions, and additions are equally apparent. Various theories have been advanced to explain the similarity and differences, so often called discrepancies, of these three Gospels. One is the theory that originally there existed a primitive Gospel, which has been lost. Out of this primitive Gospel, it is claimed, the three Gospels were constructed. Another theory is that they grew out of one another; that one wrote first and the others followed to add to it and omit what they thought best to omit. It is beyond the scope of our Bible study work to take up these attempted explanations of how the Gospels came into existence. Nor can we follow in detail the intensely interesting historical evidences, which so wonderfully demonstrate their authenticity. However, we desire to say that the last word in the controversy of the Gospels and their genuineness has been spoken. The attacks upon the historicity of the narrative, the denials which have been made, have been silenced, though infidelity cannot completely be silenced, at least not in the present age.

The well-known scholar, Dr. Schaff, made the statement, "The essential identity of the Christ of the synoptics is now universally conceded." This is true. But the differences, the divergencies in numerous things of the story the Synoptic Gospels reveal, how are they to be explained? There can be but one answer. The three persons who have written were chosen by the Spirit of God to write the narrative in exactly the way in which they did. The characteristic differences of their work is not man-made, but God-breathed. They wrote independently of each other. They did not try to improve upon a record already in existence. The Holy Spirit guided the pen of each, so that we possess in these three Gospels the testimony of the Holy Spirit concerning the Lord Jesus in a threefold aspect. The proof of this will soon be found in the careful and prayerful study of the Gospels. The truth is not discovered by learning and research in linguistic or historical lines, but by earnest searching in the Word itself. The three Gospels make the humanity of the Lord Jesus prominent, but not to the exclusion of His Deity. The full revelation of His Deity is given in the fourth Gospel, the Gospel of John, but not excluding His true humanity. The Transfiguration is given by each of the synoptics, but it is not found in the fourth Gospel. There is no room for it in the Gospel of John. Of the characteristic features of the Gospel of John and the contrast with the synoptics, we have more to say in our introduction to that Gospel.

We have already seen that Matthew describes the Lord Jesus as the King and Mark pictures Him as the obedient servant, who came not to be ministered unto, but to minister and to give His life a ransom for many. The Gospel of Luke is the Gospel of His Manhood; we behold Him in this Gospel as the Son of Man. It has often been pointed out that the early church possessed these fundamental facts concerning the synoptic Gospels and the Gospel of John and that knowledge may be traced in an outward form through centuries. It was Irenæus who, as far as we know, called first the attention to the fourfold appearances of the Cherubim and the four Gospels. He declared that the four faces of the Cherubim are images of the activity of the Son of God. The Cherubim had the faces of the lion, the ox, the man, and the eagle. The application to the four Gospels of the four faces of the Cherubim has been maintained for many centuries as the true application. Ancient manuscripts, illuminated missals, etc., bear witness to it. The Lion, the kingly animal, represents Matthew's Gospel. Mark, the Gospel of the Servant, is represented by the Ox, the burden-bearing animal. In Luke we see the Face of a Man and the Eagle, sweeping the heavens, coming from above and returning there, represents Him, who came from the Father and has gone back to the Father.

We turn now our attention to the Gospel of Luke, the Gospel of Manhood.

The Writer of the Third Gospel.

The writer of the third Gospel does not mention his name, though he speaks of himself in the opening verses of the first chapter. The first verse in the Book of Acts makes known that the same writer who wrote the Book of Acts also wrote the third Gospel and that both mention the same person, who is addressed, that is Theophilus. Furthermore, we learn from Acts i:1, that the third Gospel had been written, when the writer of Acts began his work. Inasmuch as Luke is undoubtedly the writer of the Book of Acts, he is also the penman of the third Gospel. "It has been generally and almost unanimously acknowledged that the Gospel, which we now possess is that written by Luke." (Dean Alford.)

Luke did not belong, as some hold, to the seventy our Lord sent forth to minister. His own words answer this statement. (Read Luke i:2.) The Epistles give us the only reliable information about his person. In Colossians iv:14 we read of him as "the beloved physician." In the Epistle to Philemon he is called a fellow laborer of the Apostle Paul. From Second Timothy we learn that he was in Rome when Paul was a prisoner and remained faithful to him when others forsook the Apostle. He had also joined the Apostle during his second missionary journey at Troas (Acts xiv:10). The evidence of it is found in the little word "we." He went with Paul to Macedonia and remained sometime in Philippi. In Colossians, chapter iv we find also the fact brought out that he was a Gentile. First Paul mentions those of the circumcision (Col. iv:11). Then Epaphras, a Colossian Gentile, is mentioned, followed by the names of Luke and Demas, both undoubtedly Gentiles. He is therefore the only writer in the Bible, who was a Gentile. The reason that he was selected to write the Gospel, which pictures the Lord Christ, as the perfect Man, and the Book of Acts is more than interesting. The Gospel of Luke, a Gentile, addressed to a Gentile (Theophilus) is the Gospel for the Gentiles. And the same Gentile instrument was chosen to relate the history of the Gospel going forth from Jerusalem to the Gentiles. Other critical questions, such as the time it was written, where it was written, etc., we are obliged to pass by.

The Characteristic Features of the Gospel of Luke.

We have seen from the study of Matthew that our Lord is seen in it as the King and in Mark as the Servant. The Gospel of Luke has even more characteristic features which bring out the great purpose of the last synoptic Gospel. The perfect Manhood of the Lord Jesus Christ, His moral perfections, His tender sympathies as the Saviour of man, are written here in a most precious way. The Priesthood the glorified Son of Man exercises now in behalf of His people, being touched with a feeling of our infirmities has for its foundation His true Manhood. "For every high priest taken from among men is appointed in behalf of men in things Godward, that he may offer both gifts and sacrifices for sins; Who can have compassion on the ignorant, and on them that are out of the way; since he himself also is compassed with infirmity." (Heb. v:1-2). That He was the true and perfect Man, tempted in all points like as we are, apart from sin; holy, blameless, undefiled and separate from sinners, is fully seen in the Gospel of Luke.

A glance at the beginning of the Gospel of Luke reveals at once its object. Matthew's Gospel begins with a genealogy; the genealogy of the King and is followed by the account of the wise men coming to Jerusalem looking for the new born King of the Jews. Mark begins abruptly, one might say in a hurried way, as if the writer is anxious to introduce the untiring ministry of the perfect Servant at once. And so he does.

How different is the beginning of the third Gospel! It is perfectly human. A friend writes to a friend and when he begins to tell the story he starts also in a very human way, "There was in the days of Herod the King." The two opening chapters are peculiar to Luke. All is new. We do not find anywhere else the details of John's birth, Gabriel's visit to Mary and the announcement of the coming birth of Christ, and the beautiful outbursts of praise of the two women and Zacharias. The Gospel, which is to reveal "the face of a Man" had to give these blessed facts. The second chapter, containing the most beautiful description of the birth of our Lord; bringing out the facts that He entered the world, whose Creator He is, like every other son of man, born of a woman, no room in the inn, his first resting place a manger, known to Matthew, Mark and John, were omitted by them. Luke, chosen to describe the perfect Man, had to embody these blessed details in his narrative. The babe, the child growing, the twelve year old boy in the temple, His increase in wisdom and stature, in favour with God and man, all related in the second chapter of Luke show Him forth in His true humanity. The authenticity of these two chapters has often been doubted. There can be no valid reason for it; on the contrary their genuineness are as completely proven as the rest of the Gospel. Another beautiful feature of this Gospel is that Luke speaks more of the prayers of our Lord than the others. Prayer is the expression of human dependence upon God. Inasmuch as the Son of God had taken the Creator's place, He prayed and was cast upon God. Being baptised "and praying" heaven was opened. (Luke iii, 21.) Before He called the twelve Apostles He continued all night in prayer (vi:12-13). "As He was praying" He asked the disciples, "whom say the people that I am," (ix:18). According to Luke He was transfigured "as He was praying." He also said to Peter "I have prayed for thee." All this is peculiar to this Gospel and is needed to bring out His true humanity. When Luke speaks of Him more than the other evangelists, that "He sat down to eat meat" we have the picture of a true man among men. And what more do we find in the Gospel of the beloved physician, which brings out His tender human sympathy. The story of the raising up of the widow's son at Nain is alive with tenderness and sympathy. Then there are the parables peculiar to Luke. The parable of the lost coin, the prodigal son, the parable of the importunate friend, the unjust steward, the good Samaritan, the Pharisee and the Publican praying in the temple and others are reported only by Luke. In this Gospel only we have the record of the story of the rich man and Lazarus, their life on earth, their death and their state after death; the conversion of Zacchaeus; the dying thief and his salvation; the walk to Emmaus and other incidents. How fitting that Luke, the Gentile, should also tell us what the others were not commissioned to write in reporting the prophetic utterances of our Lord, that Jerusalem should be trodden down by the Gentiles, till the times of the Gentiles are fulfilled.

All these characteristic features and many others, such as the genealogy in chapter iv, His ministry as reported by Luke, the description of His suffering, His death, and His resurrection are pointed out in the annotations. May it please the Holy Spirit to give us through the study of this Gospel a new vision of Him who was rich and who became poor for our sakes, that we through His poverty might be rich.

Events and Principal Circumstances Reported Exclusively by Luke.

It will be of much help to the student of the Gospels to possess a list of events and a number of circumstances, which are not reported by Matthew, Mark and John, but only by Luke. These interesting peculiarities of the third Gospel shed much light upon the Gospel itself. We give the list of fifty-eight items.

	CHAP.	VER.
1.—The vision of Zacharias, and conception of Elisabeth	I.	5—25.
2.—The salutation of the Virgin Mary		26—38.
3.—Mary's visit to Elisabeth		39—56.
4.—The birth of John the Baptist, and hymn of Zacharias		57—80.
5.—The decree of Cæsar Augustus	II.	1—3.
6.—The birth of Christ at Bethlehem		4—7.
7.—The appearance of angels to the shepherds		8—20.
8.—The circumcision of Christ		21.
9.—The presentation of Christ in the temple		22—24.
10.—The account of Simeon and Anna		25—38.
11.—Christ found among the doctors		41—52.
12.—Date of beginning of John's ministry	III.	1—2.
13.—Success of John's ministry		10—15.
14.—Genealogy of Mary		23—38.
15.—Christ preaching and rejected at Nazareth	IV.	15—30.
16.—Particulars in the call of Simon, James and John	V.	1—10.
17.—Christ's discourse in the plain	VI.	17—49.
18.—Raising of the widow's son at Nain	VII.	11—17.
19.—Woman in Simon's house		36—50.
20.—Women who ministered to Christ	VIII.	1—3.
21.—James and John desiring fire to come down	IX.	51—56.
22.—Mission of seventy disciples	X.	1—16.
23.—Return of seventy disciples		17—24.
24.—Parable of the good Samaritan		25—37.
25.—Christ in the house of Martha and Mary		38—42.
26.—Parable of friend at midnight	XI.	5—8.
27.—Christ in a Pharisee's house		37—54.
28.—Discourse to an innumerable multitude	XII.	1—53.
29.—Murder of the Galileans	XIII.	1—5.

	CHAP.	VER.
30.—Parable of the barren fig tree		6—9.
31.—Case of the woman diseased 18 years		10—20.
32.—Question on the few that be saved		22—30.
33.—Reply to the Pharisees' warning about Herod .		31—33.
34.—Case of a dropsical man	XIV.	1—6.
35.—Parable of the lowest room		7—14.
36.—Parable of the great supper		15—24.
37.—Difficulties of Christ's service		25—35.
38.—Parable of the lost sheep and piece of money .	XV.	1—10.
39.—Parable of the prodigal son		11—22.
40.—Parable of the unjust steward	XVI.	1—18.
41.—The rich man and Lazarus		19—31.
42.—Instruction to disciples	XVII.	1—10.
43.—Healing of ten lepers		12—19.
44.—Question and answer about the coming of God's kingdom		20—37.
45.—Parable of the importunate widow	XVIII.	1—8.
46.—Parable of the Pharisee and Publican . . .		9—14.
47.—Calling of Zacchæus	XIX.	2—10.
48.—Parable of the pounds		11—28.
49.—Christ weeping over Jerusalem		41—44.
50.—Special warning to Peter	XXII.	31—32.
51.—Direction to buy sword		35—38.
52.—Appearance of an angel, and bloody sweat in garden		43—44.
53.—Pilate sends Christ to Herod	XXIII.	6—16.
54.—Women deplore Christ's sufferings		27—32.
55.—The penitent thief		39—43.
56.—The appearance of Christ to two disciples going to Emmaus	XXIV.	13—35.
57.—Circumstances attending Christ's appearance to the eleven		37—49.
58.—Christ's departure in the act of blessing . .		50—53.

The Division of the Gospel of Luke.

As already stated, the Gospel of Luke in its beginning gives the birth and childhood of our Lord; then reveals His perfect Manhood, ministering, suffering and dying as the Saviour of men. The last chapter reveals the second Man in His resurrection glory and His ascension. All is cast in such a way as to bring out His true and perfect humanity. The best verse to quote as key for this Gospel is found in the nineteenth chapter: "For the Son of Man is come to seek and to save that which was lost" (xix:10). Various divisions have been made. Seven great parts, however, are clearly marked.

I. **The Birth and Childhood.** Chapter i-ii:52.

II. **The Beginnings of His Ministry.** Chapter iii-iv:13.

III. **The Ministry in Galilee.** Chapter iv:14-ix:50.

IV. **The Journey to Jerusalem.** Chapter ix:51-xix:27.

V. **In Jerusalem.** Chapter xix:28-xxi:38.

VI. **His Rejection, Suffering and Death.** Chapter xxii-xxiii.

VII. **His Resurrection and Ascension.** Chapter xxiv.

We give the different chapters with their contents in the Analysis.

Analysis and Annotations.

I. The Birth and Childhood.

Chapter I-II:52

CHAPTER I

1. The Introduction. 1-4.
2. Zacharias and Elizabeth; the Vision. 5-12.
3. John the Baptist, his birth and ministry announced. 13-17.
4. Zacharias' Unbelief and Punishment. 18-26.
5. The Angel's Announcement to the Virgin Mary. 27-33.
6. Mary's Question and the Answer. 34-38.
7. Mary Visits Elizabeth. 39-45.
8. The Virgin Mary's Hymn of Praise. 46-56.
9. The Birth of John. 57-66.
10. The Prophetic Song of Zacharias. 67-88.

Verses 1-4. The third Gospel begins in a way as no other Gospel does. It begins in a very human and humble way corresponding beautifully with the purpose of the Gospel. Yet it is couched in the choicest language. "Not only is it written in most classical Greek, but it reminds us by its contents of the similar preambles of the most illustrious Greek historians, especially those of Herodotus and Thucydides."* From the introduction we learn that Luke was not an eye-witness and minister of the Word; he did not belong to those who walked with the Lord during His earthly ministry. We do not know who the "many" were, who had written on the great things, which had taken place on earth and which all Christians believed. The remark has no reference to Matthew or Mark. Some have found in this simple introduction, in

* Prof. F. Godet.

which Luke has nothing to say about a divine commission to write, an evidence that he did not write by inspiration. Others have pointed out the fact that the words "from the very first" mean literally "from above" (so rendered in John iii:3) and found in these words an evidence that Luke was inspired. This, however, is incorrect; Luke does not assert his own inspiration. The entire introduction rather shows the guidance of the Spirit of God.*

Verses 5-12. For about 400 years the Lord had sent no communication to His people Israel. The silence of heaven is at last broken. The ministering Priest Zacharias beholds the Angel Gabriel, the same wonderful being, who brought heaven's messages to Daniel. The names of the aged and pious couple are significant. Zacharias means "Jehovah remembers," and Elizabeth is translated "the oath of God." If we join them together we have the sentence "Jehovah remembers the oath of God." The time of remembrance had come. Prophecy is about to be fulfilled.

Verses 13-17. John's birth and ministry are announced. "John" means "Favor of Jehovah." It fits in beautifully with the names of Zacharias and Elizabeth. "Jehovah remembers the oath of God" and the blessed result of the remembrance is "the Favor of Jehovah." Gabriel (which means: "God is mighty") announces that Zacharias' prayer had been heard and the answer was now given. The prayers of many years had not been forgotten. God's time for the answer had come. John is not Elias, but he came in the spirit and power of Elias.

---

* "It is a beautiful example of how naturally the Spirit of God works, or may work, in what we term inspiration. The instrument He uses is not like a mere pen in the hand of another. He is a man acting freely—for "where the Spirit of the Lord is there is liberty"—as if from his own heart and mind alone. He uses all the means he has got, and uses them diligently. You are quite prepared to find in his work the character of the writer: why should not He who has prepared the instrument, use it according to the quality of that which He has prepared? Why should He set aside the mind which He has furnished, any more than the affections of the heart which He has endowed?"—Numerical Bible.

Malachi iv:5-6 is yet to see its fulfillment before the coming of the great and dreadful day of the Lord.

Verses 18-26. The announcement of the birth of a son was not believed by Zacharias. Like Abraham and Sarah he looked to earthly circumstances. He did not reckon with the power of God. Disbelieving the words of Gabriel he was struck dumb. He should have shouted praises; instead, he expressed his doubt. Unbelief insults God; the character of God demands judgment upon unbelief.

Verses 27-33. Next God's messenger is sent to Nazareth of Galilee to carry the greatest message, which was ever given to an angel. He appears in Nazareth and came in to the Virgin Mary. How simple and beautiful is the narrative! Here is the woman, the Virgin of Prophecy, who is to bring forth the long promised Son. She is to conceive; bring forth a Son; His name is to be called Jesus; He shall be great and shall be called the Son of the Highest. Even so it came to pass. Then we have an unfulfilled part of the announcement. "The Lord God shall give unto Him the throne of His father David; and He shall reign over the house of Jacob forever; and of His Kingdom there shall be no end." When He comes the second time, not in humiliation, but in power and great glory, He will receive the throne of His father David and the promised Kingdom. "Let us beware of spiritualizing away the full meaning of these words. The house of Jacob does not mean 'all Christians.' The throne of David does not mean the office of a Saviour to Gentile believers. These words will yet receive a literal fulfillment, when the Lord Jesus comes a second time. The Kingdom of which he speaks is the glorious Kingdom of Daniel vii:27." (Bishop Ryle.)

Verses 34-38. The Virgin's question "How shall this be, seeing that I know not a man?"—is not the result of unbelief. She believed, presupposing the absolute reality of the promise, in asking the exact manner of its fulfillment. The blessed mystery of the incarnation, how the Son of God should take on the human form and become man, is made known. It is a great mystery. "The Holy Spirit shall come upon thee" means that the human nature of our Lord was produced in the Virgin by a creative act of the Holy Spirit. (Matt. i:18-20). And therefore He possessed an absolutely holy nature. "And the Power of the Most High shall overshadow thee." This is not a repetition of the first statement. It means that the Son of God, who is the Most High overshadowed the Virgin, uniting Himself with the miraculously prepared human nature. He is designated in His Being "that holy thing" because He cannot be classified. And because He *is* holy there could be nothing in Him, who was born of the Virgin, which is unholy. And beautiful is the submission of the Virgin to the will of God.

Verses 39-45. Mary then visited her cousin Elizabeth. How perfectly human is the whole account! And how beautiful the language of the elder woman calling the Virgin "the mother of my Lord." Surely this was a great revelation she received. With holy reverence we also should use that worthy Name. Well has it been said, "Let us remember the deep meaning of the words 'the Lord' and beware of using them lightly and carelessly." Then she blessed Mary. "Blessed is she that believed."

Verses 46-56. The marvellous outburst of praise which comes from Mary's lips is a beautiful echo of the Old Testament Scriptures. The pious Virgin knew the Word of God; her heart was filled with it and the Holy Spirit used the Word in the expression of her praise. Many Psalms are touched upon, but especially are we reminded of Hannah's inspired song. (I Sam. ii.) Notice also Mary's deep humility and her acknowledgment of the need of a Saviour. The invention of Rome, of the sinless and immaculate person of Mary, is disproved by everything in the Word of God.

Verses 57-66. When John is born Zacharias' tongue is loosed. He is a type of Israel. Now that people is dumb; some future day when "the Grace of Jehovah" is acknowledged by them, when they see and believe, the remnant of Israel will praise and bless God. No doubt Zacharias was also afflicted with deafness. The last written word of the Old Testament is a curse, Mal. iv:6; the first written word of the New Testament is "grace"* (John: Grace of Jehovah).

Verses 67-88. Zacharias prophesies. He praises God for the fulfillment of His promises spoken by the mouth of His holy Prophets. The Lord of salvation is Messiah. It denotes strength and power. He brings deliverance, salvation from enemies and the promised covenant mercies. (Ps. cxxxii:17-18). He beholds the blessings of the promised Kingdom and beholds the blessed results of the visit of the day spring from on high. The Septuagint (Greek translation of the O. T.) translates the word branch in the Old Testament with "day spring." Christ, the Branch, is also the day spring from on high. The fulfillment of Zacharias' prophecy takes place with the second coming of the Lord.

CHAPTER II

1. The Birth of Christ at Bethlehem. 1-7.
2. The Glad Tidings Announced to the Shepherds. 8-20.
3. The Circumcision and Presentation. 21-24.
4. Simeon and His Prophecy. 25-35.
5. Anna the Prophetess. 36-38.
6. In Nazareth. 39-40.
7. In the Temple. 41-51.
8. The Increase. 52.

Verses 1-7. The appointed time (Gal. iv:4) had come. According to prophecy the Saviour had to be born in Bethlehem (Micah v:1). But Mary lived in Nazareth. God in His own marvellous way ordered everything and Cæsar Augustus was directed to issue the decree of taxation at such a time and in such a way and also the journey of Joseph and his espoused wife, Mary, that she had to be in Bethlehem when the days were accomplished that she

* Bengel "Gnomen."

should be delivered. The great Roman Emperor knew nothing of what God was accomplishing by his decree. Then He was born, who left the glory of Heaven and became poor for our sakes. What condescension we behold here! The Maker of Heaven and Earth, born of a woman, taking the creature's place! The first resting place of Him, who came from the bosom of the Father is a manger! There was no room for Him in the inn.

Verses 8-20. Here not the birth of a King is announced as in Matthew, but the birth of a Saviour. The wise men from the East looking for the new-born King are not mentioned by Luke. Poor shepherds hear the glad tidings first. Heaven is opened. The Glory of the Lord shines round about; angels' voices are heard, telling out in heavenly praise, what will be the ultimate result of the work of the Second Man. "Glory to God in the highest, Peace on Earth, good will toward men." But the world rejected Him. Good will toward men sounds forth in the glad tidings, but "Glory to God in the highest and peace on earth" is yet to come, when He, the Son of Man, appears again. The shepherds were obedient. They made haste. How simple their faith; how great their reward!

Verses 21-24. And now we find that He, who came of a woman also was made under the law. The circumcision made Him "debtor to do the whole law" which He alone could fulfill; and then to redeem those upon whom the curse of the law rests, by being made a curse for us. (Gal. iii:13). The name announced before His birth is then given to the child. (Matthew i:21). Five other persons in the Bible were named before their birth: Isaac, Genesis xvii:19; Ishmael, Genesis xvi:11; Josiah, I Kings xiii:2; Cyrus, Isaiah xliv:28, and John the Baptist. As the first-born, according to His own law, He is presented unto the Lord. The required sacrifice is brought, in which is written the story of the cross. The sacrifice tells the story of poverty, for the sacrificial birds were only for the poor. "If she be not able to bring a lamb, then she shall bring two turtle doves, or two young pigeons." (Lev. xii:6).

Verses 25-35. Simeon had the divine revelation that he should not see death before he had seen the Lord's Anointed. He belonged to the faithful remnant of Israel, who in the dark days of decline and apostasy held fast the Word and waited for its promised fulfillment. The Lord had then a faithful remnant, who waited for His first coming; and now His faithful people wait for the blessed Hope, His coming again to receive them unto Himself. Simeon had the revelation that he should not see death, till He had come. This corresponds to the greater promises in 1 Cor. xv:51 and 1 Thessal. iv:17. The Spirit led him into the temple at the right moment. His waiting ended when he held the child in his arms. It was a babe, like any other babe. Yet faith saw in Him what He is, the Lord's salvation for His people; He who had come to do the great work. "A light to lighten the Gentiles, and the glory of thy people, Israel." This is prophetic. The Gentiles are put first. Even so it has come to pass; after the fulness of the Gentiles has come in all Israel will be saved. See Isaiah xlix:5-6; Rom. xi:25-26. And Simeon, holding the babe in his arms, blest the mother and Joseph, not the child, for he knew He was the Blesser.

Verse 36. Then a daughter of Phanuel, Anna, appeared to add her testimony. What a beautiful woman she must have been in her self-denying service! No sooner had she seen the Lord than she spake at once of Him to all them that looked for redemption in Jerusalem. In the midst of the wicked city, soon to become a city of murderers (Is. i:21), there was a company of men and women who looked for redemption.

Verses 39-40. They returned to Nazareth. The visit of the wise men, the flight into Egypt and the return are omitted. Twelve years passed and it did not please the Holy Spirit to give us a report of them. Spurious Gospels of the Infancy were circulated later; they are all legendary and unreliable. As the true Man He grew from infancy to boyhood. Of all the sinless conditions of the human body He was partaker. He grew both mentally and physically. His heart ever seeking God and being in subjection unto Him.

Verses 41-50. Every Jewish boy of twelve years visited Jerusalem at the time of the great festivals. He stayed behind and his anxious mother and Joseph found Him in the temple three days later. For three days He was lost to them. May this not be a reminder of the three days He was thought lost by His disciples? (Chapter xxiv:21). Here the human infirmity of Mary comes to light. She was nervously anxious. Her words have an accusing tone. The greatest mistake she committed was the mentioning of Joseph as "thy Father." In all this her human failure is in evidence. But how sublime the answer of the twelve year old boy! He is astonished that they should have sought Him; He came to seek them. He is astonished that they did not know that He had to be about His Father's business. What an answer it is! These are His first words recorded in the Gospels. He corrects His fallible mother, who had said, "thy Father and I." His Father, He declares, is He in whose house He had gone. It is the first self-witness to His Deity.

Verses 51-52. And He went down with them to Nazareth and was subject unto them. He was obedient in all things.

II. The Beginnings of His Ministry.

Chapter iii-iv:13

CHAPTER III

1. The Ministry of John the Baptist. 1-14.
2. His Testimony to Christ and his Imprisonment. 15-20.
3. The Baptism of the Lord Jesus. 21-22.
4. The Genealogy of Mary, the Mother of our Lord. 23-38.

Verses 1-14. Eighteen more years of silence follow. It is broken by the voice of the forerunner, John, who preached at Jordan the baptism of repentance for the remission of sins. He is not reported here preaching "the Kingdom of Heaven is at hand." He preached thus as the witness for the King and the Kingdom about to come. Matthew had to give the report of this preaching. Here we read that "all flesh should see His salvation." This awaits still its great fulfillment when He comes the second time. John's call to repentance is answered by the people, by the publicans and by the soldiers. They asked "What shall we do?" How different, however, the question concerning salvation and the answer. (Acts xvi: 30-31).

Verses 15-20. Then he gave witness concerning Christ. The expectation among the people was great and some thought that John might be the Messiah. The answer he gives directs the people to the coming One. Verses 16 and 17 blend together the first and second Coming of Christ. The fire-baptism takes place when He comes again; it is the fire of judgment. His first coming has brought for all who believe in Him the baptism with the Holy Spirit.

Verses 21-22. We request the reader to turn at this point to the remarks made in our annotations on Matthew and Mark. Luke omits, however, the conversation which took place between our Lord and John; then there is the additional information that our Lord was praying, when heaven opened and the Holy Spirit came upon Him. The descent into the water signified His death and as the result of His death, heaven was opened and the Holy Spirit came down. As He prayed in Jordan so He prayed in Gethsemane as He approached the cross. "Who in the days of His flesh, when He had offered up prayers and supplications with strong crying and tears unto Him that was able to save Him out of death and was heard in that He feared." (Heb. v:7).

Verses 23-38. The age of our Lord, about thirty years, is only given by Luke. In the Gospel of the Manhood this properly belongs. The annotations on the first chapter in Matthew should be carefully considered here and the two genealogies compared. The genealogy in Matthew is that of the King; Luke's genealogy is that of the Son of Man. Matthew's genealogy begins with David and Abraham and leads up to Joseph; Luke's genealogy begins with Joseph and leads up to Adam, the first man. It is a tracing backward to the head of the human race, Adam; and back of Adam is God Himself. So He who is God had come and became the Son of Man, the Second Man, the last Adam. The genealogy in Matthew is that of Joseph, a son of David, through the line of Solomon; Luke's genealogy is that of Mary, the mother of our Lord, who also is of David through the line of Nathan. Joseph is called in Luke's genealogy the son of Heli, because Mary was a daughter of Heli. Matthew's Gospel tells us that Jacob begat Joseph, the husband of Mary.

CHAPTER IV:1-13

1. The Temptation in the Wilderness. 1-12.
2. The Devil Defeated. 13.

Verses 1-13. What interests us most is the different order in which the three temptations of the Lord are reported by Luke. The second temptation the devil brings to bear upon Him (in the high mountain) is the last in the Gospel of Matthew. Why did Luke change the order and put the second temptation last and the last temptation into the second place? Matthew gives, no doubt, the correct order. The Lord's word to Satan, "Get thee behind me, Satan," proves this.* The order in Luke corresponds to the nature of man. Man is composed of Body, Soul and Spirit. The first temptation concerns the body; the second the soul, and the third the spirit. The temptations man has to go through in life are clearly seen here. In youth it is the lust of the flesh; in manhood the lust of the eyes, to possess and to enjoy; in old age the pride of life. The change in the order is made to correspond to this. But "the holy thing," the holy Son of God, had nothing in Him which could ever respond to this trinity of evil. He did not sin, nor could He ever sin. The devil departed from Him for a season.

* These words must be omitted in the 8th verse. They are not found in the best manuscripts.

III. The Ministry in Galilee.

Chapter iv:14-ix:50

CHAPTER IV:14-44

1. In the Synagogue of Nazareth. 14-21.
2. Unbelief and Rejection of Christ. 22-32.
3. A Demon Cast Out in Capernaum. 33-37.
4. Peter's Wife's Mother Healed; Many Healed. 38-44.

Verses 14-21. And now the description of the ministry of the Son of Man begins. The beginning is in His own city. How all written here is again in a very human manner. He had been brought up in that city and as His custom was "He went into the synagogue," and as He had done, no doubt, before, He stood up to read and like a man finds the place in the scroll which the servant had handed Him. Isaiah lxi:1-2 is read by Him and then applied to Himself. The Spirit of the Lord was indeed upon Him to preach the Gospel to the poor. But He stopped in the middle of a sentence. The acceptable year of the Lord, is the last word He read. In His Person all this had appeared. He came to preach the Gospel, to heal the broken-hearted, to preach deliverance to the captives, recovering of sight to the blind and to set at liberty them that are bruised. He did not read "the day of vengeance of our God." That too is His work, but not as long as the acceptable year of the Lord lasts.

Verses 22-32. "Is not this Joseph's son?" It is the first hint of the coming rejection. Then when He declared that God's grace is not to be confined to Israel, but that it will, as in days of old, in the case of the widow of Sarepta and Naaman, go out to the Gentiles, they were filled with wrath. They were ready to kill Him. What happened? "But He, passing through the midst of them, went His way." Was it a miracle? Is it the same as when He passed through shut doors? It was the result of His own dignity as the perfect Man, which awed the crowds, so that no one dared to touch Him.

Verses 33-37. The same incident is reported in Mark i:21-28. The demons knew Him but He had come to spoil the enemy and here He manifested His power.

Verses 38-44. Many works of power followed. As the seeker of the lost to preach the good tidings, He went from city to city.

CHAPTER V

1. The Miraculous Draught of Fishes. 1-11.
2. The Leper Healed. 12-16.
3. The Paralytic Healed. 17-26.
4. The Call of Matthew and the Feast. 27-29.
5. The Scribes and Pharisees Answered. 30-35.
6. The Parable of the Garment and the Bottle. 36-39.

Verses 1-11. Two miraculous draughts of fishes are found in the Gospels. The one here at the beginning of His ministry; the other after His resurrection. (John xxi). Both demonstrate His power as Lord over the animal creation. Here the net broke (or began to break), in the other miracle it did not break. Peter is prominent in both. Here he falls at His feet crying out, "Depart from me, for I am a sinful man, O Lord." The divine presence, made known by the miracle, showed Peter his own condition. The Lord graciously calms his fear. The soul that sinks down at the blessed feet of the Lord and owns his sinfulness is safe. He came to seek and to save what is lost. And more than that. He calls into service. "Fear not, from henceforth thou shalt catch men." They left all and followed Him. It would have been strange if they had done anything else. The highest and best besides knowing the Lord as our Saviour is to follow Him and to be obedient to His call.

Verses 12-16.—Luke describes the leper as being full of

leprosy. The terrible disease had advanced so as to cover the entire body. Leprosy is the most awful, incurable disease. It is a living death and one of the best illustrations of sin and its ravages. He has the power, and He alone, to heal the leper, as He is the only One who can heal the spiritual leprosy. Then great multitudes came together to hear and to be healed. How men were attracted to Him and sought Him! But He went instead into the wilderness to pray. He felt the need as the perfect man to seek the Father's presence. He has given us an example. It is the pattern we should follow.

"Why is it that there is so much apparent religious working, and yet so little result in positive conversions to God,—so many sermons, and so few souls saved,—so much machinery, and so little effect produced,—so much running hither and thither, and yet so few brought to Christ? Why is all this? The reply is short and simple. There is not enough private prayer. The cause of Christ does not need less working, but it does need among the workers more praying. Let us each examine ourselves, and amend our ways. The most successful workmen in the Lord's vineyard, are those who are like their Master, often and much upon their knees." *

Verses 17-26. The same miracle is reported by Matthew and Mark. (Matthew ix:2-8; Mark ii:1-12). See annotations there.

Verses 27-29. The Publican Levi is Matthew, the writer of the Gospel of Matthew. He was a taxgatherer and as such despised by his own brethren, because he was serving the hated Roman government. Taxgatherers and sinners the Son of Man came to call. Levi left all and followed him. That he became at once a witness for the Lord is seen by the feast he made and the large number of taxgatherers he had invited.

The concluding verses of this chapter we have already considered in the preceding Gospels.

* Bishop Ryle.

CHAPTER VI

1. The Son of Man the Lord of the Sabbath. 1-5.
2. The Man with the Withered Hand Healed. 6-11.
3. The Twelve Apostles Chosen. 12-19.
4. Blessing and Woe. 20-26.
5. Good for Evil. 27-31.
6. Instructions to Disciples. 32-38.
7. Warnings. 39-45.

Verses 1-11. The opening verses of the chapter are nearly alike in the three Gospels. The arrangement in Matthew is different. It is used there to bring out the consummation of the rejection of the King. (Matt. xii: 1-8). Then He healed the man with the withered hand. The healing was done in their midst; it was a miracle done before their eyes. How different from the pretended healings of Christian Science and other cults. They were filled with madness and began their plotting.

Verses 12-19. Before He chose the twelve Apostles He spent the whole night in prayer. It was "in those days," the days when they were rejecting Him. The refuge of the perfect Man was then in God. He sought His presence and cast Himself upon Him for guidance. The Gospel of Luke has much to say about the prayers of the Lord Jesus. His prayers are the expression of dependence of His perfect humanity. Among the twelve is Judas the traitor. He was called to be an apostle that the Scriptures might be fulfilled. The Lord knew him from the beginning. He was not a believer in the Deity of our Lord; Judas never called Him, Lord. A very old commentary * gives the following suggestion: "Judas is chosen that the Lord might have an enemy among His attendants, for that man is perfect who has no cause to shrink from observation of a wicked man, conversant with all his ways."

Verses 20-45. Certain parts of the Sermon on the Mount. In Matthew it occupies the most prominent

* Anselim, who lived from 1033-1109.

place, for in the Gospel of the King it is the great proclamation He utters in the beginning of His ministry. See the Study pamphlet on Matthew. Luke reports only a part of the great discourse. A comparison will show that Luke gives a number of additions, which are all in line with the purpose of the Gospel. There is no allusion made as in the Gospel of Matthew to the Law, nor is there given in Luke the expansion of the Law. The instructions concerning alms and prayer are likewise omitted. In Luke's Gospel the words are reported which touch upon the wants of the disciples as men, who are in the world. Their separation from the world, their conduct, besides warnings are fully given. In Matthew we read, "Be ye therefore perfect as your Father in heaven is perfect." Luke changes by divine guidance the word perfect to "merciful." The correct rendering is "Become ye merciful." The Son of Man came to this earth in mercy to meet man; the disciple is to manifest the same mercy. The word "perfect" given by Matthew is the larger description; it includes "mercifulness," which Luke is led by the Spirit of God to emphasize.

CHAPTER VII

1. The Centurion's Servant Healed. 1-10.
2. The Widow's Son Raised from the Dead. 11-17.
3. John's Questions and the Answer. 18-23.
4. The Testimony Concerning John. 24-29.
5. The Unreasonableness of Unbelief. 30-35.
6. The Woman With the Alabaster Box. 36-40.
7. The Parable of the Two Debtors. 41-50.

Verses 1-10. In Matthew the healing of the Centurion's servant comes after the healing of the leper. It teaches there the dispensational lesson, that the Gentiles would enter the Kingdom and the children of the Kingdom would be cast out into the outer darkness. As Luke writes for another purpose he omits Matthew viii:11-12. Luke tells us that the Centurion sent the Jewish Elders first; when on the road to the Centurion's house, the friends of the Centurion with the message of unworthiness, met the Lord. Some have tried to explain these differences by making the two accounts, two different miracles. This is not the case at all. The account given by Matthew is more fully explained by Luke. The Centurion first sent messengers to our Lord, and afterwards he came to speak to Him in person. Matthew relates the personal interview and Luke the message. "Speak the word only, and my servant shall be healed," is a marvellous utterance of faith. The Centurion owned Him as Lord of all, with power over all. To him He is the Creator with omnipotent power. And the Lord marvelled at him. It is an evidence of His true humanity. Twice He marvelled; here at faith and in Mark vi:6 at unbelief.

Verses 11-17. The account of the raising of the widow's son is peculiar to Luke. The story brings out the deep compassion of the Son of Man and that is why it is exclusively reported in the third Gospel. The only son of a widow had died. Here is human sorrow in the fullest sense. A widow losing her only son, her only support. He had compassion on her. How human and filled with sympathy were His words "Weep not." And the second Word He spoke in touching the bier was "Arise." And when the young man came back to life, He delivered him to his mother. "Weep not!" the word of His sympathy; "Arise" the word of His power. No wonder that the people declared, "God hath visited His people." Elijah raised the son of a widow, but he had to humble himself and had to cry to the Lord. Elisha also raised the son of the Shunamite, but only after having stretched himself over the child. But the Lord commands and death has to release its prey at the one word. The Second Man has power to deal with sin and death and man's need is fully met.

Verses 18-35. John, perplexed with doubt, sends to Him two of his disciples. "Honest doubt never stays away from Christ, but comes to Him for solution." The disciples beheld the miracles the Lord did at that time. Then when John had evidently made shipwreck of his witness bearing, the Lord bears witness to him. He declares the greatness of his person. (Verses 27-28). All this is recorded in Matthew xi:2-15; but Luke gives an interesting addition. Two classes of people stood there. The people who had heard John, accepted his message of repentance and who had been baptized. They and the taxgatherers justified God. The leaders of the nation rejected the counsels of God against them, they had testified to that by not being baptized by John.

Verses 36-50. The balance of this chapter is again peculiar to Luke. He is seen as the friend of sinners, who had come to seek and save that which is lost. Beautiful sight this woman so sinful, standing behind Him at His feet, weeping, so that she wet His feet with her tears! This incident must not be confounded with the similar one reported by Matthew, Mark and John; nor was the woman Mary Magdalene. She seeks shelter with her burdened soul at the feet of Him, whom the proud Pharisees called "a friend of publicans and sinners." How great must have been His compassion, how marvellous His lovingkindness, that a woman could come thus in His presence. The loveliness and attractiveness of the perfect Man as the friend of sinners is here fully seen. And the proud host, the Pharisee Simon, doubts that He is a prophet, for would He then not know what kind of a woman she is! The Son of Man at once gives him the evidence of His omniscience. Not alone does He know who the woman is, but He also knows the unspoken thoughts of Simon. The parable the Lord gives to Simon explains the great love of the woman, much had been forgiven her. The consciousness of that forgiveness had produced these blessed actions of the woman. And once more she hears from the lips of the Friend of Sinners, what countless thousands have heard spoken to their hearts by His Spirit: "Thy faith hath saved thee; go in peace."

CHAPTER VIII

1. The Ministering Company. 1-3.
2. The Parable of the Sower. 4-15.
3. The Parable of the Lighted Candle. 16-18.
4. The Declaration of a New Relationship. 19-21.
5. The Storm on the Lake. 22-25.
6. In the Country of the Gadarenes; the Maniac Healed. **26-36.**
7. His Rejection by the Gadarenes. 37-40.
8. The Woman With the Issue of Blood Healed. 41-48.
9. The Daughter of Jairus Raised. 49-56.

Verses 1-3. This also is reported exclusively by Luke. What wonderful preaching it must have been when He with the Apostles went about preaching! And the trophies of His power and grace were also with Him. Here we read that women ministered unto Him of their substance. What privilege was theirs to minister to Him!

Verses 4-18. The parables which follow are known to us from the Gospels of Matthew and Mark. The parable of the Sower is here not in the dispensational setting in which it appears in Matthew (Chapter xiii). The parables of the mustard seed and the leaven are reported later by Luke. The parable of the Sower is linked here with the preaching of the Word in verses 1-3.

Verses 19-56. The events which follow are also found in the synoptics. The Storm on the Lake shows His true humanity. He is asleep. But in the threatening danger, when the helpless vessel fills with water, He knows no fear. They have to wake Him. The wind and waves obey His Word. And blessed be His Name! He is still the same. Then there is the man in his fallen, pitiful condition, under the complete dominion of Satan, both in body and in soul. And once more the Son of Man shows His absolute power over Satan. The sufferer is completely healed. What a transformation took place! "The 'many devils' by whom he had been possessed were compelled to leave him. Nor is this all. Cast forth from their abode in the man's heart, we see these malignant spirits beseeching our Lord that He would 'not torment' them, or 'command them to go out into the deep,' and so confessing His supremacy over them. Mighty as they were, they plainly felt themselves in the presence of One mightier than themselves. Full of malice as they were, they could not even hurt the 'swine' of the Gadarenes until our Lord granted them permission."

CHAPTER IX:1-50

1. Christ Sends Forth the Twelve Apostles. **1-6.**
2. Herod Perplexed. 7-9.
3. The Return of the Apostles. 10.
4. The Feeding of the Five Thousand. 11-17.
5. Peter's Confession of Christ. 18-21.
6. The Son of Man Announces His Death and Resurrection. **22.**
7. Necessity of Self-Denial. 23-26.
8. The Transfiguration. 27-36.
9. The Demon Cast Out. 37-43.
10. The Second Prediction of His Rejection. 44-45.
11. Disciples Rebuked. 46-50.

Verses 1-9. The sending out of the twelve is briefly given by Luke. The full account is in Matthew. All this shows the guidance of the Holy Spirit. Matthew writing concerning the King must needs give all the details of the sending out of the Kingdom messengers. In the foreground is put here the power and authority which the Lord gave to the Apostles over all demons and to cure all diseases. Did Judas also have this power? Assuredly, for he was an Apostle. The authority and power was conferred upon them and not for any faith, virtue or merit on the Apostle's side. They went forth preaching the gospel and healing everywhere. They are the messengers of the compassionate friend of sinners. Herod here fears Him and desires to see Him, who was greater than John, whom he had beheaded. Herod saw Him later. He had desired to see Him for a long time. At last He stood before Him bound, the willing sacrifice to be led away to the cross. Herod never heard a single word from His lips. Then the wicked King mocked. (Chapter xxiii:8).

Verses 10-26. The compassion and tenderness of the Lord is blessedly revealed throughout these verses. The Apostles returned and He took them away for rest. The multitude followed Him "and He received them, and spake unto them of the Kingdom of God, and healed them that had need of healing." The miracle of the feeding of the five thousand is reported in all the Gospels including John. He graciously supplied their need. Peter's confession is preceded by prayer. In Matthew we read the fuller confession, "Thou art the Christ, the Son of the living God." There also the Lord saith that it was revealed unto Peter by His Father. Luke alone tells us He prayed before. May we then not look upon the confession as an answer to the Lord's prayer?

Verses 27-50. In the transfiguration scene we see Him again in prayer. "And as He prayed the fashion of His countenance was altered, and His raiment was white and glistening." Luke tells us of the subject of the conversation between the Lord, Moses and Elijah. They spoke of His decease, which He should accomplish in Jerusalem. He had announced for the first time His coming suffering and death (verse 22) and that death demanded by the Law (Moses) and predicted by the prophets (Elijah), which must needs be and precede His glory, is the great theme. Another statement is found in Luke, which is absent in Matthew and Mark. Moses and Elijah "appeared in glory"; not their own glory, but His glory. Luke also informs us that when they entered the overshadowing cloud, they feared. The Transfiguration is prophetic. Some day the Second Man, the last Adam, the head of the new creation, will appear in His Glory, and all His Saints will share that coming Glory.

IV. The Journey to Jerusalem.

Chapter ix:51-xix:27

CHAPTER IX:51-62

1. His Face Set Toward Jerusalem. 51-52.
2. The Rejected Messengers and His Rebuke. 53-56.
3. Tests of Discipleship. 57-62.

The fifty-first verse marks a new part in this Gospel. The time was come; His hour was approaching. As the perfect Man we have seen Him. As babe, as child, as man in all His loveliness we have seen Him and now the compassionate, loving One, He, who always pleased God in a perfect obedience "steadfastly set His face to go up to Jerusalem." Coming from Galilee the messengers entered into a village of the Samaritans, who would not receive Him because His face was set toward Jerusalem, the city the Samaritans hated. James and John asked the Lord to command fire to come down from heaven to consume them as Elias did. They believed the Lord had the power to do this. They had been with Him and had seen His deeds of love and kindness and yet they could make so strange a request. He then rebuked them. Later John went again into Samaria, but manifested a far different spirit (Acts viii).

CHAPTER X

1. The Seventy Appointed. 1-16.
2. The Return of the Seventy and the True Rejoicing. 17-20.
3. Jesus Rejoiced in Spirit. 21-24.
4. The Question of the Lawyer. 25-29.
5. The Parable of the Good Samaritan. 30-37.
6. Martha and Mary. 38-42.

Verses 1-24. Seventy others are commissioned by Him to be His heralds. They were to visit every city and place, which He would visit. How great and extended the labors of the Son of Man must have been. The Gospel of the Kingdom was then heralded as a witness. And He knew that the message would be rejected. The meek and lowly One, the friend of sinners pronounces as Judge the woes upon the cities, who had already rejected the message. When the messengers returned He said unto them, "I beheld Satan as lightning fall from heaven." According to Revelation xii, he is still occupying the heavens and the casting out of Satan is still future. The Lord beheld this complete downfall of Satan; the work the seventy had done was but a little anticipation of that which is yet to come. Then He rejoiced. Three times we read of Him that He wept, but only once that He rejoiced. He uttered concerning Himself a great declaration, which reveals His glory. "All things are delivered to me of my Father: and no man knoweth who the Son is but the Father, and who the Father is but the Son, and he to whom the Son will reveal Him." Only He who is very God could utter such a declaration.

Verses 25-37. The lawyer's question leads to the utterance of the parable of the good Samaritan, to answer the question, "Who is my neighbour?" The parable answers the question fully, but it also contains the most blessed Gospel truths. Jerusalem is the city of God; Jericho represents the world. The traveller is the type of humanity. Man has fallen in the awful road which leads down, fallen among thieves, naked, wounded, helpless and hopeless. The failure of the Priest and the scribe to help illustrates the inability of the law and the ordinances to save man out of his deplorable condition. The good Samaritan is the Lord Jesus Christ. He came to the place where the lost are and He alone could have compassion on him. The wine typifies His precious blood He shed to save us. The oil is the type of the Holy Spirit, who applies the blood. He takes care of fallen man found by Him. The inn is typical of the church, where the Lord through His Spirit cares for His own. The two pence are not typical of "two sacraments" but speak of the reward, which those receive, who, under the Holy Spirit, care for souls. The promised coming again with a greater reward offered is the Second Coming of our Lord. The Gospel of the Manhood records this parable exclusively.

In **verses 38-42** we find another incident reported exclusively by Luke. The story of Martha and Mary is closely linked with the preceding paragraph. Martha and Mary were both disciples. Martha was busy serving the Lord, while Mary took her place at His feet and let the Lord serve her. In this He delights.

"Martha has received Christ into her house, and surely into her heart. If she is busy, she is busy serving *Him;* yet that does not prevent her being distracted by it. She is more: she is vexed and irritated. Mary her sister is sitting quietly at the feet of Jesus, listening to His word; and she blames even the Lord for permitting it, while she needs her help so much. But the Lord asserts that Mary has chosen the good part, and it is moreover the only needful thing: it shall not be taken from her.

But is learning of Jesus, then, the one needful thing? Is activity nothing? is service nothing? We may be sure the Lord is very far from meaning that. But if a man brings me, let us say, an apple, I do not despise it when I say, "The one thing is the tree that bears the apples." *

Twice more we find in the Gospels Mary at the feet of the Lord. When her brother Lazarus had died, she wept at His feet and He comforted her. When she anointed Him, Mary again was at His feet. She owned Him as Prophet (Luke x); as Priest (John xi) and as King (John xii).

* Numerical Bible.

CHAPTER XI

1. The Prayer Given to the Disciples. 1-4.
2. The Friend at Midnight. 5-10.
3. Encouragement to Pray. 11-13.
4. A Demon Cast Out and the Blasphemous Accusation. 14-23.
5. The Return of the Unclean Spirit. 24-26.
6. The Blessedness of Hearing the Word. 27-28.
7. The Sign of Jonas. 29-32.
8. The Single Eye. 33-36.
9. The Pharisees Exposed and Denounced. 37-44.
10. The Lawyers Exposed and Denounced. 45-54.

Verses 1-13. Prayer is here more fully dealt with. We have learned how the perfect Man, the Son of God, who had taken the creature's place, made use of prayer. Again we see Him praying and when His disciples request Him to teach them to pray, He gives them the form of prayer, commonly known as "the Lord's prayer." But the better name is "the Disciples prayer," for the Lord Jesus had no need to pray, "forgive us our sins." Many teach that this form of prayer was given twice, once in the Sermon on the Mount and the second time here. This is of course not impossible, but far from probable. If the prayer had been previously given, why should the request be made again? The ending which appears in Matthew, "For thine is the kingdom, etc.," is omitted here as it ought to be in the Gospel of Matthew, for it was undoubtedly added by someone else. The parable which follows is peculiar to Luke. The parable was spoken to encourage perseverance in prayer, to pray without ceasing, continue in prayer, to always pray and not faint, which are all exhortations to His people. The promise contained in the thirteenth verse was fulfilled when the Holy Spirit was given on the day of Pentecost. To plead this promise now is unscriptural. The Holy Spirit has been given; He has come and dwells in the believer.

The story of His rejection is followed much in

the same way as in Matthew. Verses 24-26 are in Matthew's Gospel applied to the nation. The unclean spirit of idolatry had left them and is to return with seven others. But here the words of the Lord have a wider application, for He speaks of the state of a man. Outward reformation without true conversion and the reception of the nature from above, but brings Satan back with seven other spirits. Self-reformation cannot save.

The chapter closes with the judgments pronounced upon the Pharisees and Lawyers. Verses 37-54. He had entered the lawyer's house as his guest. When the Pharisee marvelled, that He had not washed His hands in the ceremonial way, as commanded by the traditional law, the Lord uttered these solemn woes. They remind us of Matthew xxiii, but a closer study reveals the fact that the words of judgment Luke reports here were uttered at another occasion entirely. The words in Matthew were uttered in Jerusalem, while the words in Luke were spoken when He was journeying towards Jerusalem.

CHAPTER XII

1. Warning Against Hypocrisy. 1-3.
2. Encouragements. 4-14.
3. Warning Against Covetousness. 15-21.
4. Warning Against Anxiety. 22-31.
5. The Disciples Comfort and Hope. 32-40.
6. The Parable of the Steward. 41-48.
7. The Purpose of God and the Resulting Division. 49-53.
8. Concerning Signs. 54-57.
9. The Failure of Israel. 58-59.

Verses 1-31. Nearly all of the entire twelfth chapter is not found in the other Gospels. Perhaps the largest multitude, which ever gathered to hear the Lord is seen here. He speaks to His disciples first of all and warns of the leaven of the Pharisees. But the warning was also meant for all who heard Him. He declares a coming day, when the hidden things shall be uncovered. Then

He gives encouragement to His friends, "Be not afraid." What meaning these words have, coming from such lips! The entire first half of the chapter is taken up with warnings and encouragements to those who heed the warnings and are His friends.

Verses 32-48. He speaks of His own coming again. The little flock is assured of the kingdom. Everything else is uncertain, insecure and passing away. He is coming again and His return will bring the reward to His friends, who are obedient to His Word. They are to wait for Him. "From the wedding" is better rendered by "because of the wedding." The wedding, the marriage-feast does not precede His return, but follows that event. "He shall gird Himself, and make them to sit down to meat, and will come forth and serve them." This is a wonderful statement. What service that will be, when He has His faithful people with Him! The Romans divided the night into four watches. The Lord speaks of the second and third watches, but does not mention the fourth. However in Matthew xiv we read that He came to His toiling servants in the fourth watch.

> "He says nothing of the fourth, simply for the reason that the disciples, from that, should note that His return was by no means to be expected as late as possible; even as He does not name the first, because it would weaken the whole representation of the watchful servants. The Parousia does not come so quickly as impatience, nor yet so late as carelessness supposes, but in the very middle of the night, when the temptation to fall asleep is great and therefore must be most vigorously combated. It may even tarry longer than the servants think; but, grant that it should not take place even till the third, or should come even in the second watch of the night, whosoever perseveres faithfully at his post shall in no wise lose his reward." *

He assures them that He will come "at an hour when ye think not." The parable of the Steward is closely linked with all this. A solemn declaration is made, found only in Luke, concerning the penalties. (Verses 47-48.) The punishment is according to the knowledge of

* Van Oosterzee.

the Lord's will. His rejection by Israel has brought for the world the results of which He speaks next.

CHAPTER XIII

1. The Necessity of Repentance. 1-5.
2. The Barren Fig-Tree. 6-9.
3. The Healing of a Daughter of Abraham. 10-17.
4. Parable of the Mustard-seed. 18-19.
5. Parable of the Leaven. 20-21.
6. Solemn Teachings. 22-30.
7. The Answer to Herod. 31-33.
8. Lament over Jerusalem. 34-35.

Verses 1-9. Luke alone gives the parable of the fig tree as well as the historical incidents preceding the parable. The absolute necessity of repentance is emphasized by the Lord. The fig tree is the nation Israel; but the individual application must not be eliminated. When there is no repentance, after God's merciful patience, the delayed judgment will be executed. Israel illustrates this fully. The tree was hewn down, though the root remains. In Matthew we read of the budding fig tree, the sign that the summer is nigh.

Verses 10-17. The healing of the daughter of Abraham, whom Satan had bound for eighteen years, is reported only by Luke. Attention has been called to the significance of the number 18. Upon 18 fell the tower of Siloam and the woman, who was bound for 18 years. "The number 18, which is 3 x 6 (six the number of man) speaks of evil manifested in its highest uprise."* Satan had manifested his dreadful power over this daughter of Abraham but the Son of Man, who came to seek and to save that which is lost, has the power to deliver her. She was made straight and glorified God. The expression "daughter of Abraham" signifies that she was a believer. Satan was permitted to afflict her body; it was the same with Job. See also I Cor. v:5.

* Numerical Bible.

Verses 18-21. The parables of the mustard seed and the leaven appear in Luke in an entirely different setting than in Matthew. We have already seen in our annotations of Matthew xiii, what these two parables teach. Here in Luke they are evidently closely linked with the parable of the barren fig tree, showing that when Israel has failed and passed under the national judgment, the Kingdom of God, as resting in the hands of man, becomes like any other kingdom of the world, sheltering the unclean (fowls), and internally it is corrupted by leaven.

Solemn teachings follow in answer to the question "Lord, are there few to be saved?" The door is open, but narrow. And the door to salvation will one day be shut for those who refused to enter in. And here we find the words which were omitted by Luke in the account of the healing of the Centurion's servant. The application to the Jews, who rejected Him, and the acceptance of the Gospel by the Gentiles is self-evident. The person, whom our Lord calls "fox," most likely was Herod himself. The "to-day and to-morrow" refer to His great work in bearing testimony and working miracles; the third day, when He would be perfected, is the day of resurrection. Then follows His lament over Jerusalem. The consecutive teachings of this chapter, beginning with the necessity of repentance, Israel's failure, the demonstration of His power, His solemn words and finally His lament over Jerusalem are intensely interesting.

CHAPTER XIV

1. The Man with the Dropsy Healed on the Sabbath. 1-6.
2. The Wisdom of Humility. 7-11.
3. Recompensed in Resurrection. 12-14.
4. The Parable of the Great Supper. 15-24.
5. Conditions of Discipleship. 25-35.

Verses 1-6. Again He heals on the Sabbath. In the house of a ruler, a Pharisee, they were watching Him.

He had gone there to eat bread. What condescension! They were His enemies, yet He loved them. He healed the man with the dropsy. The question, "Is it lawful to heal on the Sabbath day?" was answered by the very power of God.

Verses 7-14. The parable which follows, also peculiar to Luke, emphasizes the wisdom of humility. The natural man with the pride of life as a governing principle loves self-exaltation. Abasement for him follows in judgment to come; but if man humbleth himself before God, exaltation will follow. He, the Son of Man, had humbled Himself and taken the lowest place. How great is His exaltation! Then He exhorts to seek recompense at the resurrection of the just. Here is a hint on the two resurrections, which are so clearly distinguished in Scripture. The first resurrection is the resurrection of the just and includes all the Saints of God. In that resurrection there will be a reward according to works, but no sinner can work to make himself worthy of that resurrection.

Verses 15-24. The parable of the great supper is distinct from the similar one in Matthew xxii:1-14. They were spoken at different occasions. The parable in Matthew has clearly marked dispensational aspects, such as the twofold offer to Israel, before and after the cross, the judgment upon Jerusalem and the calling of the Gentiles, etc. The primary object of the parable in Luke is also to show the unbelief of the Jews, especially the self-righteous Pharisees and the call of the publicans and harlots. God has mercifully provided the feast. The Kingdom had come nigh. All things are now ready. The Son of God had come in their midst. But the parable also looks forward to the finished work of the Cross. That work has made all things ready. The self-righteous among the Jews refused and brought their excuses. Then exactly that came to pass of which the Lord had spoken (verses 12-14). The publicans and harlots, the poor, maimed, blind and lame came. They could not have the excuses of the self-righteous of the nation. The call of the Gentiles is also seen in this parable: "Go out into the highways and hedges, and compel them to come in, that my house may be filled." The doom of the rejectors is seen in verse 24. The great multitude, which followed Him then hears from His lips the conditions of true discipleship. Let no one say, as it has been said, that they are not binding to-day.

CHAPTER XV

1. The Murmuring Pharisees. 1-2.
2. The Parable of the Lost Sheep. 3-7.
3. The Parable of the Lost Coin. 8-10.
4. The Parable of the Prodigal Son and the Elder Brother. 11-32.

Verses 1-10. A blessed climax of the teaching of our Lord as the Saviour and the friend of sinners is reached with this chapter, a chapter which the Saints of God have always loved and will always love. Here we find the completest illustration of the key text of Luke "For the Son of Man is come to seek and to save that which is lost." The taxgatherers and sinners, after hearing His words and knowing the welcome which awaited them, drew near to Him in large numbers. The murmuring of the Pharisees and scribes and their words "This man receiveth sinners and eateth with them" is answered by the Lord with three parables. The parables of the lost sheep, of the lost coin and of the prodigal son belong together. The lost coin parable and the parable of the prodigal are peculiar to Luke. The Trinity is revealed in these parables seeking that which is lost. The Son is seen in the Shepherd; the Holy Spirit in the parable of the lost coin and the Father in the parable of the prodigal.

In the study of these parables it must not be overlooked that the Lord answers in the first place the murmuring Pharisees. This however does not exclude the wider application on Gospel lines. Bengel states that in the first parable the sinner is sin as stupid; in the second as totally ignorant of himself and in the third as the daring, wilful sinner. In the parable of the Shepherd the ninety and nine do not represent the unfallen angels, nor, as it has been suggested, inhabitants of other worlds, but the self-righteous Pharisees, who think they need no repentance. The one sheep, lost and helpless, pictures the taxgatherers and sinners, who owned their lost condition. All must first be applied on this ground. The Son of Man had come to seek and to save. He looked for the lost; He followed them and sought them out at their tables; He ate and drank with them, so that He was called a wine-bibber. The found sheep He puts on His own shoulders; He would not leave this to a servant. The care of the saved sheep is all His own. And there is joy in heaven over one repenting sinner. It was a severe rebuke to the Pharisees, who did not rejoice when the taxgatherers and sinners came, but murmured. The second parable is of much interest and has been interpreted in various ways. We quote here the exposition as given in the "Numerical Bible" as the most satisfactory one.

"The second parable is that of the woman, in the Scripture the figure of the Church, the instrument of the Spirit. The lamp of the Word is in her hand, and she needs it in the darkness of the night, while Christ is absent. The 'house' is the circle of natural ties and relationships; for it is not just a question of public preaching, but of that testimony upon which the success of the preacher after all so much depends, and for which the whole Church, and not any class or section of it, is responsible. Good it is to realize that every soul of man, covered with the dust of sin as he may be, and hidden in the darkness of the world, belongs of right to the King's treasury, and has the King's image stamped on him, though with sore disfigurement. Claim him we may, wherever we may find him, for God to whom he belongs. This general evangelism, we may learn from the parable here, is what is the mind of the Spirit for the Church indwelt of Him. Here too there must be friends and neighbors summoned to rejoice,—angelic onlookers who are in sympathy with Him who is always the glorious Seeker, and who sets in motion all the springs of love and pity that flow anywhere in unison with His own."

In the Parable of the prodigal son is brought out again the two classes of men before whom the Lord spoke these parables. The prodigal represents the publicans, the elder son the ritualistic Pharisees. The application in the Gospel, which this parable so blessedly reveals, the condition of man as a sinner, the true repentance, the Father's joy, the welcome the returning one receives, etc., all is so well known that we need to make no further annotations. The elder son's character clearly shows that the Pharisee, self-righteous and self-sufficient, is completely in view. He has never transgressed a commandment and therefore considers himself above the poor, lost wanderer, who has returned home; he was angry. Thus the Pharisees were angry, when the Lord received the outcasts. It is strange that this parable should have been explained to mean, that our Lord endorses worldly amusements and that a Christian may dance and make merry. There is no reason whatever that He has done so. The parable has, no doubt, a national meaning as well. The elder son represents the Jews and their unwillingness to see the Gentiles converted. The prodigal then is a picture of the degradation of the Gentiles.

CHAPTER XVI

1. The Unjust Steward. 1-12.
2. The Impossible Service. 13.
3. The Deriding Pharisees Answered. 14-17.
4. Concerning Divorce. 18.
5. The Rich Man and Lazarus. 19-31.

Verses 1-12. Let us notice that this story was spoken to the disciples. It contains a number of difficulties. It has well been said "there are knots in it which perhaps will never be untied, until the Lord comes again. We might reasonably expect that a book written by inspiration, as the Bible is, would contain things hard to be understood. The fault lies not in the book, but in ourselves." The story of the unjust steward is used to teach wisdom in the use of earthly things. What the steward did was an unjust thing, but he acted wisely. "The lord commended the unjust steward because he had done wisely." Then our Lord makes the statement that "the children of this world are in their generation wiser than the children of light." But what is the application? "And I say unto you, Make yourselves friends of the mammon of unrighteousness; that when it (not ye) fails, they may receive you into everlasting habitations." Pages could be filled with interpretations which have been given of this statement. Many of these have been made at the expense of the grace of God, which alone fits a sinner for glory.* Heaven cannot be bought by the rightful use of earthly things. Man as God's steward has failed and has wasted His goods. But the disciple is to use earthly things, the mammon of unrighteousness, to a wise and advantageous purpose. The Lord's word may be paraphrased in this wise: "Use the temporal things, the mammon of unrighteousness with an eye to the future, as the steward did his, so that it will be like friends you have made." "That they may receive you" is indefinite and must be regarded to signify rather "Ye may be received." We leave this difficult passage by quoting a valuable comment on it: "On the one hand let us beware of supposing that by any use of money we can purchase to ourselves God's favour and the pardon of our sins. Heaven is not to be bought. Any such interpretation of the verse is most unscriptural. On the other hand, let us beware of shutting our eyes against the doctrine which the verse unmistakably contains. That

* Godet gives a novel interpretation: "May not the disciple who reaches heaven without having gained here below the degree of development which is the condition of full communion with God, receive the increase of spiritual life, which is yet wanting to him, by means of those grateful spirits with whom he shared his temporal goods here below?"

doctrine plainly is, that a right use of our money in this world, from right motives, will be for our benefit in the world to come. It will not justify us. It will not bear the severity of God's judgment, any more than other good works. But it shall be an evidence of our grace, which shall befriend our souls. There is such a thing as 'laying up treasure in heaven,' and 'laying up a good foundation against the time to come.' (Matt. vi:20; I Tim. vi:19.)"* That the whole story has a meaning connected with the elder son the Pharisee in the preceding parable must not be overlooked. The Pharisees were avaricious. After the Lord had declared the impossible service, not alone then, but in all times, "Ye cannot serve God and mammon," the Pharisees, who heard all these things and who were covetous, derided him.

Verses 19-31. A solemn paragraph closes the chapter. Avoid the use of the word "parable" in connection with these verses. The Lord said, "There was a certain rich man." It is history and not a parable. The derision of the Pharisees on account of the Lord's words about the unjust steward must have been based upon their trust in the law and the promise of the law, that temporal blessings and riches were in store for all who keep the law. The story our Lord relates is aimed once more at the sneering, unbelieving, self-righteous Pharisees. The rich man had great riches. But his riches were not the evidences of divine favor and blessing. Lazarus, the poor man, had no earthly possessions. Was his poverty an evidence of divine displeasure? Then the Lord, the omniscient Lord, draws aside the veil and reveals what is hidden from the sight of man. Both die. Lazarus is carried by the angels into Abraham's bosom. He had no means to make friends for himself by using the mammon of unrighteousness, so as to be welcomed in the everlasting habitations. And yet he is there. God had in His infinite grace carried him so high. Lazarus' name means "God is Helper." The rich man also died and is

* Bishop Ryle.

in hades.* He is in torment and sees Lazarus in Abraham's bosom. He hears that there is no relief, no hope. An impassable gulf is fixed, which separates *forever* the lost and the saved. Not a ray of hope is given by the Lord, that there is the slightest possibility after death for another chance. Death fixes forever the eternal condition of every human being. Whoever meddles with this solemn truth, whether a Russellite, or Restorationist or whatever name he may bear, rejects the testimony of the Son of God and charges Him with not having spoken the truth. We cannot follow the solemn story in all its details. Future punishment of the wicked, the future conscious punishment of the wicked, the future conscious and *eternal* punishment of the wicked is denied and sneered at to-day by the majority of professing Christians. But the Lord Jesus, the friend of sinners, the One who came to seek and to save what is lost, teaches *beyond controversy* in this solemn story, the future, conscious and eternal punishment of the wicked.

Of late one hears much that the story is a parable, that the rich man typifies the Jew, his torment, their persecutions; the poor man is the Gentile. It is an invention. The story must be forced to mean this. The careful student will soon see how impossible such an application is. Nor is the view new. It was taught by many errorists of past generations.

CHAPTER XVII

1. Concerning Offences and Forgiveness. 1-4.
2. Increase of Faith and Lowly Service. 5-10.
3. The Ten Lepers. 11-19.
4. Concerning the Kingdom and His Second Coming. 20-37.

Verses 1-19. The story of the ten lepers is only found in Luke. All were cleansed by the power of God and the nine obeyed the Word of the Lord and went to the priests

* Not in hell; the lake of fire opens after the judgment.

(Leviticus xiii-xiv). But the tenth did not go but instead, turned back and glorified God with a loud voice and fell on his face at the feet of the Lord. He took the attitude of a worshipper; and he was a Samaritan. He turned his back upon the ceremonial law and owned the Giver of the blessing he had received. We have in this healed, worshipping Samaritan, who does not worship in the mountain of Samaria, nor in the temple in Jerusalem, an earnest of the new dispensation to come. (John iv:22-24.)

Verses 20-37. The question "when the Kingdom of God should come" is answered by the statement "the Kingdom of God is within you." The translation is faulty. The "within" means "among"; so that we read "the Kingdom of God is among you." It had appeared in their midst in the Person of the King. Then He spoke of His second coming. He reminds them of the days of Noah and the days of Lot. His coming here is His visible coming at the end of the age and not His coming for His Saints, which is a subsequent revelation. (I Thess. iv:13-18.) Then one will be taken (in judgment as the people perished in Noah's and Lot's day) and the other left (on the earth to be in the Kingdom).

CHAPTER XVIII

1. The Unjust Judge and the Avenging of His Elect. 1-8.
2. The Parable of the Pharisee and the Publican. 9-14.
3. The Little Children and the Required Lowliness. 15-17.
4. The Rich Young Ruler. 18-27.
5. Rewards Promised. 28-30.
6. The Renewed Prediction of His Suffering, Death and Resurrection. 31-34.
7. The Blind Man near Jericho Healed. 35-43.

Verses 1-8. The parable of the unjust judge is closely connected with the preceding announcement of His second coming. "When the Son of Man cometh, shall He find faith on the earth?" Apostasy and darkness will rule the day. But a faithful remnant of His people, His elect, will suffer and cry day and night to Him for help and deliverance. His coming will avenge them. The resources in those days will be prayer, as prayer is always the resource of the Saints of God. In the Psalms the Spirit of God has recorded the prayers of the suffering Jewish Saints during the great tribulation.

Verses 9-14. This parable also is found only in Luke. It is a continuation of the great subject of this Gospel, that the lost are saved and the self-righteous rejected. "Every one that exalteth himself shall be abased; and he that humbleth himself shall be exalted." The self-righteous Pharisee trusted in himself; pride and self-conceit are expressed in his prayer. He speaks of a negative goodness "not as other men" and then he speaks of his good works, which are even more than God demanded in His law. God did not demand tithes of all possessions. The Publican did not lift his eyes to heaven. His prayer was more than asking for mercy. It means literally translated "God be propitiated towards me, the sinner." He felt the need of a sacrifice. It is interesting to note that the Greek word "be merciful to" is found only once more in the New Testament. In Heb. ii:17 it is applied to our Lord "making reconciliation."

CHAPTER XIX:1-27

1. The Salvation of Zacchæus. 1-10.
2. The Parable of the Ten Pounds. 11-27.

Verses 1-10. When He drew near to Jericho the Lord healed the blind beggar. The reader will find hints on the meaning of this miracle in the annotations of the Gospel of Mark. (x:46-52.) The story of Zacchaeus is not found in the other synoptics. The Lord is now in Jericho. Zacchaeus (meaning: clean) was the chief tax-gatherer and a rich man. "He sought to see Jesus"; his desire and faith overcame all hindrances which were in his way. The rich man climbing into a sycamore tree must have brought him ridicule. Little did he know that He, whom he sought, was seeking him. The Lord knew him and called him by name. And so Zacchaeus received Him joyfully into his house, while others murmured because He was to be a guest of a sinner. But Zacchaeus, though the chief publican, was an honest man. His confession shows that. He did not say what he intended to do, but what he had done already in his past life. It was not the result of having received the Lord in his house, but Zacchaeus answered by it the accusation of those who had murmured. He was a son of Abraham, yet destitute of salvation, which he knew not with all his honesty. But the Lord had brought now salvation to his house. Zacchaeus was lost but the Son of Man had found him.

Verses 11-27. The parable of the ten pounds was occasioned because they that heard Him thought the Kingdom of God should immediately appear. He speaks of Himself in the parable as going to a far country to receive a Kingdom and to return. In the interval His servants are to be faithful with the entrusted pounds. "Occupy till I come." The ten servants represent Christendom in the same way as the ten virgins. The one who had hidden the pound in the sweat cloth (*soudarion*) is called a wicked servant and represents a mere professing believer, an unsaved person. The citizens mentioned in the parable, who hated the nobleman are the Jews. (Verse 14.) The parable teaches definitely that when the Lord returns He will reward His faithful servants for their faithfulness. May it be an incentive for us to occupy till He comes.

V. In Jerusalem.

Chapter xix:28-xxi-38

CHAPTER XIX:28-48

1. The Triumphal Entry in Jerusalem. 28-40.
2. Weeping over Jerusalem. 41-44.
3. The Purification of the Temple. 45-48.

Verses 28-40. The triumphal entry of the Lord into Jerusalem has been before us already in Matthew and Mark. He is presented as King. Luke gives an interesting addition. The multitude of disciples rejoiced and praised God for all the mighty works they had seen. "Blessed be the King that cometh in the name of the Lord; peace in heaven and glory in the highest." The angelic announcement was "peace on earth"; here the disciples say "peace in heaven." Such will be the ultimate and glorious effect of the work of Christ, when Satan will be cast out of heaven, the heavenly inheritance redeemed (Ephes. 1:13), and the reconciliation of things in heaven (Col. i:20) accomplished. All this and much more will surely come, when the King-Messiah comes again. Then there will be peace on earth, peace in heaven and glory in the highest.

Verses 41-48. What a scene it must have been when He saw the great city and wept over it! Before He utters the great prophecy announcing the doom of the city, He weeps. What a glimpse it gives of the loving heart of the Saviour-King, the friend of sinners! And all came as He announced. The second cleansing of the temple took place after that. See annotations on Mark xi:15-18.

CHAPTER XX

1. His Authority Demanded and His Answer. 1-8.
2. Parable of the Wicked Husbandmen. 9-19.
3. Question about Tribute to Cæsar. 20-26.
4. The Question Concerning Resurrection. 27-40.
5. The Question Christ Asked. 41-44.
6. Beware of the Scribes! 45-47.

The events in this chapter are found in both Matthew's and Mark's Gospels. The parable of the vineyard foretells His death. He is the son, the beloved son, whom the husbandman cast out of the vineyard and killed. The rejected stone, which becomes the head of the corner (Psalm cxviii:22) is likewise Christ. Verse 18 shows the judgment which came upon the Jews nationally. Rejecting Christ, stumbling and falling upon that stone they were broken. It also shows the future judgment which will strike the Gentile world-powers at the close of the times of the Gentiles, when the Stone shall fall out of heaven and smite the image, which represents Gentile dominion (Daniel ii). Inasmuch as we have followed the different questions in Matthew and Mark, put to the Lord by the chief priests, scribes, Sadducees and Pharisees, to ensnare Him, no further annotations are needed here.

CHAPTER XXI

1. The Widow's Mite. 1-4.
2. The Destruction of the Temple Predicted. 5-6.
3. The Disciple's Question Concerning the Future. 7.
4. Things to Come. 8-19.
5. The Destruction of Jerusalem and the World-wide Dispersion of Israel. 20-24.
6. The Return of the Lord with Power and Great Glory. 25-28.
7. The Fig Tree and Warnings. 29-38.

This entire chapter with the exception of the incident of the widow's mite is prophetic. Luke's account however differs in many ways from the account given of the prophetic Olivet discourse in Matthew and also that in Mark. Matthew gives the Olivet discourse in its completest form. (See Matthew xxiv and xxv.) He reports what the Lord had to say concerning the end of the age, the great tribulation, which concerns the Jewish believers living at that time; then in three parables He revealed the moral conditions existing in Christendom and how He will deal with them and finally He revealed, as reported by Matthew, the judgment of the Gentile nations. The characteristic feature of Luke's report is that he has little to say about the details of the end of the age, such as the great tribulation and what will take place during that period of time (Matthew xxiv:4-42). Instead of this he was led by the Spirit of God to record in the fullest way what our Lord had said concerning the fall of Jerusalem, the fate of Jerusalem, the dispersion of the nation and the duration of all this. The Lord announced that Jerusalem would be compassed by armies and that days of vengeance would come. (Verses 20-23.) There would then be great distress in the land and wrath upon this people. This great prophecy was fulfilled in the year 70 A. D., when the Romans besieged Jerusalem and a million perished, besides 100,000 who were made slaves. It is one of the most awful pages in human history. So has verse 24 been fulfilled. The Jewish nation has been scattered among all the nations; Jerusalem has been trodden down by the Gentiles and is still in that state. But the times of the Gentiles will be fulfilled in the future and when that comes, deliverance and restoration for Jerusalem and the nation are promised. Luke significantly tells us about the fig tree, "and all the trees." (Verse 29.) They are to shoot forth and that would be a sign of His Return. The fig tree is Israel. Who are the other trees? Other nations, who are to see a revival before the Lord comes, such as the centers of the Roman empire, Italy, Greece and Egypt. Israel and these other nations indeed "shoot forth"; from this we are to learn that great events in connection with the Kingdom of God are at hand. May we also heed the warnings with which this chapter closes.

VI. His Rejection, Suffering and Death.

Chapter xxii-xxiii

CHAPTER XXII.

1. The Betrayer. 1-6.
2. Preparation for the Passover. 7-13.
3. The Last Passover. 14-18.
4. The Lord's Supper Instituted. 19-20.
5. The Betrayal Announced. 21-23.
6. Strife for Honor; True Greatness. 24-27.
7. Rewards Promised. 28-30.
8. Peter and the Disciples Warned. 31-38.
9. The Agony in the Garden. 39-46.
10. The Betrayal and the Arrest. 47-53.
11. Peter's Denial. 54-62.
12. The Son of Man Buffeted and Before the Council. 63-71.

And now we reach the story of His Rejection, Suffering and Death. What pen is able to describe it all! What mind can fathom it! We shall again confine ourselves to those things which are peculiar to Luke and not repeat annotations as given in Matthew and Mark. Notice the difference in the words of the institution of the Lord's supper. Matthew and Mark have "My blood shed for many." In Luke we find the words "My body which is given for *you*"; "My blood which is shed for *you.*" His love shines out fully in these words. In Luke alone we have His loving request "this do in remembrance of Me." Oh! that His people for whom He shed His blood may never forget this beautiful word and remember Him in this simple way.

And Luke shows us the contrast between Himself and His disciples. He was about descending into the deepest depths of humiliation; sorrow and shame were before the willing victim, yea the greatest agony and death.

Among them was strife, who of them should be accounted the greatest. This was the second instance of contention for pre-eminence recorded by Luke. (See ix:46.) Then He announced the denial of Peter. Verses 31-32 are peculiar to Luke. Satan was to sift him as wheat, but the Lord knew all about it and had prayed for him and therefore Peter could not succumb and be lost. And the Lord is the same to-day. He knows His own and prays for them before Satan can ever come near with his temptations. The word "when thou art converted" does not mean that Peter was unconverted. It has the meaning "when thou hast returned back."

There is also a marked difference in the account Luke gives of Gethsemane from the accounts in Matthew and Mark. Luke tells us of an angel who strengthened Him. How could an angel strengthen Him, who is the Creator of the angels? He certainly could not strengthen His holy soul. That an angel strengthened Him must belong to His deep humiliation.

> "But the body suffers, and presently the strain upon it is seen in the 'sweat, as it were great drops of blood,' that fall down upon the ground. Laborer for God and man as He is, His labor is a warfare also: the enemy is here, as He presently says to those who come to apprehend Him: 'This is your hour, and the power of darkness.' The Seed of the woman is planting His heel upon the head of the old serpent, but His heel is bruised in doing this. In the weakness of perfect Manhood He suffers, and conquers by suffering." *

Then follows the Betrayal with a kiss, the arrest of the Son of Man, Peter's Denial. Luke alone tells us that the Lord looked upon denying Peter; what look that must have been! The chapter ends with the cruel treatment of the Son of Man, the Friend of sinners, who had come to seek and to save that which is lost, received from man, His glorious self-witness and unjust condemnation by the council.

---

* F. W. Grant.

CHAPTER XXIII

1. The Son of Man before Pilate and Herod. 1-12.
2. Pilate Yields to the People's Will; Barabbas Freed and the Son of Man Condemned. 13-26.
3. The Crucifixion of the Son of Man. 27-38.
4. The Penitent Thief. 39-43.
5. The Death of the Son of Man. 44-46.
6. The Testimony of the Centurion. 47-49.
7. The Burial. 50-56.

Verses 1-12. Before Pilate the Son of Man is accused as a perverter of the nation and as an enemy of the Roman government. They had attempted to ensnare Him with the question of the tribute money and failed so miserably in it. Their motive stands now uncovered. Pilate asks Him concerning His Kingship, which the Lord answered affirmatively. Thus He witnessed to two facts, His Sonship and His Kingship. Luke tells us what Matthew and Mark omit, that Pilate sent Him to Herod. The silence of the Son of Man standing before that wicked king is very solemn. Then He is mocked by Herod and his soldiers. Herod and Pilate became united in rejecting Christ. See how this fact is used in the first prayer meeting after the church had been formed. Acts iv:23-30.

Verses 13-38. The weakling Pilate is helpless. Their voices prevail. "Away with this man!"; "Release unto us Barabbas!"—"Crucify Him! Crucify Him!" These are the cries now heard. Pilate then gave the awful sentence, that it should be done to Him as they required. The lamenting women and the Lord's answer is peculiar to Luke. "Weep not for me!" Blessed words of His great love. He looked for no sympathy from man. Frail women were moved to pity. He is the green tree; they were the dry wood. The people's wrath fanned by Satan's power was spending itself upon Him, the green and fruitful tree. How awful it would be when the dry wood, the unsaved masses, would be exposed to the fires of wrath and persecution. Forty years later the "dry wood" burned fiercely in the siege of Jerusalem. When they reach the place called "Calvary" (the skull), the Latin, Gentile name for Golgotha,* they crucified Him. Luke omits much which is more fully given in the other synoptics; we read nothing of the cry of the forsaken One. But Luke tells us of the blessed prayer which Matthew and Mark omit, "Father, forgive them for they know not what they do." And His last word, "Father, into Thy hands I commit My Spirit," is also given exclusively by Luke. All this is in blessed keeping with the character of this Gospel.

Verses 39-56. The story of the dying thief and his salvation is also characteristic to Luke. The great lesson of the three crosses is so familiar that it needs no lengthy annotations. The two classes, the saved and the unsaved, are represented by the two thieves. He, the Lamb of God paying the penalty of sinners, is in the midst. The way the penitent was saved is the only way in which man can be saved. He could do no good works; he could not get baptized or perform anything else. All he could do was to cast himself in faith as a lost sinner upon the Lord. Nor was his salvation a life-long, progressive work (as some teach on salvation); it was instantaneous. Nor was there any "purgatory" for him. He expected to be remembered in the Kingdom to come. Instead of that he hears, "Verily I say unto thee, to-day thou shalt be with me in paradise." The attempt by soul-sleepers, restorationists and others to put the comma after "to-day" is a deceptive invention to bring the Word of God into line with their evil doctrines.

"This short prayer contained a very large and long creed, the articles whereof are these. 1. He believed that the soul died not with the body of man;—2. That there is a world to come for rewarding the pious and penitent, and for punishing the impious and impenitent;—3. That Christ, though now under crucifying and kill-

---

* Luke only gives the name "Calvary" because it is the Gentile Gospel.

ing tortures, yet had right to a kingdom;—4. That this kingdom was in a better world than the present evil world;—5. That Christ would not keep this kingdom all to himself;—6. That He would bestow a part and portion hereof on those that are truly penitent;—7. That the key of this kingdom did hang at Christ's girdle, though he now hung dying on the cross;—8. That he does roll his whole soul for eternal salvation upon a dying Saviour." *

Then the Son of Man cried with a loud voice ere He dismissed His spirit and the Centurion, in keeping with this Gospel, bears witness, that He was a righteous Man.

* Ness.

VII. His Resurrection and Ascension.

CHAPTER XXIV

1. The Resurrection. 1-12.
2. The Walk to Emmaus; the Appearance of the Risen Son of Man. 13-35.
3. The Appearance to the Eleven. 36-45.
4. The Commission. 46-48.
5. The Ascension. 49-53.

The account of the Resurrection in Luke's Gospel has also its characteristic features. He alone reports the full account of the walk to Emmaus. It is a precious story showing forth the fact that the risen One is the same tender, loving, sympathizing friend of His own. He joined Himself to the two disciples, who had left Jerusalem. Their hearts were filled with sadness and perplexity. He Himself drew near and their eyes were holden that they could not recognize Him. In a perfectly human way He joined Himself to them and asked them about their troubles. Then He reproved them for their unbelief and opened the Scriptures unto them. Constrained by them, He abides with them, as He always will with those who belong to Him. In the breaking of bread, their eyes were opened and they knew Him and He vanished from them. They returned to Jerusalem where they found abundant proof that the Lord is risen indeed. The appearance to Simon is not fully made known. What took place between the Lord and the disciple who failed Him is a blessed secret between them. He then appeared again with His gracious "Peace be unto you." He showed them His hands and feet. He had a body of flesh and bones. He was not a phantom, but a real man. His body was real for He ate fish and honeycomb. All this belongs properly to the Gospel of the Manhood. It is the fullest demonstration of His physical resurrection. All the wicked "isms," including Russellism and Christian Science, which deny His physical resurrection stand here fully convicted.

It may be well to mention here the twelve distinct appearances of our Lord after His resurrection. He appeared:

1. To Mary Magdalene alone. Mark xvi; John xx:14.

2. To the women returning from the sepulchre. Matt. xxviii:9, 10.

3. To Simon Peter alone. Luke xxiv:34.

4. To the two disciples going to Emmaus. Luke xxiv: 13, etc.

5. To the apostles at Jerusalem, except Thomas, who was absent. John xx:19.

6. To the apostles at Jerusalem, a second time, when Thomas was present. John xx:26, 29.

7. At the sea of Tiberias, when seven disciples were fishing. John xxi:1.

8. To the eleven disciples, on a mountain in Galilee. Matt. xxviii:16.

9. To above five hundred brethren at once. 1 Cor. xv:6.

10. To James only. 1 Cor. xv:7.

11. To all the apostles on Mount Olivet at His ascension. Luke xxiv:51.

12. To Paul as an untimely birth. 1 Cor. xv:8-9.

Three times we are told that His disciples touched Him after He rose. Matt. xxviii:9; Luke xxiv:39; John xx:27. Twice we are told that He ate with them. Luke xxiv:42; John xxi:12, 13.

The Gospel of Luke ends with the commission given to His disciples and the ascension of the Lord "while He blest them."

THE GOSPEL OF JOHN

The Gospel of John.

Introduction.

The fourth Gospel has always been ascribed to the beloved disciple, the Apostle John. He was one of the sons of Zebedee. His mother Salome was especially devoted to the Lord. (See Luke viii:3; xxiii:55 and Mark xvi:1.) He knew Him from the beginning of His ministry and had followed Him with much love and faithfulness, and seems to have been the most beloved of the Lord. He never mentions himself in the Gospel by name, but nevertheless speaks of himself, as the disciple whom Jesus loved (Chapters xiii:23; xix:26; xx:2; xxi:7, 20, 24). With James and Peter he was singled out to witness the transfiguration and to go with the Lord to the garden of Gethsemane. The three also were present when the Lord raised the daughter of Jairus from the dead (Mark v:37). John was likewise an eye-witness of the sufferings of Christ (xix:26, 35).

The Johannine Authorship.

The Johannine Authorship of the fourth Gospel is proven by the testimony of the so-called church-fathers. Theophilus of Antioch, Tertullian, Clement of Alexandria, Hippolytus, Origen, Dionysius of Alexandria, Eusebius, and above all, Irenæus, all speak of this Gospel as the work of the Apostle John. Other ancient authorities might be added. Of great value is the testimony of the two most pronounced enemies of Christianity, Porphyry and Julian. Both speak of the Gospel of John and neither one doubted that the Apostle John wrote this last Gospel. Had there been any evidence against the Johannine authorship we may rest assured that these two prominent adversaries would have made good use of it to reject the authenticity of the Gospel which emphasizes the absolute Deity of Christ.

The most interesting and conclusive evidence for the Johannine authorship is furnished by Irenæus and Polycarp. Polycarp had known the Apostle John personally and Irenæus knew Polycarp. In a letter to his friend Florinus, Irenæus wrote as follows:—

"I can describe the very place in which the blessed Polycarp used to sit when he discoursed, and his goings out and his comings in, and his manner of life, and his personal appearance, and the discourses which he held before the people, and how he would describe his intercourse with John and with the rest who had seen the Lord, and about His miracles, and about His teaching, Polycarp as having received them from eye-witnesses of the life of the Word, would relate altogether in accordance with the Scriptures."

Now Irenæus who had known Polycarp the friend and companion of the Apostle John, speaks of the Gospel of John as the work of the Apostle John; he treats the entire fourth Gospel as a well-known and long used book in the church. He does not mention what authority he had for doing this. There was no need for it in his day, for everybody knew that this Gospel had been written by John. "When Irenæus who had conversed with Polycarp, the friend of the Apostle John, quotes this Gospel as the work of the Apostle, we may fairly presume that he had assured himself of this by the testimony of one so well capable of informing him." * This strongest evidence for the Johannine authorship has been ably stated by R. W. Dale of Birmingham in the following words:—"Irenæus had heard Polycarp describe his intercourse with John and the rest who had seen the Lord; this must have been long after John's death, perhaps as late as A. D. 145, or even A. D. 150, for Irenæus lived into the third century. Was the Fourth Gospel published before that time? Then Polycarp must have spoken of it; if John had not written it, Polycarp would have denied that it was genuine; and Irenæus, who reverenced Polycarp, would never have received it. But if it was not published before that time, if it was unknown to John's friend and disciple forty or fifty years after John's death, then, again, it is incredible that Irenæus should have received it.

"Polycarp's martydom was in the year A. D. 155 or A. D. 156. He had known John; and for more than fifty years after the death of John he was one of the trustees and guardians of John's memory. During a great part of that time he was the most conspicuous personage among the Churches of Asia Minor. Nor did he stand alone. He lived to such an advanced age, that he probably survived all the men who had listened with him to John's teaching; but for thirty or forty years after John's death there must have been a large number of other persons who would have associated themselves with him in rejecting a Gospel which falsely claimed John's authority. While these persons lived, such a Gospel would have had no chance of reception; and for thirty years after their death, their personal friends, who had heard them speak of their intercourse with John, would have raised a great controversy if they had been asked to re-

* Dean Alford, Greek N. T.

ceive as John's a Gospel of which the men who had listened to John himself had never heard, and which contained a different account of our Lord from that which John had given. But within thirty years after the martyrdom of Polycarp our fourth Gospel was universally regarded by the church as having a place among the Christian Scriptures, and as the work of the Apostle John. The conclusion seems irresistible; John must have written it."

The Defeat of the Critics.

The Johannine authorship of this Gospel was first doubted by an English clergyman by name of Evanson, who wrote on it in 1792. In 1820 Prof. Bretschneider followed in the history of the attack upon the authorship of this Gospel. Then came the Tübingen school, Strauss and Baur. Baur, the head of the Tübingen school gave the year 170 as the date when the Gospel of John was written; others put the date at 140; Keim, another critic, at 130; Renan between 117 and 138 A. D. But some of these rationalists were forced to modify their views. The Tübingen school was completely defeated and is now the dead thing of the past. We could fill many pages with the views and opinions of these critics and the answers, which able scholars who maintain the orthodox view, have given to them. This, we are sure, is not needed for true believers. The ripest and the best scholarship declares now that the fourth Gospel was written by John. Well said Neander, "this Gospel, if it be not the work of the Apostle John, is an insoluble enigma."

While the correct year in which the Gospel of John was written cannot be given, it seems quite evident that it was about the year 90 A. D.

The Purpose of the Gospel of John.

Modern critics of this Gospel have opposed the genuineness of it on the ground of the radical diversity between the views of the Person of Christ and His teachings as presented in the Gospel of John and the Synoptics. Such a diversity certainly exists, but it is far from being an evidence against the genuineness of this Gospel. It is an argument for it.

The synoptic Gospels, Matthew, Mark and Luke, were already in existence for several decades and their contents known throughout the church. If an uninspired writer, some other one than John the Apostle, had undertaken to write another Gospel, such a writer would, in some way at least, have followed the story, which the synoptics so closely follow. But the Gospel of John is, as already stated, radically different from the three preceding Gospels, and yet no critic can deny that the Gospel of John reveals the same wonderful Person who is the theme of the other Gospel records. As we have seen Matthew wrote the Jewish Gospel, describing our Lord as the King; Mark makes Him known as the true Servant, and Luke pictures the Lord as the perfect Man. Thus the Synoptics emphasize His true humanity and show Him forth as the minister of the circumcision. The first two Gospels at least belong as much to the Old Testament as they belong to the New. True Christianity is not fully revealed in these Gospels. They move on Jewish ground. And what had taken place when finally the Holy Spirit moved the Apostle John to write his Gospel? The nation had completely rejected their Lord and King. The doom predicted by the Lord Jesus had fallen upon Jerusalem. The Roman army had burned the city and the temple. The Gentiles had come into the vineyard and the nation's dispersion among all the nations had begun. These facts are fully recognized by the Spirit of God in John's Gospel. This we find on the very threshold of this Gospel. "He came unto His own, and His own received Him not" (John i:11). That Judaism was now a thing of the past is learned from the peculiar way in which the Passover-feast is mentioned. "And the Passover, a feast of the Jews, was nigh" (vi:4; also ii:13; xi:55). The Sabbath and the Feast of Tabernacles are spoken of in the same way (v:1; vii:2). Such statements, that the divinely given feasts were but "feasts of the Jews," are not found in the Synoptics. In John's Gospel these statements show that we are outside of Judaism. Hebrew names and titles are translated also and the Gentile meaning is given. (Messiah, which is interpreted Christ. i:41. Rabbi, which is to say, being interpreted, Master. i:38. The place of a skull, which is called in Hebrew, Golgotha. xix:17, etc.) This is another evidence that Judaism is no longer in view.

But something else had happened since the three first Gospels had been written. The enemy had come in perverting the truth. Wicked apostates and anti-Christian teachers asserted themselves. They denied the Person of the Lord, His essential Deity, the virgin birth, His finished work, His physical resurrection, in one word, "the doctrine of Christ." A flood of error swept over the church. (*)

"Gnosticism" was corrupting the professing church everywhere. This system spoke of the Lord Jesus as occupying the highest rank in the order of spirits; they also denied the redemption by His

---

* The Epistles of John, besides the early Christian literature, bear witness to this fact. See I John ii:18-23; iv:1-6. Men were scattering the anti-Christian doctrines everywhere so that the Spirit of God demanded the severest separation from such. "If there come any unto you, and bring not this doctrine, receive him not in your house, neither bid him God speed. For he that biddeth him God speed is partaker of his evil deeds" (II John:10-11). **An exhortation which is in force for all times.**

HE MAN WHO KNEW HOW TO MAKE EASY MONEY

Jesus: "Will you please give me few moments time to consider our soul's salvation?"

Mr. O. U. Foolish Man: "I posi-ively can't do it; I'm too busy."

You're STRONG and WELL—That's Fine
You HOPE to Remain So —That's Natural
You MAY BE Disappointed —That's Possible.

E THE OTHER SIDE FOR NEXT PICTURE

GRIM TRACT SOCIETY, Inc., Randleman, N. C.
cts free, as the Lord supplies the means. Send
tage for over 100 samples.

BUT—

Mr. O. U. Foolish Man: "O horrors! I never expected you s soon! Wait until I repent and ge ready to die!"

Death: "I positively can't do it I'M TOO BUSY."

You WILL DIE —That's SURE.
You Better Start to Get Ready— That's Wisdon
GOD WANTS TO SAVE YOU

"Repent ye therefore and be converted, that you sins may be blotted out." Acts 3:19.

"Believe on the Lord Jesus Christ, and thou sha be saved, and thy house. Acts 16:31.

blood and the gift of God to believing sinners, that is, eternal life. God in His infinite wisdom held back the pen of the Apostle John till these denials had matured and then he wrote under divine guidance the final Gospel in which the Lord Jesus Christ, the Son of God, the Only-Begotten, the Second Person of the Godhead, is made known in the fulness of His Glory. Linked with this marvellous picture of Him, Who is the true God and the Eternal Life, is the other great truth made known in the fourth Gospel. Man is dead, destitute of life; he must be born again and receive life. And this eternal life is given by the Son of God to all who believe on Him. It is communicated as a present and abiding possession, dependent on Him, Who is the source and the Life as well. At the same time the Third Person of the Godhead, the Holy Spirit, is revealed in this Gospel as He is not revealed in the Synoptics. The Gospel which reveals the Eternal Life is necessarily the Gospel in which the Holy Spirit as the Communicator, Sustainer and Perfecter is fully made known. The Gospel of John is therefore the New Testament Gospel, the good news that Grace and Truth have come by Jesus Christ. It makes known what is more fully revealed in the doctrinal Epistles.

The last chapter in which we hear the Lord Jesus Christ speak, before His passion, is the seventeenth chapter. He speaks to the Father in the great prayer rightly called "the highpriestly prayer." In it He touches upon all the great truths concerning Himself and His own made known in this Gospel, and we shall also find that all the great redemption truths given in their fulness by the Holy Spirit in the Epistles, are clearly revealed in this prayer.

John's Own Testimony.

At the close of the twentieth chapter of this Gospel we find John's own testimony concerning the purpose of this Gospel. "And many other signs truly did Jesus in the presence of His disciples, which are not written in this book. But these are written that ye might believe that Jesus is the Christ, the Son of God, and that believing ye might have life through (in) His Name." Thus the twofold purpose of the fourth Gospel is given by the Apostle:—Christ the Son of God and the Life He gives to all who believe.

The characteristic features of this Gospel are too numerous to mention in this introductory word. We shall point them out in the annotations.

The Division of the Gospel of John.

"For God so loved the world that He gave His only begotten Son, that whosoever believeth in Him should not perish, but have everlasting life." (iii:16). This verse may be given as the key-text of this Gospel, while the prominent words are: Life; Believe; Verily.

Different divisions of this Gospel have been suggested. In its structure it has been compared to the three divisions of the temple. The outer court (Chapter i-xii); the Holy Part (xiii-xvi); the Holiest (xvii-xxi). Others have used chapter xvi:28 to divide the Gospel; "I came forth from the Father, and am come into the world; again I leave the world and go to the Father." This is unquestionably the order of events in the Gospel of John. He came forth from the Father (i:1-18); He came into the world (i:19-xii); He left the world and has returned to the Father (xiii-xxi). Keeping the great purpose of this Gospel in view we make a three-fold division.

I. The Only-begotten, the Eternal Word; His Glory and His Manifestation. Chapter i-ii:22.

II. Eternal Life Imparted; what it is and what it Includes. Chapter ii:23-xvii.

III. "I lay down My life, that I might take it again" Chapter xviii-xxi.

First then we behold Him, the Only Begotten, the Creator of all things, the Life and the Light of men, in His full glory. The Eternal Word was made flesh and manifested Himself among men. This is followed by the main section of the Gospel. It begins with the story of Nicodemus in which the absolute necessity of the new birth, the reception of eternal life by faith in the Son of God, is emphasized; it ends with the great summing up of all He taught concerning eternal life and salvation, in the great prayer of Chapter xvii. Chapters iii-xvii contain the progressive revelation concerning eternal life. The Reception and assurance of it, the Holy Spirit as the Communicator, the provisions for that life, the fruits of it, the goal of it, etc., we can trace in these chapters. In the third part we find the description of how He laid down His life and took it again in resurrection.

Analysis and Annotations.

I. The Only-begotten, the Eternal Word; His Glory and His Manifestation.

Chapter i-ii:22

CHAPTER I

1. The Word: the Creator, the Life and the Light. 1-4.
2. The Light and the Darkness. The Light not Known. 5-11.
3. The Word Made Flesh and Its Gracious Results. 12-18.
4. The Witness of John. 19-34.
5. Following Him and Dwelling With Him. 35-42.
6. The Next Day. Nathanael's Unbelief and Confession. 43-49.
7. The Promise of Greater Things. 50-51.

Majestic is the beginning of this Gospel. Hundreds of pages might be written on the opening verses and their meaning would not be exhausted. They are inexhaustible. The name of our Lord as "the Word" (Logos) is exclusively used by the Apostle John. The Jewish philosopher Philo of Alexandria, who lived in the days of the Apostle John, also speaks of the Word. Critics have therefore claimed that the Apostle copied from Philo and reproduced his mystical Jewish philosophy. However, this theory has been exploded. Prof. Harnack, the eminent German scholar, states "the Logos of John has little more in common with the Logos of Philo than the name." It is significant that the rabbinical paraphrases on the Old Testament (Targumim) speak hundreds of times of the Lord as "the Word" (Memra). These ancient Jewish paraphrases describe Jehovah, when He reveals Himself, by the term "Memra," which is the same as the Greek "Logos"—"the Word." Genesis iii:8 they paraphrased "they heard the

Word walking in the garden." These Jewish comments ascribe the creation of the world to the Word. It was "the Word" which communed with the Patriarchs. According to them "the Word" redeemed Israel out of Egypt; "the Word" was dwelling in the tabernacle; "the Word" spake out of the fire of Horeb; "the Word" brought them into the promised land. All the relationship of the Lord with Israel is explained by them as having been through "the Word." In the light of the opening verses of the Gospel of John these Jewish statements appear more than interesting.* The Only Begotten is called "The Word" because He is the express image of God, as the invisible thought is expressed by the corresponding word. He is the revealer and interpreter of the mind and will of God.

"In (the) beginning was the Word, and the Word was with God, and the Word was God." Three great facts are made known concerning our Lord. 1. He is eternal. He did not begin to exist. He has no beginning, for "in the beginning *was* the Word." He ever was. Before time began and matter was created, He was. 2. He was and is a Person distinct from God the Father, yet one with Him. "The Word was with God." 3. The Lord Jesus Christ *is* God, for we read "The Word was God." He could therefore not be a being, a creature like the angels. The verses which follow add to this the fact that He is the Creator of all things and the Source of all light and life. Here is the most complete refutation of the wicked teachings concerning the Person of our Lord, which were current in the days of the Apostle, which have been in the world ever since and which will continue to exist till the Lord comes. Arianism, which makes our Lord a Being inferior to God, is answered. So is Socinianism, Unitarianism, Russellism, International Bible Student Assoc., which teach that Christ was not very God, but a man. Well has it been said in view of the revelation contained in the first verse: "to

* These paraphrases in the form we possess them were written in Aramaic about 300 A. D. But long before they were written they must have existed as traditions among the Jewish people.

maintain in the face of such a text, as some so called 'Christians' do, that our Lord Jesus Christ was only a man, is a mournful proof of the perversity of the human heart." And in Him was life, which must be applied to spiritual life. Spiritual life and light is impossible apart from the second Person of the Godhead. The commentator Bengel makes a helpful statement on the opening verses of this chapter. "In the first and second verses of this chapter mention is made of a state before the creation of the world; in the third verse, the world's creation; in the fourth, the time of man's uprightness; in the fifth, the time of man's decline and fall."

John the forerunner is in this Gospel presented to bear witness of the Light. How this reveals the darkness which is in the world that He, Who is the Life and the Light, needed one to announce His coming! "The true light was that which, coming into the world, lighteth every man." (Verse 9; correct translation.) And when He came into the world He had made, the world knew Him not. Even His own, to whom He came, received Him not. This is His rejection by Israel, which in detail is described in the first three Gospels.

Verses 12 and 13 make known the gracious results for those, who receive Him, who believe on His name. The world had not known its Creator; Israel had rejected Him. After the great work of the Cross had been accomplished, the work done for guilty man, the good news is made known. As many as receive Him, to them He gives the right to be the children of God. The new birth is here mentioned for the first time; it is the communication of the divine nature by believing on His name. Believing on Him, receiving Him, we are begotten again and are therefore the children of God. Of this nothing is said in the preceding Gospels. The Gospel of John begins where the others end. The authorized version is incorrect in having "sons of God."* John always speaks of "children"

* The same error appears in I John iii:3.

not of "sons." The expression "children of God" denotes the fact that we are God's born ones, born by the new birth into the family of God. "Sons of God" we are called in view of our destiny in Christ and with Him. As sons of God we are also the heirs of God and fellow-heirs of Jesus Christ. Nowhere is it said that we are heirs of God because we are children of God. Our Lord is never called a child of God, for He is not born of God as we are; He is "Son." (Acts iv:30 is incorrect; not "holy child Jesus," but "holy servant.") Verse 14 gives the fact of His incarnation. Here then we read what the Word became. It is almost impossible to believe that men who claim scholarship, who deny the fact of the incarnation, can state as they do, that the Gospel of John has nothing to say on this great foundation truth of our faith. These apostates must be blinded. The great mystery is made known here as it is in Matthew and in Luke. The Eternal Word, the Word which ever was, the Word which is God, became flesh. He became so by the union of two perfect and distinct natures in one Person. His Person however cannot be divided. And when He became flesh, took on the creature's form, He did not cease to be very God; He emptied Himself of His outward glory, but not of His Deity. He became truly man, but He was holy, sinless; not alone did He not sin, but He could not sin. There is an ancient Latin statement which is worth repeating. It represents "the Word having become flesh as saying: "I am what I was, that is *God*"—"I was not what I am, that is *Man*"—"I am now called both, *God and Man*." In Him they beheld His glory, the glory of the Only Begotten, full of grace and truth. Grace and truth came by Him. The only begotten Son, who is in the bosom of the Father, declared Him, Whom no one hath seen at any time. These are great statements. The word "grace" is found here for the first time in the New Testament. And He, the Incarnate Word, and He alone is full of Grace and Truth. Out of His fulness have we all received, and grace upon grace. It is all grace, that those receive from Him who believe on His name.

The witness of John the forerunner is different from his witness and preaching as given by the synoptics. They report mostly his testimony to the nation. Here we read when he saw Jesus coming to him, he saith, "Behold the Lamb of God who taketh away the sin of the world." * He knew that He Who came to him was to be the Sin-bearer. He knew that He is the true Sacrifice for sin, the true Passover-Lamb, the Lamb which Isaiah predicted. And he testified that the Lamb of God was to take away (not taking away then, or has taken away) the sin of the world. The Lamb of God had to die and the ultimate results of His death are announced in this testimony. They have not yet come, but will be realized in the new heaven and the new earth, when all things are made new.

Beginning with **verse 35** we read what happened the next day after John had given his testimony concerning the Lamb of God. The results of that testimony now appear. Once more John points to Him: "Behold the Lamb of God." He, who was the greatest prophet of the Old Testament, directs his disciples to the Lord. The two disciples heard him speak and followed Jesus. These are the blessed steps: speaking the message, hearing (and in hearing believing) then following the Lord. And He knew them and their hearts' desire. His grace was drawing them to Himself. Their question, "Rabbi, where dwellest Thou?" is answered by that most blessed invitation, "Come and see." These are the first words of our Lord besides His question, written in this Gospel. He wanted them to know Him, to be in communion with Himself. They abode with Him that day. It foreshadows the results of the Gospel of Grace. The unmentioned place where they dwelt with Him is typical of the heavenly

* Often Christians quote "sins of the world." If our Lord had taken away the *sins* of the world, the whole world would be saved. Our Lord only bore the *sins* of those who believe on Him. All who do not believe die in their sins and are lost.

place where He is now. In faith we see where He abides, and by faith we know we are there in Him. It is a beautiful picture of the gathering which takes place throughout this Gospel-age. He is the Center, and "Come and see" are still His gracious words to all who hear and believe. And how Andrew at once testified and brought his brother Simon to Jesus!

Verses 43-49 unfold another picture. Nathanael (gift of God) would not believe. Philip had testified to him "We have found Him of whom Moses in the law, and the prophets did write, Jesus of Nazareth, the son of Joseph." Nathanael under the fig-tree, where the Lord had seen him, is the type of the remnant of Israel. When the Lord spoke to him he owned Him as the Son of God, the King of Israel. So all Israel in a future day will confess Him. Notice the first day, when the first company is gathered to abide with Him (typical of this age and the gathering of a heavenly company); then the second day, when the Lord reveals Himself to unbelieving Nathanael (typical of the conversion of the remnant of Israel).

The last two verses of this marvellous chapter will find their fulfillment in that day when heaven is opened. Then greater things will take place. The angels of God will be seen ascending and descending upon the Son of Man. It will take place when He comes the second time, when Israel acknowledges Him as their King and as the Son of God.

CHAPTER II:1-22

1. The Marriage in Cana. 1-11.
2. The Temple Cleansed. 12-22.

The second chapter gives the record of the first miracle reported in this Gospel. He manifested His omniscience in the previous chapter and here, in turning water into wine, He reveals Himself as the omnipotent Creator. What harmony there is between the opening of the first two chapters of the Gospel of John. The first chapter speaks of Him as the Creator of all things and in the second chapter He manifests the power of the Creator. He needed no wine, no grapes, no mellowing process, to furnish the best wine. He but commanded and it was so. This is omnipotence. In verse 17 of the previous chapter there is a contrast between Moses representing the law dispensation and our Lord Jesus Christ through whom grace and truth have come. The first miracle Moses did, was turning water into blood, typical of the ministration of the law unto death; the first miracle of our Lord turns water into wine, which is typical of joy and the ministration of Grace which is unto life.

The many applications and lessons of the marriage in Cana and the changing of water into wine we have to omit. But we call attention to the dispensational aspect. The third day * mentioned connects with the preceding chapter. On the first day the two disciples abode with the Lord. On the second day unbelieving Nathanael confessed Him as Son of God and King of Israel. On the third day there was a marriage. The third day clearly indicates the time of Israel's blessing and restoration. Beautiful is the predicted and still future confession of Israel: "After two days will He revive us, in the third day He will raise us up and we shall live in His sight." (Hos. vi:1-3). The marriage typifies the restored relationship of the Lord with Israel. That is why the mother of Jesus (type of Israel) and His disciples (those who come with Him to the marriage) are mentioned. And this miracle is spoken of as the "beginning of miracles," when He manifested His glory. When He comes again and changes existing conditions, when Israel enters into the promised and blessed relationship, when He manifests His glory, then the wine of joy will not fail. Better things are promised and better

* The numbers 3 and 7 are prominent in this Gospel. Three times the Lord went into Galilee, three times into Judea; three passovers are mentioned, etc. There are seven signs or miracles, seven times the Lord speaks "I am"; seven times the phrase "These things have I spoken unto you, etc." is used.

things will come, when that blessed day appears. But "His hour is not yet come." It will surely come.

The words of rebuke to Mary clearly show that she erred and was as fallible as any other woman. The Lord rebuked her because He did not want her to interfere with Him and His work. "She erred here, perhaps from an affectionate desire to bring honour to her Son, as she erred on other occasions. The words before us were meant to remind her that she must henceforth leave our Lord to choose His own times and modes of acting. The season of subjection to her and Joseph was over. The season of His public ministry had at length begun. In carrying on that ministry, she must not presume to suggest to Him. The utter contrariety of this verse to the teaching of the Roman Catholic Church about the Virgin Mary is too palpable to be explained away. She was not without error and sin, as Romish writers have dared to assert, and was not meant to be prayed to and adored. If our Lord would not allow His mother even to suggest to Him the working of a miracle, we may well suppose that all Roman Catholic prayers to the Virgin Mary, and especially prayers entreating her to 'command her Son,' are most offensive and blasphemous in His eyes." *

The purging of the temple is closely connected with the marriage and miracle of Cana. When He comes again the Father's house, the temple, will be cleansed. "Yea every pot in Jerusalem shall be holiness unto the Lord of hosts . . . and in that day there shall be no more the Canaanite (which means translated: merchantman) in the house of the Lord of Hosts." (Zech. xiv:21). This is the first cleansing of the temple, mentioned exclusively by John. The synoptic Gospels report the cleansing which occurred at the close of His ministry. He manifested in it His authority as the Son of God, and Psalm lxix:9 was fulfilled in His action.†

---

* J. C. Ryle.

† The whole transaction is a remarkable one, as exhibiting our Lord using more physical exertion, and energetic bodily action, than

Then He spoke of His coming death and resurrection in a veiled form. The Jews and His disciples did not understand what temple He meant. He spoke of His own body. "In three days I will raise it up." His resurrection was both through the power of God and by Himself. God raised Him up and He raised Himself up. This statement properly belongs to this Gospel in which we behold Him as the Son of God. The same statement we find in chapter x:18—"I have power to lay down my life, and I have power to take it again."

---

we see Him using at any other period of His ministry. A word, a touch, or the reaching forth of a hand, are the ordinary limits of His actions. Here we see Him doing no less than four things:—(1) Making the scourge;—(2) Driving out the animals;—(3) Pouring out on the ground the changers' money;—(4) Overthrowing the tables. On no occasion do we find Him showing such strong outward marks of indignation, as at the sight of the profanation of the temple. Remembering that the whole transaction is a striking type of what Christ will do at His second coming, we may get some idea of the deep meaning of that remarkable expression, "The wrath of the Lamb." (Rev. vi:16)—Expository Thoughts on John.

II. Eternal Life Imparted: What it is and What it Includes.

Chapter ii:23-xvii

The second part of this Gospel contains the blessed teachings the Son of God gave concerning eternal life, how it is imparted and what it includes. Everything in these chapters is new. The story of Nicodemus, the woman at Sychar's well, the healing of the impotent man, the discourses of our Lord, etc., are not reported by the synoptic Gospels. There is not a word of the Sermon on the Mount reported by John; the many miracles, so significantly arranged in Matthew, are omitted (except the feeding of the 5000); nor do we find a single parable concerning the Kingdom of Heaven. The progressive revelation concerning eternal life will be brought out in the annotations. As already stated the teachings begin with the new birth, in which eternal life is imparted, and end with the destiny of those who are born again. This is revealed in His high priestly prayer, "Father, I will that they also whom thou hast given me be with me where I am, that they may behold my glory."

CHAPTER II:23-III:36

1. The Many Who Believed on Him. ii:23-25.
2. Nicodemus and the New Birth. iii:1-8.
3. How the New Birth is Accomplished. 9-21.
4. The Last Testimony of John. 22-36.

He worked many miracles in Jerusalem, which are unreported by John. Many therefore believed in His name, but the Omniscient One knew that they were only convinced, but their hearts had not been touched and so they did not receive Him as the Son of God. But there was one who was more deeply exercised, an earnest, seeking soul, Nicodemus. He came to Jesus by night and addressed Him as Rabbi, acknowledging that He was a teacher come from God. The Lord did not permit him to go on with his address nor to state the object of his visit. The Lord treated him in an abrupt, almost discourteous, way and informed him at once of the absolute necessity of the new birth. "Verily, verily, I say unto thee, except a man be born again (literally: born from above) he cannot see the Kingdom of God." Not teaching, mere knowledge, was the need Nicodemus had to see the Kingdom, but to be born from above.

But what Kingdom does our Lord mean? It refers primarily to the Kingdom of the Old Testament, promised to Israel. When that Kingdom comes, with the Return of the Lord, only those of Israel will enter in who are born again. The unbelieving and apostate mass of Jews will be excluded from that earthly, millennial Kingdom. Only the believing remnant inherits that Kingdom to come. This may be learned from Ezekiel xxxvi and Isaiah iv:3, and other passages. That is why the Lord said to Nicodemus: "Art thou the teacher of Israel, and knowest not these things?"

But the truth our Lord gave to Nicodemus has a wider application. Man is spiritually dead, destitute of spiritual life. In order to enter the Kingdom of God, to be in the presence of God, man must be born anew. Such a statement is nowhere found in the preceding Gospels. In the Gospel of John, the Gospel of Eternal Life, it is put into the foreground. Nicodemus is the only person to whom the Lord spoke of the absolute necessity of the new birth. He never made such a statement to the publicans and the harlots. And who was Nicodemus? A Pharisee, and therefore an extremely religious man. A ruler of the Jews, which necessitated a moral life. The teacher of Israel, one who possessed much learning. Religiousness, morality, education and culture are insufficient to save man and give him a place in the Kingdom of God. The new birth is the one thing needed. "That which is born of the flesh is flesh." The flesh is the old nature which every human being brings into the world; it is a fallen, a corrupt nature and can never be anything else. And "they that are in the flesh cannot please God." (Rom. viii:8). The natural man may do anything he pleases, become religious and philanthropic, but he cannot please God. What then is the new birth? It is not reformation. Nor is it, as so often stated, an action of the Holy Spirit to make an evil nature good. The flesh cannot be changed into something better. The new birth is the impartation of a new nature, the divine nature, by the Holy Spirit. "That which is born of the Spirit is spirit." This new nature is absolutely holy, as the old nature is absolutely corrupt. This new nature is the only thing which fits man to be in the presence of God.

But what is the meaning of "water" in verse 5? "Except a man be born of water and of the Spirit, he cannot enter the Kingdom of God." The water is claimed by ritualists to mean baptism. If a little water is put upon the head of an infant, they would have us believe, regeneration takes place. Others hold upon this statement of our Lord that the water is Christian baptism, and that therefore water-baptism is necessary to salvation. But the words of our Lord have nothing whatever to do with baptism.* The water cannot mean Christian baptism. Christian baptism (an entirely different thing from the Jewish baptism of John) was not instituted till after His death and resurrection. If it meant Christian baptism, the Lord's rebuke to Nicodemus would be unjust. How could he know something that was still undivulged? Water in this passage is the figure of the Word of God, which the

---

* Ezekiel xxxvi:25-27 must be linked with John iii:5 and must be considered here as a national promise to Israel, how they will enter the Kingdom. But the verses in Ezekiel have absolutely nothing whatever to do with baptism. To apply them thus is ridiculous.

Spirit of God uses for the quickening of souls. The following passages will demonstrate this fact: Eph. v:25-26; 1 Cor. iv:15; 1 Peter i:23; James i:18. Begotten again by the Word of God, and water is the figure of that Word.

The Lord speaks next of revealing heavenly things (in distinction from earthly things relating to Israel). Then the Cross is revealed by which the heavenly things are realized, and how lost man is to be saved and receive eternal life (the new nature). The Son of Man must be lifted up. He Who knew no sin was made sin for us. "God so loved the world that He gave His Only-begotten Son, that whosoever believeth on Him should not perish but have everlasting life."—"In this was manifested the love of God toward us, because God sent His Only-begotten Son into the world, that we might live through Him. Herein is love; not that we loved God, but that He loved us, and sent His Son to be the propitiation for our sins." (1 John iv:9-10). Blessed words these! It is by believing on the Son of God, who died for our sins, that we are saved and are born again.

John bears his final testimony in verses 23-26. He testifies of Christ as the bridegroom, who is to have the bride. John calls himself the friend of the bridegroom. "He must increase, but I must decrease." Note the three "must's" in this chapter. "Ye must be born again"; the necessity of the new birth. "The Son of Man must be lifted up"; the necessity of the death of the Lord to make salvation possible. "He must increase, but I must decrease"; the result of salvation. The final testimony of John the Baptist takes us beyond the cross. (Verse 35-36). Blessed assurance! He that believeth on the Son hath everlasting life.—Solemn declaration! He that believeth not the Son shall not see life; but the wrath of God *abideth* on him.

CHAPTER IV

1. He Must Needs Pass Through Samaria. 1-5.
2. At Sychar's Well; Jesus and the Samaritan Woman. 6-26.
3. The Woman's Witness and the Believing Samaritans. 27-42.
4. His Return to Galilee. 43-45.
5. The Second Miracle, the Healing of the Nobleman's Son. 43-54.

In the Gospel of Matthew the Lord told His disciples not to go into the way of the Gentiles and not to enter into any city of the Samaritans. (x:5). He sent them to preach the nearness of the Kingdom. Here He must needs go through Samaria. He had left Jerusalem and was on His way to Galilee and passing through Samaria He manifested His marvellous Grace. Tired on account of the way, an evidence of His true humanity, "He sat thus on the well." There He rested in unwearied love, waiting for the poor, fallen woman, whose sad story He knew so well.

To follow the beautiful account of His dealings with the Samaritan woman in all its blessed details is impossible in our brief annotations. What mercy and grace He exhibited in seeking such a one! What wisdom and patience in dealing with her, bearing with her ignorance! And what power in drawing her to Himself and making her a messenger to bring others to Him! How different He treated her in comparison with Nicodemus in the preceding chapter.

The Lord speaks to the Samaritan woman concerning the living water, which He can give to all that ask Him. The central verse of His teaching is the fourteenth, "But whosoever drinketh of the water that I shall give him shall never thirst; but the water that I shall give him shall be in him a well of water springing up into everlasting life." The well or fountain of water in the believer is the indwelling Spirit. In chapter vii:37-39 the Lord speaks also of living water and there the interpretation of it is given. "This He spake of the Spirit, whom they that believe on Him should receive; for the Holy Spirit was not yet given, because that Jesus was not yet glorified." The believer has therefore not only eternal life, but also the gift of the Spirit, Who dwells in him as the spring of living water.

The new worship is next revealed in answer to the question of the woman. Verses 21-24. The Samaritans worshipped on a mountain (Gerizim); the Jews in the temple, but the hour was coming when the true worshippers would worship the Father in the Spirit. No longer would true believers worship God as the God of Israel, but as Father. It is to be a worship in the Spirit and not confined to a locality. Christian worship has for its foundation the possession of eternal life; the indwelling Spirit is the power of that worship. Only true believers, such who are born again and possess the gift of the Spirit, can be worshippers. "For we are the circumcision who worship God in the Spirit and rejoice in Christ Jesus, and have no confidence in the flesh." (Phil. iii:3). And such worshippers the Father seeketh. In Old Testament times the Jews worshipped in an earthly place. In the coming, the millennial age, nations will go up to Jerusalem to worship the Lord of hosts in the great millennial Temple. (Is. ii:1-4; Zech. xiv:16, etc.) This present dispensation is the dispensation of Grace, and the Father seeketh worshippers who worship Him in Spirit and in Truth. Thus we are brought in the Gospel of John altogether upon the ground of grace.

Then He revealed Himself to the woman. "Jesus saith to her, I that speak to thee am He." She was face to face with the Messiah; she stood in the presence of Jehovah. She left her waterpot to tell others the good news of the living water. The earthly things were forgotten. And what a messenger she became! How her simple testimony was blessed in the conversion of souls! He abode there two days and is owned and proclaimed not alone as the promised Messiah but as the Saviour of the world. (Verse 42).

Once more we see Him at Cana of Galilee, and the nobleman's son, who was sick at Capernaum, is healed by the Lord. The nobleman represents typically Israel. The word the Lord addressed to him fits that nation. "Except ye see signs and wonders, ye will not believe." How different from Samaria, where He did no miracle and yet they believed. And as the nobleman and his whole house believed, so will Israel believe in a future day.

CHAPTER V

1. The Healing of the Impotent Man. 1-9.
2. The Opposition of the Jews. 10-18.
3. His Unity with the Father. 19-23.
4. The Present Hour. Believers Delivered from Death and Judgment. 24-25.
5. The Future Hour. His Power to Raise the Dead. 26-29.
6. Witness Concerning Himself. 30-32.
7. The Witness of John. 33-35.
8. The Witness of His Works. 36.
9. The Witness of the Father. 37.
10. The Witness of the Scriptures, and the Unbelief of the Jews. 39-46.

The teachings contained in this chapter are closely linked with the third and fourth chapters. He went up to Jerusalem again. In the foreground stands the healing of the impotent man at the pool of Bethesda with its five porches. An angel troubled the water at certain seasons, so that some were healed. We believe that it was actually so, though we cannot explain it. Many critics attack this occurrence and reject its genuineness.* But the impotent man could not avail himself of the opportunity for he was helpless. Such was Israel's condition under the law. The

* "After all there is no more real difficulty in the account before us, than in the history of our Lord's temptation in the wilderness, the various cases of Satanic possession, or the release of Peter from prison by an angel. Once admit the existence of angels, their ministry on earth, and the possibility of their inter-position to carry out God's designs, and there is nothing that ought to stumble us in the passage. The true secret of some of the objections to it, is the modern tendency to regard all miracles as useless lumber, which must be thrown overboard, if possible, and cast out of the Sacred Narrative on every occasion. Against this tendency we must watch and be on our guard."

thirty-eight years point back to Israel's wandering in the wilderness. Furthermore the impotent man presents a striking picture of the utter helplessness of man as a sinner. By His word the Lord Jesus made him perfectly whole, so that he took up his bed and walked.

Opposition and objection from the Jews followed at once. They accused the healed man of breaking the Sabbath. He evidently did not know the Lord at all; only after He had spoken to him (Verse 14) did he find out that it was Jesus. Then he told the Jews. Their hatred was turned at once against the Lord. They persecuted Him and sought to slay Him because He had done this miracle on the Sabbath. The Lord's answer is most blessed. "My Father worketh hitherto, and I work." It is the first time in this Gospel that He speaks of God as "My Father." He, the Son, was in their midst to make the Father known. He told them that His Father works and that the Son works. Sin made this work necessary. He stood in their presence and claimed perfect and unbroken fellowship with His Father.

The Jews knew what He meant. Had He said "Our Father" instead of "My Father" no word of protest would have escaped their lips. They knew His words could mean but one thing, that He is equal with God, by saying that God was His Father. Augustine remarked on this verse: "Behold the Jews understood what the Arians (deniers of His Deity) would not understand." And He accepted the charge of the Jews as a correct one. "He thought it not robbery to be equal with God." (Phil. ii:6). His words which follow declare His perfect unity with the Father in His work; He is the Beloved of the Father; the Father raiseth up the dead, so does He; judgment is committed unto the Son; He is to be honoured as the Father is honoured. "Whosoever does not honour the Son with equal honour to that which he pays to the Father, however he may imagine that he honours or approaches God, does not honour Him at all; because he can only be known by us as 'the Father who sent his Son.' "* Unitarianism, Russel-

* Dean Alford.

lism, the new theology and a host of other "isms," which deny the absolute Deity of our Lord, stand condemned and convicted in the presence of these wonderful words, "He that honoureth not the Son honoureth not the Father." All worship apart from the Son of God is idolatry. He claims the unity in Godhead; and such belongs to Him.

Verse 24 is a blessed Gospel text. Hearing and believing are the conditions to receive eternal life. There is no mention made of repentance. The word "repent" so prominent in the Gospel of Matthew in the Kingdom offer is not found once in the fourth Gospel. Faith and repentance, however, are inseparable. He that hears His words and believeth Him that sent the Son also repents. Again eternal life is spoken of as a present possession, "hath" not "shall have" or "shall receive later," but "hath eternal life." And with that gift comes deliverance from judgment. The reception of eternal life is a full acquittal; passed from death and all it means, into life.

"The coming hour" in verse 25 is the present dispensation. The dead are the spiritually dead. They that hear the voice of the Son of God shall live; they receive His life. Then He speaks of an hour which was to come and which has not yet come. Two resurrections are revealed by Him; the resurrection of life and the resurrection of judgment. This does not mean that these two resurrections are to take place the same time, in, what is termed, a general resurrection. Elsewhere we find the full revelation concerning these two resurrections. There is the first resurrection, the resurrection of the just, and a thousand years later the resurrection of the wicked dead. (Rev. xx.) All the wrong teachings concerning the wicked dead, such as Annihilation, Restitution, Restoration, Second Chance, etc., as taught by Seventh Day Adventism, Millennial Dawnism,* Universalism and others, are completely refuted by the words of our Lord in verse 29.

*** Now called "International Bible Students' Association."**

The five witnesses who testify concerning Himself, that He is the Son of God, are of much importance and should be carefully studied.

CHAPTER VI

1. The Feeding of the Five Thousand Men. 1-14.
2. The Attempt to Make Him King. 15.
3. The Stormy Sea. "It is I, be not afraid." 16-21.
4. The Discourse on the Bread of Life. The Food of the Believer. 22-59.
5. The Falling Away of Disciples. 60-66.
6. Peter's Confession. 67-71.

The events which are recorded in this chapter happened at the Sea of Galilee, the Sea of Tiberias. John exclusively uses this name, an evidence that he wrote after the fall of Jerusalem. By this name the lake had become known to the Gentiles. The feeding of the five thousand is the same mentioned by the Synoptics. This great sign showed that Jehovah was in their midst, He Who had fed His Israel with manna in the wilderness and promised to satisfy the poor with bread. (Ps. cxxxii:15.) When they had seen the great sign they acknowledged Him to be the promised Prophet who should come (Deut. xviii:15) and wanted to make Him King. But He departed into a mountain. He knew that all they meant by making Him King was to become the leader of a carnal movement to overthrow the hated Roman government.

The storm on the sea and His coming across the stormy sea we have had in the other Gospels.

The great discourse on the Bread of Life follows. It is connected with the sign of the feeding of the multitude. When He speaks of being the Bread from Heaven He refers to His incarnation. "For the bread of God is He which cometh down from heaven, and giveth His life for the world." They rejected that Bread. Then He speaks of eating His flesh and drinking His blood both for the reception of life and for the sustenance of that life. These words have nothing whatever to do with the Lord's Supper. Bishop Ryle, who was a leader in a ritualistic church, repudiated this wrong interpretation in the following words: "For one thing, a literal 'eating and drinking' of Christ's body and blood would have been an idea utterly revolting to all Jews, and flatly contradictory to an often-repeated precept of their law.—For another thing, to take a literal view of 'eating and drinking,' is to interpose a bodily act between the soul of man and salvation. This is a thing for which there is no precedent in Scripture. The only things without which we cannot be saved are repentance and faith.—Last, but not least, to take a literal view of 'eating and drinking,' would involve most blasphemous and profane consequences. It would shut out of heaven the penitent thief. He died long after these words were spoken, without any literal eating and drinking. Will any dare to say he had 'no life' in Him?—It would admit to heaven thousands of ignorant, godless communicants in the present day. They literally eat and drink, no doubt! But they have no eternal life, and will not be raised to glory. Let these reasons be carefully pondered.

"The plain truth is, there is a morbid anxiety in fallen man to put a carnal sense on Scriptural expressions, wherever he possibly can. He struggles hard to make religion a matter of forms and ceremonies,—of doing and performing,—of sacraments and ordinances,—of sense and of sight."

The Bread of God, He Himself, gave His life for the world. He gave His body and shed His blood on the cross. It is His sacrificial, atoning death. By faith we partake of it. Without it there is no life. Note the difference in verses 53 and 54. In verse 53 He speaks of those who have eaten His flesh and drunk His blood, apart from which there is no life. By faith the sinner appropriates Him, Who gave His body and shed His blood, and then receives eternal life. In verse 54 He speaks of a continuous eating and drinking. He is the Source of eternal life. The believer feeds on Him; the eternal life the believer has must be sustained, nourished and kept by Himself, by ever feeding on His dying love. "The life that I now live in the flesh I live by the faith of the Son of God, who loved me and gave Himself for me." (Gal. ii:20.) And the believer eating and drinking becomes one with Him. "He that eateth my flesh and drinketh my blood dwelleth (literally: abideth) in Me and I in him." It is a wonderful discourse on His incarnation, His sacrificial, atoning death, and the blessed assurances given to those who believe on Him. Precious are the promises of this great chapter. "He that cometh to me shall never hunger, and he that believeth on me shall never thirst." (Verse 35.) "Him that cometh unto me I will in no wise cast out." (Verse 37.) "Every one who seeth the Son, and believeth on Him, may have everlasting life; and I will raise him up at the last day."* (Verse 40.) "Verily, verily, I say unto you, he that believeth on me hath everlasting life." (Verse 47.)

CHAPTER VII

1. My Time is not Yet Come. 1-9.
2. Departure from Galilee; Sought by the Jews. 10-13.
3. In the Temple Teaching. 14-29.
4. Opposition to Him. 30-36.
5. The Indwelling Spirit Promised. 37-39.
6. The Division Among the People Because of Him. 40-44.
7. The Returning Officers and the Defence of Nicodemus. 45-53.

The Lord tarried in Galilee. How He must have sought souls there as He walked in Galilee! He would not walk in Judea (not "Jewry," as in the Authorized Version) because the Jews, that is the leaders of the people, sought to kill Him. The Feast of Tabernacles was at hand and what

* "The last day" does not mean a day of a final and universal judgment followed by the end of the world. It is the end of the Jewish age to which our Lord refers (the age which is yet to be completed in great tribulation.—Matt. xxiv). The first resurrection includes Old Testament saints, New Testament saints and the Jewish believers, who are martyred during the great tribulation. The first resurrection will be completed at the close of the tribulasion period and followed by the setting up of the Kingdom.

we find written in this chapter happened during that Feast. His brethren, no doubt sons born to Mary after His own birth, urged Him to go to Judea. Their motives were selfish. They did not believe on Him. However, later they believed, for we find them among those who waited in Jerusalem for the promise of the father. (Acts i:14.) The Feast of Tabernacles typifies the millennial blessings for Israel and the Gentiles, the great consummation. The world hated Him and He declared that His time had not yet come. We cannot follow at length the interesting account of His coming to Jerusalem, the words He spake, the answers He gave to those who hated Him. He taught and they marvelled. He declared that the doctrine He preached was of Him that sent Him. What a challenge He gave them! "If any man will do His will, he shall know of the doctrine, whether it be of God, or whether I speak of myself." Then He told them that they tried to kill Him. "Thou hast a demon," was their reply, while others said: "Is not this He whom they seek to kill?" They sought to take Him and the Pharisees and Chief Priest sent officers to arrest Him. Thus the hatred against Him is manifested. His hour had not yet come; no one could touch Him. When the hour came He yielded Himself.

The great center of this chapter is found in verses 37-39. The last day of the Feast of Tabernacles was the greatest. It was the eighth day, a day of rest and holy gathering together. During the seven days of the feast water was daily drawn from the pool of Siloam and then poured out. On the last day this ceremony did not take place. The seven days typified their wilderness journey; the eighth day the entrance into the land. For seven days they drew the water and poured it out, commemorating the water the Lord had supplied to Israel during the wilderness journey. On the eighth day they enjoyed the springs of the land itself; an emblem of the living waters which the Lord had promised to His people. Israel has these promises. "And it shall be in that day that living waters shall go out from Jerusalem." (Zech. xiv:8.) The same promise we find elsewhere. (See Ezek. xlvii; Isaiah xii.) And He Who had given to His people these promises, Who had come to fulfill them, stood in their midst. They hate Him. They tell Him to His face, "Thou hast a demon." They seek to kill Him.

On the last day of the feast, typical of Israel's promised blessing and glory, He stood and cried: "If any man thirst let him come unto Me and drink." He offers now upon the rejection of Himself something new to "any man who thirsts"; the national promises of living water pouring forth from Jerusalem cannot be fulfilled now. They will be fulfilled when He comes again. It is an individual invitation, an individual promise, He gives. "He that believeth on Me, as the Scripture hath said, out of his belly shall flow rivers of living water." We are then told that this means the gift of the Holy Spirit, which they were to receive who came to Him and believed on Him. The promise was fulfilled on the day of Pentecost. Then the Holy Spirit came to dwell in believers. The overflow, the streams of living water to flow from the believer, is the type of the Spirit, the Spirit of power manifesting Himself through the believer in bearing testimony for Christ. In the third chapter we saw the Holy Spirit communicating life; He is the Life-giving Spirit. In the fourth chapter the Lord spoke of the Spirit as the well of living water; He indwells the one who is born again to make communion and worship possible. Then followed His teaching in chapters v and vi, again concerning the life the believer hath in Him and how it is sustained. In the present chapter the indwelling Spirit, Who is the well of living water in the believer, is seen flowing forth to others, just as a spring will overflow.

CHAPTER VIII

1. The Woman Taken in Adultery. 1-11.
2. The Light of the World. 12.
3. His Testimony Concerning Himself and the Father. 13-20.
4. His Solemn Declarations. 21-47.
5. Before Abraham Was, I Am. 48-59.

The first verse belongs to the preceding chapter. The officers returned without Him, bearing their testimony that "never man spake like this man." Nicodemus ventured his timid defence. Then every man went to his own house while the Lord went to the Mount of Olives.

The story of the woman taken in adultery has been rejected by many leading scholars. It is claimed that it is nothing less than a forgery. The chief arguments against it are the following: That the story is missing in some of the oldest manuscripts and earlier translations; that some of the Greek Fathers never refer to it; that it differs in style from the rest of the Gospel of John, and that the incident ought to be discredited on moral ground. However all these arguments have been proven invalid. Many old manuscripts have the story as well as some of the oldest translations. Others of the so-called church-fathers speak of it. There can be no question whatever of its genuineness. It was omitted on purpose in certain manuscripts. The Grace, which shines forth so marvellously in the Lord's dealing with the woman, was unpalatable to teachers who mixed Law and Grace. They left it out for a purpose.*

It was a clever scheme from the side of the Scribes and Pharisees to tempt Him. The Law of Moses demanded her death by stoning. If He gave as an answer "let her be stoned!" He would contradict His own testimony that He

* "The argument from alleged discrepancies between the style and language of this passage, and the usual style of St. John's writing, is one which should be received with much caution. We are not dealing with an uninspired but with an inspired writer. Surely it is not too much to say that an inspired writer may occasionally use words and constructions and modes of expression which he generally does not use, and that it is no proof that he did not write a passage because he wrote it in a peculiar way."

came not to judge, but to save. If He declared that the guilty woman was not to be stoned, then would He break the law. They appealed to Him as teacher, not as judge. He was silent and stooped down and wrote with His finger in the ground.* It is the only time we read of our Lord that He wrote. The finger which wrote in the ground was the same which had written the law in the tables of stone. What He wrote we do not know; but it was symbolical of the fact that the law against man is written in the dust, the dust of death. Not alone had the woman deserved death, but all were equally guilty. After His demand, "He that is without sin among you, let him first cast a stone at her," the oldest in the company left first till the Lord was alone with the guilty woman. He did not set aside the law, and yet He manifested His marvellous Grace. The self-righteous accusers were condemned and sneaked into darkness, away from Him Who is the Light. The woman addressed Him as Lord, showing she believed on Him; and He told her to go and sin no more. The Grace He shows demands holiness.

The scene occurred in the Temple and the words He spoke following this incident were likewise spoken there. A great testimony again follows, which He gives concerning Himself. He is the Light of the world; it is not confined to Israel, but the light is to reach the Gentile nations. This is revealed in the Prophet Isaiah. After Messiah's complaint, "I have laboured in vain," the rejected One is to be the light to the Gentiles. "I will also give thee for a light to the Gentiles that thou mayest be my salvation unto the ends of the earth." (Is. xlix:1-6.) Then follows an individual promise. He that followeth Him walks not in darkness, but has the light of life. In Him is life as well as light; there is then fellowship with God for the child of life, fellowship one with another if we walk in the light.

He then bore additional testimony concerning Himself.

---

* The words, "as though He heard them not" are in italics and must be omitted.

He knew where He came from and whither He went. The blind Pharisees did not. And when He spoke of the fellowship of Himself and the Father, they asked, "Where is thy Father?" They were blind and blinded, and knew neither Him nor the Father.

Very solemn are the declarations in verses 21-29. They are as solemn and as true to-day as when they were uttered by the lips of the Son of God. "I said therefore unto you that ye shall die in your sins; for if ye believe not that I am He, ye shall die in your sins." Rejecting Christ, not believing on Him, means to die in sin. When they ask Him again, "Who art thou?" He answered, "Absolutely* what I am also speaking to you." He is the Word, the Truth, the Life, the Light. He is, in the principle of His being, what also He speaks. Essentially, precisely, what He is, He also speaks. The phrase "lifting up" means His crucifixion. (See iii:14 and xii:32.) After that event His vindication would come. He is the "I am." Many believed on Him. Were they true believers or the same class as we find at the close of the second chapter? Most likely they misunderstood His statement of being lifted up. They may have thought of Him becoming King; they certainly knew nothing of the Cross.

More teaching follows. To be a true disciple means to abide in His Word. By the Word and the Spirit we are begotten, and to live as a disciple needs abiding in His Word. The Son is the Deliverer Who makes free from the power of Satan and of Sin, of which He bears witness.

This interesting chapter ends with a startling self-revelation of His absolute Deity, that He is the Eternal Jehovah. Eleven times the name "Abraham" is found in the eighth chapter of John. At the close the Lord speaks of Abraham having seen His day and rejoiced. He saw it in faith. Then when the Jews expressed their astonishment He answered, "Before Abraham was, *I AM!*" It is the most positive, the clearest declaration of our Lord of His Eter-

* The rendering of the Authorized Version is incorrect.

nity, that He is God. He is the "I AM"—Jehovah. Thus this great testimony has always been received. We let a few of the ancient teachers speak:

Chrysostom observes: "He said not before Abraham was, I was, but, I AM. As the Father useth this expression I AM, so also doth Christ, for it signifieth continuous being, irrespective of all time. On which account the expression seemed to the Jews blasphemous."

Augustine says: "In these words acknowledge the Creator and discern the creature. He that spake was made the Seed of Abraham; and that Abraham might be, He was before Abraham."

Gregory remarks: "Divinity has no past or future, but always the present; and therefore Jesus does not say before Abraham was I *was*, but I *am*."

The Unitarians try to explain this away by saying, "Jesus only meant that He existed as Messiah in God's counsels before Abraham." Astonishing! How do they know what He meant? It is a satanic invention. The Jews knew better. They understood what He meant. They took up stones to stone Him, because they knew He claimed absolute Deity. A miracle followed. The Greek means literally "He was hid." Their eyes must have been holden as He went out of the Temple and passed by.

CHAPTER IX

1. The Man Born Blind, Healed. 1-7.
2. The Healed Man Questioned. 8-26.
3. Reviled and Cast Out. 27-34.
4. Jesus Reveals Himself to Him. 35-41.

The healing of the man born blind is a type and an illustration of how Christ, the Light, communicates light and how he who follows the Light walks no more in darkness, but has the light of life. (Chapter viii:12.) And before He healed the man He testified that His day of activity on earth as Man was rapidly drawing to its close. (Verses 4 and 5.) The clay and the spittle did not effect the opening of the eyes; it was the power of Christ. The blind man went and washed in the pool of Siloam and came seeing.

The conflict the blind man had is interesting and instructive, but too lengthy to follow in our annotations. The Pharisees exhibit their hatred against Him Who healed the blind man and they did all in their power to discredit the miracle and Him Who performed it. They questioned the man to confound him, but did not succeed. Then they questioned the parents, but they were afraid to say how their son had received his sight, for the Jews had agreed that if any man confessed Him as Christ he should be put out of the synagogue. Then they questioned the man again and he gave them an excellent testimony. "Whether he be a sinner or no, I know not; one thing I know, that, whereas I was blind, now I see." And when after repeated questionings the healed one expressed his firm belief that He Who gave him sight was of God, they cast him out.

But they only cast him into the arms of the loving Lord. He heard of what had been done to the man, and He sought for him. Then He revealed Himself to him as the Son of God. The man believed and worshipped Him. He was thrust outside of Judaism and in that outside place Christ found him, and he believed on Christ. Like everything else in the Gospel of John this anticipates the position of true Christianity. It is outside of the camp of Judaism, outside of that which has rejected Christ. "Let us go forth therefore unto Him without the camp, bearing His reproach." (Heb. xiii:13.)

CHAPTER X

1. The Shepherd of the Sheep. 1-5.
2. The Good Shepherd, His Sheep and His Work. 6-21.
3. At the Feast of Dedication; the Repeated Testimony. 22-30.
4. Accused of Blasphemy and His Answer. 31-39.
5. Beyond Jordan; and Many Believed on Him. 40-42.

The teaching of this chapter is closely linked with the preceding event. It has become evident that the true sheep of Christ, belonging to His flock, would be cast out of the

Jewish fold. The healed man cast out had become one of His sheep. Therefore He teaches now more fully concerning Himself as the Shepherd and about His sheep. The Old Testament speaks often of Israel as the sheep of Jehovah, and of Jehovah as the Shepherd. (Ps. lxxx:1; xcv:7; xxiii:1; Ezekiel xxxiv; Zech. xi:7-9; xiii:7.) The true Shepherd had come through the appointed door into the sheepfold, that is among Israel. He is the only One, and the porter (the Holy Spirit) opened to Him. He came and called His own sheep by name to lead them out. And the sheep hear His voice and follow Him. All is Jewish. He came, the true Shepherd, into the sheepfold to lead them out to become His flock.

It was a parable He spoke in these opening verses, but they did not understand it. What follows is a fuller revelation of Himself as the good Shepherd, and the sheep who belong to His flock. Judaism was a fold out of which the Shepherd leads His flock. He is the Door of the sheep. He is the means of getting into the flock, as a door is the means of getting into a house. Through Him all His sheep must enter by faith into the flock. There is no other door and no other way. He came into the fold by God's appointed way and He is God's appointed way. "I am the door, by Me if any man enter in, he shall be saved, and shall go in and out and find pasture." A most blessed promise. He is the door. Any man, it does not matter who it is, any man may enter in by Him and then having entered in by Him, that is believed on Him, He promises salvation, liberty and food. These three things are bestowed upon all who believe on Him. Salvation is in Him and it is a present and a perfect salvation; liberty, freed from the bondage of the law which condemned the sinner, a perfect liberty; pasture, food, which He supplies; He Himself is the food, a perfect food. It is all found outside of the fold, the fold of Judaism, and in Christ. He came that they might have life and that they might have it more abundantly. The abundant life He speaks of here is the life which comes from

His death and resurrection. The good Shepherd had to give His life for the sheep. How different from the hireling, who fleeth and careth not for the sheep. The hirelings were the faithless shepherds. (Ezek. xxxiv:1-6.) Again He said: "I lay down my life for the sheep."*

In verse 16 our Lord speaks of other sheep, which are not of this fold. These are the Gentiles. He leads out first from the Jewish fold His sheep; then there are the other sheep whom He will bring and who will hear His voice. The result will be one flock and one Shepherd. The Authorized Version is incorrect in using the word "fold." Judaism was a fold, the church is not. The ecclesiastical folds in which Christendom is divided have been brought about by the Judaizing of the church. The fold no longer exists. There is one flock as there is one Shepherd; one body, as there is one Lord. All who have heard His voice, believed on Him, entered in by Him, are members of the one flock.

At the Feast of Dedication, commemorating the cleansing of the Temple and re-dedication by Judas Maccabæus after the desecration by Antiochus,† the Lord continued His blessed teaching, ending it once more with a great revelation of Himself. He makes a most blessed addition to His previous instructions concerning Himself and His sheep. "I give unto them eternal life and they shall never perish, neither shall any man pluck them out of my hand. My Father, which gave them me, is greater than all; and no man is able to pluck them out of my Father's hand." Here we have the comforting assurance of the absolute security of every sheep of Christ. Eternal life is a present and personal possession, not something which comes after death. It is therefore an abiding possession and cannot be lost. Then He Who is the Life and the Light, the Way

* "The expression, 'laying down the soul or life' for any one, does not occur anywhere else independently in the New Testament. It is never found in profane writers. It must be referred back to the Old Testament, and specially to Isai. liii. 10, where it is said of Messiah, 'He shall make, or place, His soul an offering for sin.'"
—*Hengstenberg.*

† See Daniel viii:9-14.

and the Truth, assures us that His sheep shall never perish. Some say that He said "no one can pluck them out of His hand" but we can do it ourselves by living in sin, etc. This is fully answered by the correct rendering of His words, "they shall never perish." It means literally: "they shall in no wise ever perish." This is absolute; it covers everything.

Then His great revelation: "I and the Father are one." Again the Jews understood what He meant, for they wanted to stone Him. After His answer they wanted to take Him, but He escaped out of their hands. His hour had not yet come.

CHAPTER XI

1. The Sickness of Lazarus Announced. 1-4.
2. The Delayed Departure and the Death of Lazarus. 5-11.
3. The Arrival at Bethany. 17-27.
4. Weeping with Them That Weep. 28-38.
5. The Resurrection of Lazarus. 39-46.
6. The Prophecy of Caiaphas. 47-52.
7. Seeking to Kill Him. 53-57.

The resurrection of Lazarus is the final great sign or miracle in this Gospel. It is the greatest of all. Some critics have discredited it by saying that, if it had really taken place the Synoptics would have something to say about it. The Gospel of John is the Gospel in which this miracle properly belongs. As we have seen, the Gospel of John is the Gospel in which our Lord as Son of God is fully revealed. The resurrection of Lazarus proves Him the Son of God, Who can raise the dead. The philosopher and sceptic Spinoza declared that if he could be persuaded of the historicity of this miracle he would embrace Christianity. The miracle is supported by the most incontrovertible evidence; it requires more credulity to deny it than to believe it.

A German Expositor * put together the evidences of this great miracle in the following way:

---

* Dr. Tillmann.

"The whole story is of a nature calculated to exclude all suspicion of imposture, and to confirm the truth of the miracle. A well-known person of Bethany, named Lazarus, falls sick in the absence of Jesus. His sisters send a message to Jesus, announcing it; but while He is yet absent Lazarus dies, is buried, and kept in the tomb for four days, during which Jesus is still absent. Martha, Mary, and all his friends are convinced of his death. Our Lord, while yet remaining in the place where He had been staying, tells His disciples in plain terms that He means to go to Bethany, to raise Lazarus from the dead, that the glory of God may be illustrated, and their faith confirmed. At our Lord's approach, Martha goes to meet Him, and announces her brother's death, laments the absence of Jesus before the event took place, and yet expresses a faint hope that by some means Jesus might yet render help. Our Lord declares that her brother shall be raised again, and assures her that He has the power of granting life to the dead. Mary approaches, accompanied by weeping friends from Jerusalem. Our Lord Himself is moved, and weeps, and goes to the sepulchre, attended by a crowd. The stone is removed. The stench of the corpse is perceived. Our Lord, after pouring forth audible prayer to His Father, calls forth Lazarus from the grave, in the hearing of all. The dead man obeys the call, comes forth to public view in the same dress that he was buried in, alive and well, and returns home without assistance. All persons present agree that Lazarus is raised to life, and that a great miracle has been worked, though not all believe the person who worked it to be the Messiah. Some go away and tell the rulers at Jerusalem what Jesus has done. Even these do not doubt the truth of the fact; on the contrary, they confess that our Lord by His works is becoming every day more famous, and that He would probably be soon received as Messiah by the whole nation. And *therefore* the rulers at once take counsel how they may put to death both Jesus and Lazarus. The people, in the meantime hearing of this prodigious transaction, flock in multitudes to Bethany, partly to see Jesus, and partly to view Lazarus. And the consequence is that by and by, when our Lord comes to Jerusalem, the population goes forth in crowds to meet Him and show Him honour, and chiefly because of His work at Bethany. Now, if all these circumstances do not establish the truth of the miracle, there is no truth in history."

To follow the historical account in all its details would take many pages. It reveals the glory, the sympathy and the power of our Lord as perhaps no other Scripture does.

The heart of the chapter is found in His words to Martha: "I am the resurrection, and the life: he that believeth in Me, though he were dead, yet shall he live. And whosoever liveth and believeth in Me shall never die.'' (Verse 25-36.) In the first place these words anticipate His death and resurrection. He Who laid down His life and took it again, *is* the resurrection, and the life. He can raise the dead, the spiritually and physically dead. But these words take us also forward to His coming again, when they will find their great fulfillment, and when the crowning proof is given that He is the resurrection and the life. The Saints, who believed on Him and died in Christ, will be raised first. This truth is expressed in His words: ''He that believeth in Me, though he were dead, yet shall he live.'' And all who live when He comes for His Saints, when His shout opens the graves, will be caught up in clouds, changed in a moment, in the twinkling of an eye, passing into His presence without dying. Of this He speaks in His last statement: ''He that liveth (when He comes) and believeth on Me shall never die.'' (I Cor. xv:51; I Thess. iv:16-18.)

Who is able to describe the scene as He goes to the cave where His friend Lazarus had been laid away four days previous! Mary sank weeping at His feet. When He saw her weeping, the Jews weeping, then He groaned in the spirit and was troubled. Jesus wept! Oh, precious words! Conscious of His Deity and of His power, He enters with deepest sympathy into the sorrows and afflictions of His people. Such He is still, our great High-priest, Who is touched with the feeling of our infirmities. The cave was covered with a stone. When He commands that stone to be removed, Martha interrupted Him by saying, ''By this time he stinketh, for he has been dead four days.'' It was unbelief. After He had lifted His eyes to heaven and had spoken to the Father, He uttered His majestic ''Lazarus, come forth!'' It was the word of omnipotence to manifest now fully that He is the Son of God, Who hath the power to raise the dead. Who can describe the solemn moment and what happened immediately! Perhaps there was a faint echo out of the cave, for He had cried His command with a loud voice. All eyes were looking towards the dark entrance of the cave, when lo! the dead man was seen struggling forward, bound by the grave clothes. Lazarus, who had been dead four days, whose body had already entered into decomposition, came forth a living man.* "He came back, a challenge thrown in the face of Christ's would-be murderers, of the possibility of success against One to Whom death and grave are subject." † A second word He spoke: "Loose him and let him go." Lazarus is the type of a sinner who hears His Word. We are dead in trespasses and sins. Spiritually man is in the grave, in death and in darkness. He is in corruption. The Lord of Life gives life. And besides this He gives with that life—liberty. He looses from the bondage of the law and of sin. In the next chapter we read of Lazarus again. He is in fellowship with the Lord Who raised him from the dead. Life, Liberty and Fellowship are the three blessed things which he receives who hears and believes. Compare this great chapter with the teachings of the fifth chapter. And Lazarus is also a fit type of Israel and her coming national resurrection.

Then many believed on Him, while the Pharisees and chief priests, acknowledging the fact that He did many miracles, plan His death. Remarkable is the prophecy of Caiaphas. He was used as an instrument to utter a great truth. Christ was indeed to die for that nation, and also that He should gather together in one the children of God that were scattered abroad.

---

* A more plain, distinct, and unmistakable miracle it would be impossible for man to imagine. That a dead man should hear a voice, obey it, rise up, and move forth from his grave alive is utterly contrary to nature. God alone could cause such a thing. What first began life in him, how lungs and heart began to act again, suddenly and instantaneously, it would be waste of time to speculate. It was a miracle and there we must leave it.—*C. Ryle.*

† Numerical Bible.

CHAPTER XII

1. The Feast at Bethany. 1-8.
2. The Entrance into Jerusalem. 9-19.
3. The Inquiring Greeks and His Answer. 20-33.
4. His Final Words. 34-50.

From the close of the previous chapter we learn that the Lord had gone with His disciples to a city called Ephraim. Six days before the Passover He came to Bethany again. They made Him a feast. Lazarus is especially mentioned as well as Martha, who served; Mary also was present with others who were of His disciples. It is a beautiful type of the Marriage Supper of the Lamb, when He will have His own with Him. Lazarus represents the Saints risen from the dead, the others represent the Saints who never died, but are changed in a moment. Service is represented in Martha. Fellowship they had together in the feast with the Lord, and worship in Mary, who anointed His feet. The Synoptics record the fact that she also anointed His head; she did both and there is no discrepancy. She was deeply attached to Him and knew of the threatening danger which hung over Him as Man. She did not know the full meaning of her beautiful act, but the Lord knew and said: "Against the day of my burying hath she kept this." And how He appreciated her love and devotion, though she had not the full intelligence of all it meant. It is devotion to Himself our Lord appreciates most in His people. Well has it been said, "She learned at His feet what she poured out there."

A large number of Jews came to Bethany to see Him, while others came out of curiosity to see Lazarus. Then the wicked chief priests held a consultation that they might put Lazarus also to death. We do not hear another word about Lazarus after this.

His triumphant entrance into Jerusalem followed. The account of it in John's Gospel is very brief. The people welcome Him with the Messianic welcome, "Hosanna! (Save now.) Blessed is the King of Israel that cometh in the name of the Lord." That shout will be heard again in Jerusalem and then it will not be followed by the awful cry, "Crucify Him!" When He comes in power and glory as Israel's King the believing remnant of His people will welcome Him by the same word. (See Matthew xxiii:39.) Zechariah's prophecy (Zech. ix:9) is quoted in part, and that which was unfulfilled is omitted. But the disciples did not understand it, nor did they know that they were fulfilling prophecy. Only after "Jesus was glorified" (John xii:16) did they remember these things. The resurrection of Lazarus played an important part in His triumphant entrance into Jerusalem. Those who stood by and saw the miracle done, bore witness, and others met Him because they heard of the miracle. The testimony of His enemies was: "Behold the world is gone after Him."

Then Greeks (Gentiles) inquired after Him, "Sir, we would see Jesus." How great was His triumph! There was no answer to those Greeks. Before the Gentiles could come to Him, He would have to die. The hour then had come when He, the Son of Man, should be glorified. He meant the Cross and that which follows the suffering, His resurrection and ascension. By His death as Son of Man He acquired Glory and receives ultimately the Kingdoms of this world, the nations and the uttermost parts of the earth for His inheritance. He, therefore, speaks of Himself as the grain of wheat. If there is to be fruit from the one grain of wheat it must fall in to the ground and die. The grain of wheat has life in itself and when it is put into the ground that life is carried through death, to be reproduced in the many grains of wheat. The Life had to pass through death so that it might be communicated to others. The fruit springs from His death and resurrection. What a wonderful sacrifice He brought in giving His life! Believers possess the life of the grain of wheat, which passed through death and therefore are to follow Him and manifest it in a practical way. That is why He adds: "He that loveth his life shall lose it; and he that hateth his life in this world shall keep it unto life eternal.

If any man serve Me, let him follow Me; and where I am, there shall also my servant be; if any man serve Me, him will My Father honour." Giving up, self-denial, the path He went is our path. But how glorious the promised reward!

Then He looked forward to the Cross and His soul was troubled. "Father, save Me from this hour!" This was His prayer, much like that in Gethsemane. But He also adds at once, "for this cause came I unto this hour." He had come to die. The next request, "Father, glorify Thy Name," is at once answered by the voice from heaven. The Father's Name had been glorified by the Son, in a special manner the Father's Name was glorified in the resurrection of Lazarus. The glorification in the future, "and will glorify it," took place "when Christ was raised up from the dead through the glory of the Father." (Rom. vi:4.)

The chapter closes with the final words of our Lord to the people. Many of the chief-rulers believed on Him without making an open confession. The last words He speaks before He gathers His own around Himself are concerning the Father Who sent Him.

CHAPTER XIII

1. The Washing of the Disciples' Feet. 1-11.
2. Instructions given; to Wash One Another's Feet. 12-17.
3. The Betrayal Foretold. 18-30.
4. His Own Departure and the New Commandment. 31-35.
5. The Denial of Peter Foretold. 36-38.

We reach with this chapter the most precious portion of this Gospel. The multitudes are left behind. Israel has completely rejected Him and now He gathered His own beloved disciples around Himself and gave them the sweet and blessed words of instruction, of comfort and cheer, His farewell. A little while and He would leave them to return to the Glory from which He came. "He is leaving upon earth the chosen companions of His path; those indeed that have hardly ever understood Him,—whose lack of sympathy has been itself one of the bitterest trials, of those that made Him the "Man of Sorrows" that He was. Yet they are his hard-won spoils from the hand of the enemy,—the first-fruits of the spiritual harvest coming in. They are His own, the gift of His Father, the work of His Spirit, the purchase of His blood, by and by to tell out, and, for the ages to come, divine love and power to all His intelligent creation. Nor, spite of their feebleness, can He forget how their hearts awakened by His call, have clung to Him in the scene of His rejection, how they have left their little all to follow Him. Now He is going to leave them in that world whose enmity they must for His sake incur, and in which they would fill up that which was behind of His afflictions for His body's sake, which is the Church (Col. i:24). In human tenderness His heart overflows towards them, while in divine fulness; and this is what we find before us now. It is peculiar to John, and furnishes them for the way, and arms them for the impending conflict."*

Our brief annotations are not sufficient to cover all the blessed teachings of these chapters. What a great assurance is given in the first verse of this chapter! He knew that His hour had come to depart out of this world. He knew because He is the Son of God. Then follows the assurance of His love for His own; even unto the end. His love knows no change. His tender, loving words addressed to His own in these chapters fully manifest that love which passeth knowledge.

The washing of the disciples' feet was a great symbolical action to teach His own the gracious provision made for them during His absence. Some well meaning Christians have applied the words of our Lord, "ye also ought to wash one another's feet," in a literal way, and teach that the Lord meant this to be done literally. The words of our Lord to Peter, "What I do thou knowest not now; but thou

---

* F. W. Grant.

shalt know hereafter" (Verse 7), show that underneath the outward action of the Lord in washing the disciples' feet there is a deeper spiritual meaning. We see Him girded, with a basin of water in His blessed hands, to wash the disciples' feet. The water explains the spiritual meaning. We have seen that the water in the third chapter is the type of the Word of God. It has the same meaning in this chapter. Peter first refused to have his feet washed; then when the Lord had said unto him, "If I wash thee not thou hast no part with Me," he asked Him to wash his hands and his head as well. "Jesus saith to him, He that hath been bathed * needeth not save to wash his feet, but is clean every whit: and ye are clean, but not all." When the Lord spoke of His disciples being bathed and clean every whit, He had reference to the new birth by the water and the Spirit. They were all bathed, born again, except Judas, whom the Lord meant when He said "but not all." Titus iii:5 reads, literally translated: "Not by works of righteousness which we have done, but according to His mercy He saved us by the *bath of regeneration* and renewing of the Holy Spirit." This great work is done once for all and cannot be repeated, just as the natural birth cannot be repeated with the same individual.

The Lord washed the disciples' feet, not their hands. Hands are for work and the feet for walking. His action has a meaning in connection with our walk in the world. We contract defilement as we pass on through this world. And defilement severs communion with the Lord. We need therefore cleansing. All disciples need it. This He has graciously provided, and the washing of the disciples' feet typifies that needed cleansing. He uses His Word to bring this about. This is "the washing of water by the Word." He is the Advocate with the Father to restore us to fellowship. We must come to Him with our failures, our stumbling, imperfect walk, our defilement, and place

* Verse 10 contains two different words for washing; the one is "bathed" and the other "wash." This difference is not made in the Authorized Version.

ourselves into His hands as the disciples placed their soiled feet in His loving hands. His own perfect light will then search our innermost beings and bring to light what has defiled us, so that, after cleansing, we can enjoy His fellowship and have part with Him. This necessitates confession and self-judgment from our side. If this blessed truth is not realized and enjoyed in faith, if we do not come to Him for this service of love, we are at a distance from Him.

And we are also to walk in the same spirit of serving and wash one another's feet. As He lovingly deals with us, so we are to deal with one another. The one that is overtaken in a fault is to be restored by him that is spiritual in the spirit of meekness. "He that would cleanse another's feet must be at his feet to cleanse them." How little of all this in a practical way is known among God's people.

The betrayal by Judas is announced, and he goes into the night. The Lord announces also His imminent departure and gives them the new commandment "love one another." The chapter closes with the prediction of Peter's denial.

CHAPTER XIV

1. Let not Your Heart be Troubled! 1-7.
2. I Am in the Father and the Father in Me. 8-14.
3. The Other Comforter Promised. 15-27.
4. I Go unto the Father. 28-31.

There is no break between these two chapters. The Lord continues His discourse to the eleven disciples. "Let not your heart be troubled!" What precious words of comfort! How many hearts have been soothed by them and how many tears they have dried! And after His loving words He said again: "Let not your heart be troubled, neither let it be afraid." (Verse 27.) He speaks first of all of the Father's house with its many abodes. The Father's house is no longer the temple, but the blessed home where the loving Father dwells and to which the Son of

God was about to return in the form of man, after His death and resurrection. And the Father's house with its many abodes belongs to all who belong to Him; and all who are His, whom He is not ashamed to call brethren (John xx:17; Hebrews ii:11 and Psalm xxii:22) belong to the Father's house. He has gone there to prepare a place. The ark of the covenant of the Lord went before Israel to search out a resting place for them (Numbers xi:33) and so He has gone before as our forerunner. What it all means "to prepare a place for you" we cannot fully know, but we know that His great work has removed every barrier for all who believe on Him, and in God's own time the full redemption of the purchased possession by the power of God will be accomplished. (Eph. i:14.) Then His unfulfilled promise, "I will come again and receive you unto myself, that where I am ye may be also," will be fulfilled. He did not mean the death of His disciples. The death of the believer is not the coming of Himself to the child of God, but when the believer dies he goes to be with Christ. "I will come again" means His coming for those who belong to Him, His Saints. How He will redeem this gracious promise and lead His own into the blessed home, is not revealed here. But He gave it in the form of a special revelation to the Apostle of the Gentiles. (I Thess. iv:13-18.) Thomas speaks first. He misunderstood the words of the Lord and was troubled with unbelief. Yet Thomas loved the Lord and was greatly attached to Him, as we learn from Chapter xi:16. Blessed answer he received. "I am the way";—He is the only way to God and to the Father's house; "the Truth";—the revelation of the Father; and "the Life" as well.

His answer to Philip's question shows that He was grieved. Yet how gentle the rebuke, "Have I been so long time with you, and yet hast thou not known me, Philip? He that hath seen me hath seen the Father." It is another great witness of His oneness with the Father. "I am in the Father and the Father in me." And His own belonging to Him, know the Father in Christ and are His.* "And ye are Christ's and Christ is God's." (I Cor. iii:23.) Verse 12 has been a difficulty to many. What did our Lord mean when He said: "He that believeth on me, the works that I do shall he do also, and greater works than these shall he do; because I go unto my Father"? Christian Scientists and extreme faith-healers claim that He meant His actual works of healing and Christians should do now the same works and even greater works. But how could a believer do a greater work than the raising of Lazarus from the dead? The promise "the works that I do shall he do also" was fulfilled immediately after the day of Pentecost. The sick were healed by Peter's shadow, the lame man was healed, demons were driven out, and the dead were raised. Were these miracles to continue to the end of the dispensation? There is nowhere a statement in Scripture that this should be the case. "If miracles were continually in the church, they would cease to be miracles. We never see them in the Bible except at some great crisis in the church's history." † The "greater works" are spiritual works. The thousands saved in the beginning of the dispensation, the preaching of the Gospel far hence among the Gentiles and the gracious results, are these greater works.

The promise of Prayer in His name follows. This is something new. It is to be addressed to the Father and the Son, and He promises, "If ye shall ask anything in my name I will do it." So far He had spoken of Himself and the Father. God the Father had been revealed in the Son, and now He speaks of the other Person of the Godhead, the Holy Spirit. He is promised to come, not to the world, but to His own as the other Comforter.†† He would come to abide in them, dwell with them and be in them. Verse

* Solemn truth it is: "Whosoever denieth the Son, the same hath not the Father." (I John ii:23.)

† "Thoughts on the Gospel of John."

†† In Greek "Parakletos," one who is alongside to help. The same word as in I John ii:1 "Advocate."

18, "I will come to you," does not mean His second coming as in Verse 3. It is Christ Himself in Spirit. The result of the coming and abiding of the Comforter is a blessed knowledge for the believer. "Ye shall know that I am in my Father, and ye in me, and I in you." Love to Him in the power of the Spirit must be expressed in obedience. Then there is the blessed legacy: "Peace I leave with you, my peace I give unto you." It is not peace with God, but the peace of Himself which He has left us. And that peace will ever be enjoyed if we believe and obey His words.

CHAPTER XV

1. The Vine and the Branch. 1-8.
2. Communion with Him and its Conditions. 9-16.
3. Love One Another! and the Hatred of the World. 17-27.

Israel is called a vine in the Old Testament (Ps. lxxx:8; Isaiah v:1-8; Jerem. ii:21; Hosea x:1) and Christ here in this parable takes the place of Israel and is the true vine. His disciples are the branches. Israel under the law covenant could not bear fruit for God, as the law cannot be the source of fruit-bearing. Fruit unto God can only spring from union with Christ. (See Romans vii:4.) He as the true vine on earth brought fruit unto God. The true believer is as closely united to Him as the branch is to the vine. The branch is in Him and He is in the branch. The life-sap of the vine circulates in the branch. And this life and nature in the believer produces the fruit. Our Lord said: "The Father who abideth in me, He doeth the works." And believers should confess: The Lord Jesus Christ Who abideth in me and I in Him, He produces the fruit. Apart from Him we can do nothing. This vital union with Christ, dependence on Him, the result—fruit unto God, is more fully revealed in the Epistles.

He told His disciples, "now ye are clean (literally: purged) through the word that I have spoken unto you." In Chapter xiii He said, "ye are clean, but not all." Judas was then present, but he had gone out to betray

Him. But what does it mean: "Every branch in me that beareth not fruit He taketh away," and again, "if a man abide not in me, he is cast forth as a branch, and is withered; and men gather them and cast them into the fire, and they are burned"? These words are often taken to teach that a believer's salvation and safety depends upon his fruit-bearing and his faithfulness. These two statements have been much perverted and misapplied as if they taught that a true branch in the vine, one who is really in Christ, may be cut off and be cast away to perish forever. If this were the meaning of these words our Lord would contradict His previous teachings. The branch in the vine which beareth not fruit is not a true believer at all, but one who by profession claims to be a branch in the vine. Note in verse 6 the change from "ye" to "a man." If our Lord had said "if *ye* abide not in me, *ye* shall be cast forth as a branch, etc.," it would mean a true believer. But the change makes it clear that no true disciple is meant, but one who makes a profession without being born again.

"These are awful words. They seem, however, to apply specially to backsliders and apostates, like Judas Iscariot. There must be about a man some *appearance* of professed faith in Christ, before he can come to the state described here. Doubtless there are those who seem to depart from grace, and to go back from union with Christ; but we need not doubt in such cases that the grace was not real, but seeming, and the union was not true, but fictitious. Once more we must remember that we are reading a parable.

After all, the final, miserable ruin and punishment of false professors, is the great lesson which the verse teaches. Abiding in Christ leads to fruitfulness in this life and everlasting happiness in the life to come. Departure from Christ leads to the everlasting fire of hell." *

The secret of true fruit-bearing (the manifestation of the new nature in our life) is abiding in Christ and Christ in us. "He that saith he abideth in Him ought himself also so to walk as He walked." The vine reproduces itself in the branch. And abiding in Christ means to walk in

* J. C. Ryle.

communion with Him and in utter dependence on Himself.

Then He declared: "As the Father hath loved me, so have I loved you; continue ye in my love." Who is able to fathom the depths of these words! As the Father loved Him so He loveth us. Continue in my love means "abide in my love." "If ye keep my commandments, ye shall abide in my love; even as I have kept my Father's commandments and abide in His love." A blessed and equally solemn contrast! When we walk in fellowship with Him, when we are obedient to Him, as He was obedient to His Father in His path down here, then we abide in His love. Obedience to His words proves our love to Him, and walking in obedience we abide in His love "and hereby we know that we know Him, if we keep His commandments." (I John ii:3.) Then He declares, "that my joy might remain in you" and "that your joy might be full." For the knowledge of His joy and the fullness of joy we need to walk in obedience.

Once more He mentions the new commandment (xiii:34) "love one another." The Holy Spirit in the first Epistle of John enlarges upon this. In the world there is no love, but hatred. It hates the true believers, as the world hated Him. The true disciple must expect the same treatment which He receives in this world. "If they have persecuted me, they will also persecute you." Israel is in view in Verse 24. They had seen and hated both Him and the Father.

Once more He announces the coming of the Paraclete, the Comforter. In Chapter xiv our Lord said, "I will pray the Father and He shall send you another Comforter." Here He promises to send Him from the Father. He is to testify of Himself, witnessing to Him as glorified in the presence of the Father. They were to be witnesses of Him.

CHAPTER XVI

1. Persecutions Predicted. 1-6.
2. The Comforter and His Demonstration. 7-15.
3. Sorrow and Joy. 16-22.
4. The Father Himself Loveth You. 23-27.
5. His Final Word before His Prayer. 28-33.

Again He announced coming persecutions. The world is the same to-day as then, and before this age ends these predictions of our Lord will be again fulfilled, during the great tribulation.

The coming of the Comforter is once more announced by Him. He could not come unless the Lord departed. He is to be sent to His own and when He comes He will make a great demonstration to the world. The word "reprove" in Verse 8 is incorrect; the Greek word is difficult to express in its full meaning. Some have translated it by "rebuke," others use the word "convince" or "convict." The word "demonstrate" seems to be the nearest to the original. "And when He is come He will bring demonstration to the world of sin, and of righteousness and of judgment." The presence of the Holy Spirit in believers is the proof to the world that the whole world is guilty of the death of Christ; the whole world is under sin and therefore not on probation but under condemnation. The Holy Spirit is also the demonstration to the world of righteousness. This does not mean that He brings righteousness to the world, or makes the world righteous, as so many erroneously believe. Our Lord adds: "Of righteousness, because I go to my Father and ye see me no more." The Holy One was rejected by the world, cast out as an unrighteous One. But He, Who owned and satisfied God's righteousness in dying as the substitute of sinners, is now exalted to the right hand of God; there He is the witness of righteousness. The presence of the Holy Spirit on earth demonstrates this fact. God raised Him from the dead and gave Him glory; the world sees Him no more as a Saviour personally on earth; but will see Him again as

Judge, when He comes to judge the world in righteousness. Righteousness is fully displayed in the glory, where He is. The hope of righteousness is to be with Him there. (Gal. v:5.) The Holy Spirit also brings demonstration to the world of judgment "because the prince of this world is judged." Sentence of judgment is pronounced against Satan, but not yet executed. He is the god of this age, but he was judged in His Cross. Judgment must come upon the world and its prince. The Holy Spirit now present upon the earth in the believers demonstrates this fact.

Many things He had to say unto His disciples, which they could not bear. The many things He mentioned were made known in due time by the Holy Spirit come down from heaven. Of this He speaks in the verses which follow. Note the seven things spoken of the Spirit of Truth: 1. He will guide you into all truth. 2. He shall not speak of Himself. 3. Whatsoever He shall hear that shall He speak. 4. He will show you things to come. 5. He shall glorify Me. 6. He shall receive of Mine. 7. He shall show it unto you. This is the work He does now among and in the Saints. In all His work His gracious aim is to glorify Christ. When we glorify Christ, exalt Him, obey Him, follow Him and are devoted to Him, the Holy Spirit fills and uses us.

Then He spoke of the little while; the little while when they would see Him not; the little while, when they would see Him again. His final words before His great prayer are full of comfort and assurance. "Verily, verily, I say unto you, Whatsoever ye shall ask the Father in my name, He will give it you."—"For the Father Himself loveth you, because ye have loved me, and have believed that I came out from God." These are words precious to faith. Once more He speaks of His leaving the world to go back to the Father. But before that homegoing takes place they all were to be scattered and leave Him alone. He added: "Yet I am not alone, because the Father is with me." Our Lord was never forsaken by His Father; He was forsaken of God, the Holy God, when He stood in the sinner's place.

The last utterance to His own is the assurance of peace in Him, the tribulation in the world, and the shout of victory: "Be of good cheer: I have overcome the world." And then His prayer.

CHAPTER XVII

1. The Finished Work. 1-5.
2. The Father's Name and the Father's Gift. 6-10.
3. Not of the World but Kept in it. 11-16.
4. Sanctification of Himself for His Own. 17-21.
5. The Glorification. 22-26.

His words were ended to the eleven disciples and next He spoke to the Father, and His disciples listened to all His blessed words. What moments these must have been! His words to the Father told them once more how he loved them, how He cared for them, what He had done and what He would do for them. Whenever we read this great Lord's prayer we can still hear Him pray for His beloved people. What a glimpse it gives of His loving heart! The prayer is His high-priestly prayer. He is in anticipation on the other side of the cross. He knows the work is finished, atonement is made; He is back with the Father and has received the glory. This anticipation is seen in His words, "I have finished the work thou gavest me to do"; "and now I am no more in the world";—"the glory thou hast given me I have given to them." It is impossible to give an exposition of this great chapter. Blessed depths are here which we shall fathom when we are with Him.

All He taught concerning Himself and eternal life, what believers are and have in Him, He mentions in His prayer. All the great redemption truths more fully revealed in the New Testament Epistles may be traced in this high-priestly prayer of our Lord. We mention seven of these great truths as made known by Him in addressing the Father.

1. **Salvation.** He has power to give eternal life to as many as the Father has given Him. "I have glorified thee on the earth: I have finished the work thou gavest me

to do." He glorified the Father in His life and He finished the work He came to do on the Cross. There alone is redemption and salvation.

2. **Manifestation.** "I have manifested thy name unto the men which thou gavest me out of the world." (Verse 6.) The Name of God, He, the Son, has made known to those who believe on Him is His Name as "Father." Such a name and relationship of the believer to God was not known in the Old Testament. The Son of God had to come from heaven's glory and declared the Father. After He gave His life and rose from the dead He spoke of "My Father and your Father." The Spirit of Sonship was given by Whom we cry: "Abba—Father."

3. **Representation.** He is our Priest and Advocate. He appears in the presence of God for us. "I pray for them; I pray not for the world but for them which thou hast given me; for they are thine." (Verse 9.) Like the High Priest He carries only the names of His people upon His shoulders and upon His heart. He prays now for His church, His body, for every member. When the church is complete and the body is united to Himself in glory, He will pray for the world. "Ask of Me," the Father has told Him, "and I will give thee the nations for thine inheritance." (Ps. ii:6.) When He asks this, He will receive the Kingdoms of this world. What comfort it should be to all His people to know He prays for us individually! His love and His power are for us.

4. **Identification.** We are one with Him, and all His Saints are one. The church is His body, an organism and not an organization. He did not pray for a unity in organization, but for a spiritual unity, which exists. "That they also may be one in us" is not an unanswered petition. The Spirit Who has come unites believers to Him and baptizes them into one body. "I in them, and thou in me, that they may be made perfect in one, that the world may know that thou hast sent me, and hast loved them as thou hast loved me"—this looks on towards the blessed consum-

mation, when the Saints will appear with Christ in glory; then the world will know.

5. **Preservation.** He prayed for the keeping of His own. He commits them into His Father's hands. The believers' keeping for eternal life and glory rests not in their own hands but in His hands. Judas is mentioned as the son of perdition; he was never born again.

6. **Sanctification.** (See Verses 17-19.) He is our Sanctification. In Him we are sanctified. We are sanctified by the Truth, by walking in obedience. Believers are constituted Saints in Christ and are called to walk in separation. The separating power is the Word and the Spirit.

7. **Glorification.** "And the glory which thou gavest me I have given them, that they may be one as we are one" —"Father, I will that they also, whom thou hast given me, be with me where I am; that they may behold my glory, which thou hast given me, for thou lovedst me before the foundation of the world." This is His unanswered prayer. Some day it will be answered and all His Saints will be with Him and share His glory.

And oh! the wealth of Grace and Truth in His wonderful words we must pass by! May His own Spirit lead us deeper and fill our hearts with joy unspeakable and full of glory.

III. "I Lay Down My Life, That I Might Take it Again."

Chapters xviii-xxi

CHAPTER XVIII

1. The Arrest in the Garden. 1-11.
2. Before Annas and Caiaphas; Peter's Denial. 12-27.
3. Before Pilate. 28-38.
4. Not this Man, But Barabbas. 39-40.

The hour of His suffering had now come. With His disciples He went across the brook Cedron into the garden. It is the Kidron mentioned frequently in Old Testament history. When David fled from his own son Absalom, he passed weeping over this brook. (2 Sam. xv:23.) See also 2 Chronicles xv:16 and 2 Kings xxiii:12. It is claimed that the way by which our Lord left the city was the way by which the scape-goat was yearly, on the great day of atonement, sent into the wilderness. The garden, though not named here, is Gethsemane. Judas knew the place, and the Lord knowing that Judas would betray Him, went deliberately there to be delivered into the hands of man. Nothing is said at all by John about the agony, the deep soul-exercise, through which our Lord passed in that night; nor is there a word about His sweat, as it were great drops of blood. All these things are recorded in the Synoptic Gospels, in which His perfect humanity is described, they are passed over in the Gospel of His Deity. But John describes a scene which the other Gospels omit. He manifests His power. When the band of men said that they sought Jesus of Nazareth, He said unto them, "I am He." Then the whole company went backward and fell to the ground. What a scene that must have been! Several hundred men with their lanterns, torches and weapons all prostrate on the ground before the One Man. They stood in the presence of Jehovah and His power and majesty was present so that the one word was sufficient to prostrate them all. It was a striking evidence that neither the treachery of Judas, nor the wicked hatred of the Jews, nor the power of Rome, could touch our Lord. But the hour had now arrived when He was ready to give Himself up. Augustine made the following comment: "What shall He do when He comes to judge, Who did this when He was about to be judged? What shall be His might when He comes to reign, Who had this might when He was about to die?" Then after His second answer He said, "If therefore ye seek me, let these go their way." Willingly He allows Himself bound, on the condition that His own must be free. It is a blessed illustration of the Gospel. The Good Shepherd gives His life for the sheep. Substitution is fully revealed in this gracious statement. He gives Himself up that His people might be free.

Then Simon Peter drew the sword and cut off the right ear of Malchus. Peter had slept; had he been watching and praying it would not have occurred. And how beautiful the words of the Lord: "The cup which my Father hath given me, shall I not drink it?" Perfect willingness and readiness to drink the bitter cup were thus expressed in the presence of His disciples and His enemies.

Then follows the account of Peter's denial, the questioning before Annas, which is only reported by John, and finally He was taken into the judgment hall before Pilate. The miserable character of the Roman Governor is brought fully to light in this Gospel. He was destitute of all moral courage; he acted against better knowledge; he knew the Lord was innocent, yet he dared not to acquit Him for fear of displeasing the Jews. Verse 32 refers to the Lord's death by crucifixion, from the hands of the Gentiles. Note the four questions of Pilate. "Art Thou the King of the Jews?"—"What hast Thou done?"—"Art Thou a King then?"—"What is truth?" The Roman historian Suetonius states that many rumors were then prevalent that a King was about to rise among the Jews who would have dominion over the whole world. No doubt Pilate knew of these rumors and therefore asked the Lord about His Kingship. The answer of our Lord, "My Kingdom is not of this world," has often been misconstrued to mean that the Lord never will have a Kingdom in this world in the sense of a literal Kingdom. Our post-millennial friends use it against a literal interpretation of the prophecies relating to the coming of an earthly Kingdom of Christ. What our Lord meant by saying "My Kingdom is not of this world" is, that His Kingdom has not its origin or nature from the world. He will receive the Kingdom promised unto Him from the Father's hands. (Daniel vii:14.)

CHAPTER XIX

1. Behold the Man! 1-7.
2. The Last Question of Pilate and Christ's Last Word. 8-11.
3. Delivered up and Crucified. 12-18.
4. The Title upon the Cross. 19-22.
5. The Parted Garments. 23-24.
6. Behold Thy Son! Behold Thy Mother! 25-27.
7. It is Finished! 28-30.
8. His Legs not Broken. 31-33.
9. The Testimony of the Scriptures. 34-47.
10. The Burial in the Garden. 38-42.

The cruel scourging, such as cruel Rome had invented, then took place. It often was so severe that prisoners died under the awful blows. What pen can ever describe the suffering and the shame He endured! Perhaps Pilate thought this awful scourging would satisfy the Jews, so that the Lord would be released. Then the mockery followed. The crown of thorns, the emblem of the curse of sin, was put upon His holy brow. The sin-bearer wore that crown for us, that we might wear a crown of glory. When He comes again He comes with many crowns. (Rev. xix:12.) They put the robe of purple, the imperial color, upon Him;

ridiculed and smote Him. Then Pilate led Him forth and said: "Behold the Man." Was it pity or contempt? Most likely both. But oh! the sight! To see Him, Who is the Life and the Light, the Holy One, the Creator, treated thus by the creature of the dust! Satan's power energized the chief priests and officers, and the answer they give as they behold "the Man of Sorrows" is "Crucify Him!" "He made Himself the Son of God" was their wicked accusation. He is the Son of God and because He had come in marvellous love to this poor lost world, He was condemned to die.

The last word the Lord Jesus spoke to Pilate is found in verse 11. The authority given from above is from God, Who spared not His own Son; but the Jews, who delivered Him up to Pilate, have the greater sin. Once more we hear Pilate's voice, "Behold your King!" They answer: "Away with Him! Crucify Him!" And then again: "Shall I crucify your King?" The answer of complete apostacy follows: "We have no King but Cæsar." Pilate is lost; he delivered Him to be crucified. We see the Lord bearing His cross to the place of the skull, Golgotha. Who can describe His agony and His sufferings as He was lifted up! Two others were crucified with Him. "He was numbered with transgressors." (Isaiah liii:12.)

Above His cross was the title written by Pilate himself. It was written in Hebrew, Latin and Greek. There is no discrepancy between the different Gospels, because they give the inscriptions in different words. Pilate worded them differently in the three languages. Matthew * and John report the Hebrew title; Mark gives the Latin and Luke the Greek inscription.

The coat (robe) without seam, woven from the top throughout, is only mentioned by John. The German expositor Bengel calls attention to the fact that our Lord never "rend" His garments in sorrow like Job, Jacob, Joshua, Caleb, Jephthah, Hezekiah, Mordecai, Ezra, Paul

* Matthew was guided to leave out "of Nazareth." This is in full accord with the purpose of his Gospel.

and Barnabas. The seamless robe is typical of His perfect righteousness, which now was stripped from Him by man's hand and thus He received the place as the evildoer. Then the prophecy of Psalm xxii:18 was literally fulfilled. Could there be anything else but a *literal* fulfillment of Prophecy?

"The importance of interpreting prophecy literally, and not figuratively, is strongly shown in this verse. The system of interpretation which unhappily prevails among many Christians—I mean the system of spiritualizing away all the plain statements of the prophets, and accommodating them to the Church of Christ—can never be reconciled with such a verse as this. The plain, literal meaning of words should evidently be the meaning placed on all the statements of Old Testament prophecy. This remark of course does not apply to symbolical prophecies, such as those of the seals, trumpets, and vials in Revelation." *

And then the loving tenderness He manifested towards His mother.†

John has nothing to say of the darkness which enshrouded the Cross. Nor do we find here the cry of the forsaken One: "My God, my God, why hast thou forsaken me?" The Father did not forsake the Son; this was His statement in Chapter xvi:32. "After this, Jesus knowing that all things were now accomplished, that the Scriptures might be fulfilled, saith, I thirst." It is not so much the awful thirst connected with crucifixion which is viewed here, as it is His perfect obedience to do the Father's will and that the Scriptures might be fulfilled. "He bowed His head

† Here, with one exception in the first chapter of Acts, we part with Mary; she is not mentioned in the after-books. In all the doctrine of the epistles she has no place. Blessed among women as she is surely by her connection with the human nature of our Lord, the entire silence of Scripture as to her in that fulness of Christian truth which it was the office of the Spirit of truth to communicate is the decisive overthrow of the whole Babel-structure of Mariolatry which Romanism has built up upon a mere sand-foundation. She remains for us in the word of God, a simple woman rejoicing in God her Saviour,—a stone in the temple to His praise, and with no temple of her own. To use the grace of the Redeemer in taking flesh among us by her means to exalt the mother to the dishonor of Christ her Lord is truly a refined wickedness worthy of the arch-deceiver of mankind.—*Numerical Bible.*

and gave up the spirit." In Luke's Gospel we read that He said: "Father, into thy hands I commend my spirit" (xxiii:46); John says nothing of Him commending His spirit, for as the Son of God He did not need to commend Himself to the Father. The final word preceding the giving up of His spirit is the majestic "It is finished." In the Greek it is but one word, "tetelestai." Never before and never after was ever spoken one word which contains and means so much. It is the shout of the mighty Victor. And who can measure the depths of this one word!

Psalm xxxiv:20 was fulfilled; "A bone of Him shall not be broken." Scripture had to be fulfilled. The spear, which pierced His blessed side, fully evidences that He had died. The blood and water have a most precious meaning. That it was a supernatural thing we do not doubt. The blood stands for the atonement, which had been made; the water for cleansing. The Jews have a strange tradition that from the rock which was smitten by Moses in the wilderness there flowed, when first smitten, blood and water.* John alone mentions this blessed fact. "It is a beautiful testimony of divine grace, answering the last insult man could heap upon Him. They drove Him outside the camp, put Him to death on the Cross, and then, to make His death doubly sure, the soldier pierced His side. Salvation was God's answer to man's insult, for the blood and water were the signs of it." John speaks of this never to be forgotten occurrence in his first Epistle (v:6). There he mentions water first. It denotes purifying which man needs, and that has come with all its attending blessings by His precious blood. But notice John writes: "And again another scripture saith, They shall look on Him whom they pierced." He does not say, another Scripture was fulfilled. Zech. xii:10 was not fulfilled when He died, but will be fulfilled when He comes again and the believing remnant of Israel mourns for Him.

Nicodemus is mentioned for the third and last time in the Gospel. He came to Jesus by night and heard the Gos-

---

* In *Shemoth Rabba.*

pel message from His lips. Later he ventured a weak and timid defence (vii:48-53); here he comes out boldly honouring the body of Jesus. Surely he believed and therefore confessed the Lord.

CHAPTER XX

1. The Empty Sepulchre. 1-10.
2. The Risen One and Mary of Magdala. 11-18.
3. The Gathered Company and He in the Midst. 19-23.
4. The Second Time. 24-29.
5. The Purpose of John's Record. 30-31.

"I lay down my life that I might take it up again." The sufferings were accomplished. The Good Shepherd laid down His life for the sheep and now we learn how He arose from the dead. Chapter ii:19 was fulfilled. "Destroy this temple and in three days I will raise it up." The stone is rolled away; the sepulchre is empty. Mary of Magdala carried the good news to Peter and John. Peter and John ran together to the sepulchre, and John outran Peter. In the sepulchre all is in order. If a thief had stolen the body he would have acted in fear and haste. A thief would not have gone about in such an orderly way. The linen clothes were lying in the proper place; the napkin (soudarion—sweatcloth) was folded inwards* in a place by itself. He had detached Himself in a miraculous way without disturbing them at all. It is an evidence of His resurrection in His own power as Son of God.

And how beautiful is the incident when Mary stood weeping and looking into the sepulchre! She beheld two angels there, yet she was not frightened when she beheld these mysterious Beings. Her heart was so occupied with her Lord that she did not even inquire of the angels. But they addressed her: "Woman, why weepest thou?" Then He came Himself. Her tears of ignorance and unbelief held her eyes that she did not recognize Him till He, Who in resurrection is the great Shepherd of the sheep, called her

* This is the meaning of "entetuligmenon."

by name. What sound that one word "Mary" must have had in her ears and heart! She would fall at His feet and hold Him, as the other women held Him by the feet and worshipped Him. (Matt. xxviii:9.) But He told her: "Touch me not; for I am not yet ascended to my Father; but go to my brethren and say unto them, I ascend unto my Father and your Father; and to my God and your God." Matthew reports how they touched Him and held Him by the feet. He is presented in that Gospel as Israel's King. Not a word is said in the first Gospel of His ascension. He is presented in Matthew as if He were to remain on earth, in an earthly relationship with His people. This is why He permitted the holding of His feet. It is symbolical of how the remnant of Israel will enjoy His presence on earth as King in the day of His Return. But John's Gospel reveals a new relationship. He is to ascend into heaven to His Father. She must not hold Him as to keep Him here.* As true believers we are linked with the glorified Lord. This higher relationship He makes known and she becomes the bearer of the great message. The relationship centers in the word "brethren." Risen from the dead He calls His own "brethren" and speaks of "My Father and your Father, my God and your God." He is not ashamed to call us brethren, because He that sanctifieth and they that are sanctified are all of one. (Ps. xxii:21-22; Hebrews ii:11-12.) Thus He, the Son of God, Who laid down His life and took it again, has brought us to God, His God and His Father. The Grain of Wheat has brought forth its blessed and gracious fruit in resurrection.

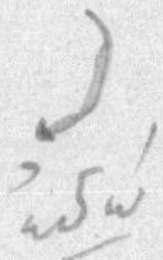

The evening scene of that wonderful day, when He stood in their midst, is very suggestive. In a measure the assembled disciples correspond to the two who, in the first chapter, on the first day abode with Him. Though John does not mention the church, here is a beautiful picture of what the church is. They are shut in and Judaism is shut out. He is in the midst. "Where two or three are gath-

* The word "touch" really means: to fasten oneself to, to hang on, to lay hold of.

ered together unto my name, there am I in the midst." Here it is fulfilled for the first time. There is the message of Peace; the sending forth; the Holy Spirit, Who comes from Him, Who as the last Adam is the quickening Spirit. He communicates spiritual life, which is divine life. And the authority of the church in discipline on earth, representing Himself, is made known by Him in verse 23. This authority is not conferred upon a priestly class, a doctrine which has produced the most obnoxious corruption of Christianity, but upon believers, who constitute a church.

Thomas corresponds to Nathanael at the close of the first chapter. Both are unbelieving. Both see first and then believe. Both acknowledge Him as God. Thomas, like Nathanael, is the type of the unbelieving Jewish remnant. The Lord comes the second time and then the remnant of His earthly people will fall at His feet and say, "My Lord and my God."

CHAPTER XXI

1. At the Sea of Tiberias. The Third Manifestation. 1-14.
2. Peter's Restoration and Ministry; the manner of His Death Predicted. 15-19.
3. Tarry Till I Come! 20-23.
4. Conclusion. 24-25.

This chapter has often been looked upon as an appendix to the Gospel of John. It is not. Quite true, John states in the last two verses of the preceding chapter the purpose of this Gospel, but that does not mean that the twenty-first chapter has no connection with the Gospel itself. Verse 14 shows that it belongs to the Gospel proper.

The third time that He showed Himself after His resurrection:—The first time on the first day of the week (Chapter xx:19); this is typical of the present age, when He is in the midst of His people. The second time, when Thomas was present; typical of His second coming and manifestation to Israel. The third time on the Lake of Tiberias; typical of the future blessings through Israel, and corresponding to the third day in Chapter ii, when there was a marriage in Cana of Galilee. The miraculous draught of fishes took place by His power, but the net did not go to pieces. It was different before His death and resurrection; then the net broke. The scene on the Lake of Tiberias foreshadows the ingathering of the nations into His Kingdom when He returns. The number of the fish caught is given, one hundred and fifty-three. The number of the nations of the world known at that time was exactly 153. How significant this is! Thus all the nations of the world will be gathered into His Kingdom.

But there are blessed spiritual lessons here. He is seen as Lord over His own. He can direct our service as He directed the disciples in casting the net at the right side of the ship. He provides for the need of His servants, as He did then in preparing a breakfast for them. (Verse 9.) He restores His servants who fail, as He so graciously restored Peter, and gives a higher and a better service. He also appoints the time and the manner of the servant's departure out of this life; He told Peter when and how he was to die. He said of John, "If I will that he tarry till I come, what is that to thee?" The Lord did not say that he should not die. John lived the longest of the disciples, and on the Isle of Patmos he beheld the events of the future and heard the voice, "Come up hither" and immediately he was in the Spirit and beheld heavenly things. The words of our Lord find likewise an application in connection with John's writings.

"It is simple enough to say that John lives on in his writings. But then it might be urged, that is only what all the inspired writers will; still it cannot but come to mind that, in fact, John's writings not only predict circumstantially the Lord's return, but stretch over all the intervening time till then. While he does not take us up into heaven, as Paul does, and show us our place in the glorified Man up there, yet all the more he seems to abide with the people of God on earth until Christ's return, as a human presence watching and caring for them. John may be thus truly said to be waiting with those on earth for his absent Lord in a way in which we could not speak of any other inspired writer.''*

The last word John reports in His Gospel, coming from the lips of our Lord, is ''Follow thou me.'' And thus He speaks to all of His people. Wonderful Gospel it is, this Gospel of the Son of God and the Eternal Life! How full and rich each portion of it! And oh! the Grace which has sought us, saved us, made us one with Him, keeps us and which will soon bring us home to the Father's house with its many mansions. May we follow Him in loving obedience, till He comes.

---

* F. W. Grant.

THE BOOK OF THE ACTS OF THE APOSTLES

CONTENTS

The Acts of the Apostles.

Introduction.

The book known by the name "The Acts of the Apostles"* follows the four Gospel records. This is its proper place. The books of the New Testament have been correctly divided into five sections, corresponding to the first five books, with which the Bible begins, that is the Pentateuch. The four Gospels are the *Genesis* of the New Testament. Here we have the great beginning, the foundation upon which the subsequently revealed Christian doctrines rest. The Book of Acts is the *Exodus;* God leads out from bondage a heavenly people and sets them free. It is the great historical book of the New Testament given by inspiration, the beginning of the church on earth. The Pauline Epistles are the *Leviticus* portion. Holiness unto the Lord, the believer's separation and standing in Christ; what the believer has and is in Christ, by whose blood redemption has been purchased, are the core truths of these Epistles. The Epistles of Peter, James, John and Jude, known by the name of the Catholic Epistles, are for the wilderness journey of God's people, telling us of trials and suffering; these correspond to the Book of *Numbers.* The Book of Revelation in which God's ways are rehearsed, and, so to speak, a review is given of the entire prophetic Word concerning the Jews, the Gentiles and the Church of God has therefore the same character as *Deuteronomy.*

By Whom was this Book Written

There is no doubt that the writer of the third Gospel record is the one whom the Holy Spirit selected to write this account of the establishment of the Church on earth and the events connected with it. This becomes clear if we read the beginning of that Gospel and compare it with the beginning of Acts. The writer in the third Gospel says: "It seemed good to me also, having had perfect understanding of all things from the first, to write unto thee in order, most excellent *Theophilus,* that thou mightest know the certainty of those things, wherein thou hast been instructed" (Luke i:3–4). The Acts of the Apostles begin: "The *former* treatise have I made, O *Theophilus,* of all that Jesus began both to do and teach." The former treatise known to Theophilus is the third Gospel, called the Gospel of Luke. The writer of that Gospel must therefore be the penman of the Book of Acts. Though we do not find Luke's name mentioned in the Gos-

*The oldest manuscript, the *Sinaiticus,* dating from the 4th century, gives the title simply as "The Acts," which is, no doubt, the better name for the book.

pel, nor in the second Book, he was entrusted to write by inspiration, there is no doubt that he wrote them both. We find his name mentioned a number of times in the Epistles, and these references give us the only reliable information we have. In Colossians iv:14 we read of him as "the beloved physician." In the Epistle of Philemon he is called a fellow laborer of the Apostle Paul, and from the last Epistle the great Apostle wrote, the second Epistle to Timothy, we learn that Luke was in Rome with Paul and was faithful to him, while others had forsaken the prisoner of the Lord. From Colossians iv we also may gather that he was not a Jew, but a Gentile, for with the eleventh verse Paul had mentioned those of the circumcision. Epaphras was one of the Colossians, a Gentile, and then follow the names of Luke and Demas, both of them undoubtedly Gentiles. The reason that the Holy Spirit selected a Gentile to write the Gospel which pictures our Lord as the Man and the Savior, and the Book of Acts, is as obvious as it is interesting. Israel had rejected God's gift, and the glad news of salvation was now to go to the Gentiles. The Gospel of Luke addressed by a Gentile to a Gentile (Theophilus) is the Gospel for the Gentiles, and Luke the Gentile was chosen to give the history of the Gospel going forth from Jerusalem to the Gentiles.

Internal Evidences.

There are numerous internal evidences which show likewise that the writer of the third Gospel is the instrument through whom the Book of Acts was given. For instance, there are about fifty peculiar phrases and words in both books which are rarely found elsewhere; they prove the same author.

Then we learn from the Book of Acts that Luke was an eyewitness of some of the events recorded by him in that book. He joined the Apostle during his second missionary journey to Troas (chapt. xiv:10). This evidence is found in the little word "*we*." The writer was now in company of the Apostle, whose fellow laborer he was. He went with Paul to Macedonia and remained some time in Philippi. He was Paul's fellow traveler to Asia and Jerusalem (ch. xxi:17). He likewise was with him in his imprisonment in Caesarea, and then on to Rome. There is no doubt that Luke had completely written and sent forth the Book of the Acts of the Apostles at the end of the two years mentioned in Acts xxviii:30, though the critics claim a much later period.

The Contents and Scope of the Book.

The first verse gives us an important hint. The former treatise, the Gospel of Luke, contains that Jesus *began* to do and teach. The Book of Acts contains therefore the continuation of the Lord's actions, no longer on earth, but from the Glory. The actions of the risen and glorified Christ can easily be traced through the entire Book. We give a few illustrations. In the first Chapter He acts in the selection of the twelfth Apostle, who was to take the place of Judas. In the second chapter He himself poured forth the Holy Spirit, for Peter made the declaration "therefore, being by the right hand of God exalted, and having received of the Father the promise of the Holy Spirit, *He* has poured out this which ye behold and hear." And in the close of the second chapter we behold another action of the risen Lord, "the Lord added to the assembly daily those that were to be saved." In the third chapter He manifested His power in the healing of the lame man. Throughout this Book we behold Him acting from the Glory, guiding, directing, comforting and encouraging His servants. These beautiful and manifold evidences of Himself being with His own and manifesting His power in their behalf can easily be traced in the different chapters.

Then on the very threshold of the Book we have the historical account of the coming of that other Comforter, whom the Lord had promised, the Holy Spirit. On the day of Pentecost the third Person of the Trinity, the Holy Spirit, came. His coming marks the birthday of the Church. After that event we see Him present with His people as well as in them. In connection with the Lord's servants in filling them, guiding them, fitting them, sustaining them in trials and persecutions, in the affairs of the church, we behold the actions of the Holy Spirit on earth. He is the great administrator in the church. Over fifty times we find Him mentioned, so that some have called this Book, "the Acts of the Holy Spirit." There are no doctrines about the Holy Spirit and His work in the Book of Acts. But we find the practical illustrations of the doctrines of the Holy Spirit found elsewhere in the New Testament.

In the third place another supernatural Being is seen acting in this Book. It is the enemy, Satan, the hinderer and the accuser of the brethren. We behold him coming upon the scene and acting through his different instruments, either as the roaring lion, or as the cunning deceiver with his wiles. Wherever he can, he attempts to hinder the progress of the Gospel. This is a most important aspect of this Book, and indeed very instructive. Aside from the human instruments prominent in this Book of Acts, we behold three supernatural Beings acting. The risen and glorified Christ, the Holy Spirit, and Satan.

Another hint about the contents of this Book and its scope we find at the close of the Gospel of Luke. There the risen Christ said "that repentance and remission of sins should be preached in His Name to all the nations beginning at Jerusalem." In the first chapter of Acts the Spirit of God reports the commission of the Lord, about to ascend, in full. "Ye shall be my witnesses both in Jerusalem and in all Judea and Samaria, and to the end of the earth." The Book of Acts shows us how this mission, beginning in Jerusalem, was carried out. The witness begins in the City where our Lord was crucified. Once more an offer was made to the nation Israel. Then we behold the Gospel going forth from Jerusalem and all Judea to Samaria, and after that to the Gentiles, and through the Apostle Paul it is heralded in the different countries of the Roman empire. The parable of our Lord in Matthew xxii:1–10 gives us prophetically the history of these events. First the guests were called to the wedding and they would not come. This was the invitation given by the Lord to His earthly people when He moved among them. They received Him not. Then came a renewed offer with the assurance that all things are ready. This is exactly what we find in the beginning in the Book of the Acts. Once more to Jerusalem and to the Jewish nation is offered the kingdom, and signs and miracles take place to show that Jesus is the Christ risen from the dead. In the above parable our Lord predicted what the people would do with the servants, who bring the second offer. They would ignore the message and treat the servants spitefully and kill them. This we find fulfilled in the persecution which broke out in Jerusalem, when Apostles were imprisoned and others were killed. The Lord also predicted in His parable the fate of the wicked City. It was to be burned. Thus it happened to Jerusalem. And after the second offer had been rejected the servants were to go to the highways to invite the guests. And this shows that the invitation was to go out to the Gentiles.

Jerusalem is in the foreground in this Book, for the beginning was to be in Jerusalem "to the Jew first." The end of the Book takes us to Rome, and we see the great Apostle a prisoner there, a most significent, prophetic circumstance.

The Division of the Book of Acts.

"But ye shall receive power after that the Holy Spirit is come upon you, and ye shall be my witnesses both in Jerusalem and in all Judea and in Samaria and unto the uttermost part of the earth" (Acts i:8). This verse in the beginning of the book is the key to the historical account it contains. The Holy Spirit came on the day of Pentecost and the witness to Christ began. We make a threefold division.

I. **The Witness to Jerusalem. The Advent of the Spirit and the Formation of the Church. The Offer to Israel and its Rejection.** Chapter i–vii.

II. **The Witness to Samaria. Saul's Conversion and Peter's Witness in Cesarea.** Chapter viii:xii.

III. **The Witness to the Gentiles. The Apostle to the Gentiles. His Ministry and Captivity.** Chapter xiii–xxviii.

While undoubtedly all witnessed, the book of Acts reports mostly the acts of Peter and Paul. The Apostle Peter is in the foreground in the first part of the book. After the twelfth chapter he is mentioned but once more. Then Paul comes upon the scene with His great testimony concerning "The Gospel of Christ, the power of God unto salvation to every one that believeth." Jerusalem is prominent in the start. Antioch, the Gentile center of Christian activity, follows, and Rome is seen at the close of the book. The witness of which the risen Lord spoke was therefore given to Jerusalem, in all Judea, in Samaria. Then to the uttermost part of the earth. Africa received a witness in the conversion of the Ethiopian Eunuch. Then followed the witness to Asia and Europe. The book of Acts ends, so to speak, in an unfinished way.

Analysis and Annotations.

Part I. The Witness to Jerusalem. The Advent of the Spirit and the Formation of the Church. The Offer to Israel and its Rejection.

Chapters I–VII.

CHAPTER I.

1. The Introduction (verses 1–3).
2. The final words of the risen Lord (verses 4–8).
3. The ascension (verses 9–11).
4. The waiting company (verses 12–14).
5. Matthias chosen in the place of Judas (verses 15–26).

The introductory words prove that Luke is the writer. In the former treatise, Luke had addressed to Theophilus (the Gospel of Luke) the beginning of the teaching, and acts of our Lord were reported. The Book of Acts reveals the same wonderful person witnessed to by the Holy Spirit. Eight things are mentioned concerning our Lord in the beginning of this book. 1. His earthly life of doing and teaching. 2. He gave them commandment. 3. He had suffered. 4. He had showed Himself after His passion by many infallible proofs. 5. He was seen by them for forty days. 6. He spoke of the things which concern the Kingdom of God. 7. He was taken up. 8. He will come again. Once more He gave to them the promise of the coming of the Holy Spirit. In verse 5 we read "ye shall be baptized with the Holy Spirit not many days hence." John the Baptist had spoken also of a baptism with fire. The Lord omits the word fire, because the baptism with fire is a judgment act linked with His second coming (See Matthew iii:12). The question they asked of Him concerning the restoration of the Kingdom to Israel was perfectly in order. This is the Hope of Israel; the Hope of the church is not an earthly kingdom, but a heavenly glory; not to be subjects in the kingdom on earth, but to reign and rule with the King.

The answer they received assured them that the kingdom was to be restored to Israel; the times and seasons for that, however, rested with the Father.

Then they saw Him ascending. What a sight it must have been! Their Lord was "received into Glory." Gradually in majestic silence He must have been lifted out of their midst. Lovingly His eyes must have rested upon them, while their eyes saw only Him. Then a cloud received Him out of their sight. "And then a cloud took Him in* out of their sight." The cloud was not a common cloud of vapor, but the glory-cloud. It was the cloud of glory which had filled Solomon's temple, which so often in Israel's past history had appeared as an outward sign of Jehovah's presence. Then angels announced His coming in like manner. And thus He will come, even back to the Mount of Olives (Zech. xiv:4).

However, we must beware of confounding this event given here with that blessed Hope, which is the Hope of the church. The Coming of the Lord here is His visible Coming as described in the prophetic books of the Old Testament; it is His coming to establish His rule upon the earth. It is the event spoken of in Daniel vii:14 and Rev. i:7. When He comes in like manner as He went up, His Saints come with Him (Col. iii:4; 1 Thess. iii:13). The Hope of the church is to meet Him in the air, and not to see Him coming in the clouds of heaven. The coming here "in like manner" is His Coming for Israel and the nations. The Coming of the Lord for His Church, before His visible and glorious Manifestation, is revealed in 1 Thess. iv:16–18. It is well to keep these important truths in mind. Confusion between these is disastrous. He left them to enter into the Holy of Holies, to exercise the priesthood which Aaron exercised on the day of atonement, though our Lord is a priest after the order of Melchisedec. And when this promise of the two men in white garments is fulfilled, He will come forth to be a priest upon His throne.

---

*This is the literal rendering.

Then we see them as a waiting company. They are not the church. Their waiting for the Coming of the Holy Spirit ended ten days after, when the Holy Spirit came. Since then He is here. To wait for another outpouring of the Holy Spirit, as so often done by well meaning people, is unscriptural. Among the waiting ones were "Mary the mother of Jesus and His brethren." The one chosen by God's grace to be the mother of our Lord; Mary, who had conceived by the Holy Spirit, is waiting with the other disciples. This proves that she has no place of superiority among God's people. When the Holy Spirit came she too was baptized by the Spirit into the one body of which, through the Grace of God, she is a member like any other believer in our Lord. After this she is not mentioned again in the Word of God. Mary, the mother of Jesus, has absolutely no relation with the redemption work of the Son of God. His brethren, according to John vii:5, were unbelieving. Since then they had also believed on Him.

The action of Peter in proposing to place another in Juda's place was not a mistake as some claim. Peter acted upon the Scriptures and was guided by the Lord. Some hold that Paul was meant to be the twelfth Apostle. This is incorrect. Paul's apostleship was of an entirely different nature than that of the twelve. Not till Israel's complete failure had been demonstrated in the stoning of Stephen was he called, and then not of men, but by revelation of Jesus Christ. There is positive proof that the Holy Spirit sanctioned this action of the disciples. See 1 Cor. xv:5-8. Furthermore, twelve apostles were needed as a body of witnesses to the entire nation. How strange it would have been if Peter and the ten, eleven men in all, instead of twelve, had stood up on the day of Pentecost to witness to Christ in the presence of the assembled multitude.

CHAPTER II.

1. The Outpouring of the Holy Spirit (verses 1–4).
2. The Immediate Effect of His Presence (verses 5–13).
3. Peter's Address (verses 14–36).
4. The Result of the Witness (verses 37–41).
5. The Gathered Company in Fellowship (verses 42–47).

This is an important chapter. The Promise of the Father was fulfilled, the Holy Spirit, the third person of the Trinity came down to earth, to be the other Comforter. He came on that blessed day.

Two things are at once apparent. He came upon the assembled believers individually, and also did a work in a corporate way. Each believer on that day was filled with the Holy Spirit. He came as the indweller to each. But He also was present as the mighty rushing wind which filled all the house. He did not only come upon each, but all were baptized with the Holy Spirit, and united into a body. In 1 Corinthians xii:13 the more complete revelation is given concerning this fact. "For by one Spirit are we all baptized into one body, whether we be Jews or Gentiles, whether we be bond or free, and have been all made to drink into one Spirit." The One Spirit is the Holy Spirit as He came on the day of Pentecost, the One Body is the church. All believers were on that day united by the Spirit into the one body, and since then, whenever and wherever a sinner believes in the finished work of Christ, he shares in that baptism and is joined by the same Spirit to that one body. A believer may be in dense ignorance about all this, as indeed a great many are; but this does not alter the gracious fact of what God has done. The believing company was then formed on the day of Pentecost into one body. *It was the birthday of the church.*

There is an interesting correspondency between the second chapter of Luke and the second chapter of Acts which we cannot pass by. In the first chapter of Luke we have the announcement of the birth of the Saviour. In the second chapter of the Gospel of Luke we read of the accomplishment of that promise given to the Virgin. And so the second chapter of Acts contains the fulfillment of a similar promise. The Holy Spirit came and the church, the mystical body of Christ, began.

But the truth concerning the church was not revealed on the day of Pentecost. The twelve apostles were ignorant of what had taken place, and that the church formed would be composed of believing Gentiles as well as believing Jews; nor did they know anything of the different relationships of the church. Through the Apostle Paul the full truth concerning the church was made known.

The Coming of the Holy Spirit was accompanied with visible signs. A new dispensation was inaugurated with outward signs, just as the giving of the law for that dispensation was accompanied with similar signs. (Hebrews xii:18–19.) The rushing mighty wind filled the house, "and there appeared unto them cloven tongues like as of fire and it sat upon each of them." The filling of the house indicated the fact that His abode would be the house; the church and the parted tongues upon each head testified to the fact that each had received Him. The Person, not a power or influence given by measure, had filled each believer. He came as the gift of God.

Then they spoke in different languages. The speaking in other languages was a miracle produced by the Holy Spirit, who had come upon them in mighty power. These Galileans spoke in different tongues, sixteen at least, if not more. "By a sudden and powerful inspiration of the Holy Spirit, these disciples uttered, not of their own minds, but as mouthpieces of the Holy Spirit, the praises of God in various languages hitherto, and possibly at the time itself, unknown to them."*

The significance of this miracle speaking in other tongues is not hard to discover. It was the oral manifestation of the parted tongues of fire, which had come upon each. Besides this it proclaimed the great fact that the Holy Spirit had come to make known the blessed Gospel to all nations

*Dean Alford in Greek Testament.

under heaven, and though no Gentiles were present when this took place, the languages of the Gentiles were heard, and that from Jewish lips, showing that the Gospel should go forth unto the uttermost part of the earth. But did they utter all an orderly discourse, preaching the truth concerning Christ, or was their speech of an ecstatic nature, in the form of praising God? We believe the latter was the case. We look in vain through this book for the evidences that these believers continued speaking these different languages.

Now, while it is true that there was such a gift as speaking in an unknown tongue in the apostolic age, and no Christian believer would doubt the power of God to impart to a person the gift to preach the Gospel in a foreign tongue, we do not believe that this gift of speaking in an unknown tongue was to abide in the church. Repeatedly claims were made in years gone by that it had been restored (for instance during the Irvingite delusion in England), but in every case it was found to be spurious or emanating from the enemy. The present day "apostolic or pentecostal movement" with its high pretensions and false doctrines, lacking true scriptural knowledge and wisdom, creating new schisms in the body, with its women leaders and teachers, has all the marks of the same great counterfeiter upon it.*

Then Peter stood up with the eleven and gave his great testimony. What boldness he manifested! What a change from the Peter before Pentecost! It was the result of the Holy Spirit he had received. His address dealt with the great historical facts of the Gospel, bearing witness to the resurrection and exaltation of the Lord Jesus. In its scope and pointedness it is a remarkable production. It has three parts. 1. He reputes the charge of drunkenness and quotes from Joel, avoiding, however, the statement that

*For a closer examination of the speaking in tongues see our larger work on Acts.

Joel's prophecy was fulfilled* (verses 14–22). 2. Next he gives a brief testimony of the life and the resurrection of the Lord Jesus. He quotes from the sixteenth Psalm (verses 23–28). 3. The last part of his address shows that the Holy Spirit had come as the result of the resurrection and exaltation of the Lord Jesus Christ. The briefest but deepest Messianic Psalm is quoted in this section (Psalm cx). The address as reported closes with the significant word: "Let the whole house of Israel, therefore, assuredly know that God has made Him, this Jesus whom you have crucified, both Lord and Christ" (verses 29–36). Notice how the Holy Spirit uses through Peter the Word of God. The Holy Spirit testifies in and through the written Word. The aim of Peter's address was to prove to the house of Israel that the crucified One is raised from the dead and that God made Him Lord and Christ, witnessed to by the presence of the Holy Spirit. The Person of Chri t and His work is still the great theme. Whenever He is preached the power of God will accompany the message.

Wonderful results followed. The Word had been preached and the power of the Holy Spirit brought the great truths to the hearts and consciences of the hearers. Their guilt in having crucified Jesus had been fully demonstrated, and now they asked, "Now, brethren, what shall we do?" Peter gives the needed answer. Repentance and baptism are the conditions. If these are fulfilled remission of sins and the gift of the Holy Spirit are promised to follow. Peter's words wrongly interpreted have led to much confusion. Upon these words doctrines, especially concerning water baptism, have been built, which are not alone nowhere else taught in the Bible, but which are opposed to the Gospel. The words of Peter to his Jewish brethren have been used to make water baptism a saving ordinance, that only by submission to water baptism, with repentance and faith in the Lord Jesus,

*Joel's Prophecy will be fulfilled in connection with the second Coming of Christ. Then the Holy Spirit, after the predicted judgments are passed, will be poured out upon all flesh. To put the fulfilment in our day is erroneous. See our Exposition of Joel.

can remission of sins and the gift of the Holy Spirit be obtained. We do not enlarge upon these unscriptural conceptions nor answer the utterly false doctrine of "baptismal regeneration," but rather point out briefly what these words of Peter mean. We must bear in mind that Peter addressed those who had *openly* rejected Jesus. They had, therefore, also openly to acknowledge their wrong and thus openly own Him as Messiah, whom they had disowned by delivering Him into the hands of lawless men. Repentance meant for them to own their guilt in having opposed and rejected Jesus. Baptism in the name of Jesus Christ (in which it differs from the baptism of John) was the outward expression of that repentance. It was for these Jews, therefore, a preliminary necessity. And here we must not forget that Peter's preaching on the day of Pentecost had it still to do with the kingdom, as we shall more fully learn from his second address in the third chapter. Another offer of the kingdom was made to the nation. The great fact that the Holy Spirit had begun to form the body of Christ, the church, as stated before, was not revealed then. In this national testimony the word "repent" stands in the foreground, and their baptism in the name of Him whom they had crucified was a witness that they owned Him now and believed on Him.

About three thousand souls were added, who repented and were baptized. Then we behold them in blessed fellowship. Doctrine stands first. It is the prominent thing. They continued steadfastly in the Apostle's doctrine. In the doctrine of the Apostles they were in fellowship together, and that fellowship was expressed in "the breaking of bread." It was not a common meal, but the carrying out of the request the Lord had made in the night He was betrayed, when He instituted what we call "the Lord's supper." Prayer is also mentioned. They had all things in common. They were like a great family, which in reality they were through the Grace of God.

And how happy they were! They had Christ, and that was enough. No system of theology, creeds, set of forms or any such thing, with which historical Christianity abounds

—"Nothing but Christ." They received their food with gladness and singleness of heart, praising God and having favor with all the people. Joy and singleness of heart are two great characteristics of the true believer.

CHAPTER III.

1. The Healing of the lame Man (verses 1–11).
2. Peter's address and appeal (verses 12–26).

The lame man, forty years old, at the gate called Beautiful is the type of the moral condition of the nation, like the impotent man whom the Lord healed (John v). Israel with all its beautiful religious ceremonies was helpless, laying outside with no strength to enter in. Peter commands the lame man in the name of Jesus Christ of Nazareth to rise up and to walk. He is instantly healed. He then walked and leaped and entered through the gate as a worshipper into the temple, praising God. This great miracle was wrought as another evidence to the unbelieving nation that Jesus of Nazareth, whom they had rejected and crucified, is their Messiah and King. It was a proof that the rejected One, who had died on a cross and had been buried, is living in Glory, and that God's omnipotent power had been revealed in answer to that name. The miracle also denoted that the promised kingdom was once more offered to the nation. Concerning that kingdom, when it comes, it is written that "the lame man shall leap as an hart." (Isaiah xxxv:6.) But the lame man, so wonderfully healed, leaping and praising God, is likewise a picture of what the nation will be in a future day, when they will look upon Him whom they have pierced (See Zech. xii:10; Ezek. xxxvi:27; Isaiah xii:1–6; xxxv:10). Peter delivers his second address. Interesting and of much importance are verses 19–21. They can only be understood in the right way if we do not lose sight of the fact to whom they were addressed, that is to Jews, and not to Gentiles. They are the heart of this discourse, and as such a God-given appeal and promise to the nation. If this is lost sight of, the words must lose their right meaning.

The repentance which is demanded of them is an acknowledgment of the wrong they had done in denying the Holy and righteous One, a confession of their blood-guiltiness in having slain the author of life. This, of course, would result in their conversion and the blotting out of their sins as a nation. This God had promised before to the nation (Isaiah xliii:25; xliv:22–23).

The "times of refreshing" and "restitution of all things" are expressions in which the Holy Spirit gathers together the hundreds of promises He gave through the different prophets of God concerning a time of great blessing for His people, and through them for the nations of the world. It would be impossible to mention all these promises and in what the times of refreshing and restoration of all things consist. These days of a coming age, the kingdom age, or as we call it because its duration will be a thousand years, the Millennium, are fully described on the pages of Old Testament prophecy. Not alone will the nation be blessed, but Jerusalem will be a great city; the land will be restored and become the great center for blessing; the nations of the earth will receive blessings, and groaning creation will be delivered from its groans and the curse which rests upon it. If we interpret the Word of Prophecy literally and cease spiritualizing it, we shall have no difficulty to behold the full meaning of the times of refreshing and the restitution of all things. The latter word does not include a restoration of the wicked dead, a second chance for those who passed out of this life in an unsaved condition. And these glorious times cannot come till the Lord Jesus Christ comes again.

CHAPTER IV.

1. Their Arrest (verses 1–3).
2. The Result of the Testimony (verse 4).
3. Peter and John before the Rulers and Elders (verses 5–7).
4. Peter's bold witness (verses 8–12).
5. The astonished Sanhedrim and their Release (verses 13–22).
6. With their own company (verses 23–31).
7. The saved multitude (verses 32–37).

The enemy begins now his acts, and the first indication is given that the offer God's mercy was making to the nation would not be accepted. The Holy Spirit was acting mightily through the spoken Word, but these ecclesiastical leaders were hardening their hearts against the Word and the Spirit of God. The hate against that blessed Name broke out anew under the satanic power to which they had yielded. And the Sadducees came too. Though not much had been said on the resurrection, yet these rationalists, or as we would call them to-day, "higher critics," were much distressed because they preached Jesus and the resurrection. The next step is the arrest and imprisonment of the two apostles. Rough hands seize them. Of the Apostles we read nothing else. They submitted. The power of the Holy Spirit now manifested itself in a new way with them. They could suffer, and perhaps with great joy; in perfect peace they allowed themselves to be taken away.

We have here also the first fulfillment of the many predictions given by our Lord that His own were to suffer persecution (Matt. x:16–17; Mark xiii:9; John xx:20). In Peter's witness we see the effect of the filling with the Spirit. What holy boldness he exhibited! He quotes the same Scripture passage to the assembled Sanhedrim, which the Lord had mentioned in their presence (See Matt. xxii:23–41).

They knew that the Lord meant them when He quoted that verse, that they were the builders, who were to reject Him. They had done so in fulfillment of that prophecy. Peter's words are directed straight at them, "He *is* the stone which has been set at naught by you, the builders."

The rejected stone had become the corner stone. The One whom they had delivered up and cast out had been given the prominent place of the corner stone upon whom, as the foundation stone, everything rests, and who unites the building.

Peter closes with the statement that salvation is only in Him whom they had set at naught. There is no other Name given to men by which man can be saved, and that is the Name of Him who had made this lame man whole.

Salvation they all needed. They, too, rulers, elders, chief priests must be saved. But only in Him God had procured salvation free and complete for all, who will have it by believing on Him. This salvation was offered to these rulers, the builders who had rejected the Lord.

They were then threatened by the astonished rulers and elders and set at liberty. We find them in their own company and after praise and prayer new manifestations of the Holy Spirit follow. In the closing verses we have another glimpse of the assembly in Jerusalem.

CHAPTER V.

1. Ananias and Sapphira (verses 1–10).
2. Signs and wonders by the Apostles (verses 11–16).
3. The second arrest of the Apostles and their Deliverance (verses 17–25).
4. Before the Council (verses 26–33).
5. Gamaliel's Advice (verses 34–39).
6. The Apostles beaten and dismissed (verses 40–42).

With this chapter the scene changes. Beautiful is the ending of the previous chapter, Barnabas having sold his land, laid the money at the feet of the Apostles. He gave by it a striking testimony how he realized as a believing Jew his heavenly portion, by giving up that which is promised to the Jew, earthly possessions.

Our chapter begins with the significant word "But." It is the word of failure and decline. All was evidently perfect; nothing marred the precious scenes of fellowship—"but," and with this little word the story of evil begins. The enemy seeing himself so completely defeated by his attacks from the outside now enters among the flock and begins his work within.

Ananias and Sapphira were lying to the Holy Spirit. Swift judgment followed as to their earthly existence. They were cut off by death. The sin they had done was "a sin unto death" and the sentence, physical death, was immediately carried out. Peter is still in the foreground.

We must remember here the words of the Lord which He spake to Peter, after this disciple had confessed Him as Son of God. "And I will give unto thee the keys of the kingdom of heaven, and whatsoever thou shalt bind upon earth shall be bound in heaven, and whatsoever thou shalt loose on earth shall be loosed in heaven" (Matthew xvi:19). The same words concerning binding and loosing the Lord addressed to all the disciples (Matthew xviii:18). The binding and loosing refers to discipline on earth. It has nothing whatever to do with forgiveness of sins or eternal salvation. Peter here exercises this authority, it was the first discipline. We must likewise remember that these events happened on Jewish, on kingdom ground. The witness was still to the nation. The sudden judgment which came upon Ananias and Sapphira was a strong witness to the nation that the Holy One of Israel, Jehovah, dwelt in the midst of this remnant, who believed in the One whom the nation had rejected. When the kingdom is established on earth and the Lord Jesus Christ rules in righteousness, then, no doubt, every sin will be swiftly judged by death.

Great things followed. Their habitual place seems to have been in Solomon's porch. No one dared to join them. They held the position of authority. Though they had been forbidden the public ministry they are back in a prominent place. The people magnified them too. Then another result was that more believers were added. Added to what? The First Hebrew Christian Church of Jerusalem? The First Jewish Christian Society? No. They were added to the Lord. The sinner believing is saved, receives the Holy Spirit, is joined to the Lord, becomes one spirit with the Lord, a member of the body of which He is the Head. Signs and wonders were done by the Apostles. The sick were healed, unclean spirits were driven out. Multitudes of people from the surrounding country flocked to Jerusalem, bringing their sick, and they were all healed. They waited even in the streets for the time when Peter walked along so that his shadow might fall on some of them. These were great manifestations of the power of God. The words spoken by the Lord were then fulfilled. They did the works He did. These signs and wonders, however, are nowhere mentioned as to their permanency throughout this age. They were only for the beginning of this age; after the Gospel of Grace and the mystery hidden in former ages had been fully made known they disappeared.

All the Apostles were then arrested and put into the common prison. During the night an angel of the Lord opened the prison door and led them out. Such a manifestation was perfectly in order at that time, and fully corresponds with the other kingdom characteristics in the beginning of this book. But these supernatural manifestations have ceased. Peter once more with the other Apostles bears witness to the resurrection and exaltation of the rejected Christ. On the advice of Gamaliel they were released after they had been beaten. With rejoicing that they had been counted worthy to suffer shame for His Name, they departed and continued in their great ministry.

CHAPTER VI.

1. The Murmuring of the Grecians against the Hebrews (verses 1–7).
2. Stephen; His Ministry and Arrest (verses 8–15).

Another failure is brought before us. The enemy acts again. From without and from within Satan pressed upon that which was of God. While the Lord Jesus Christ and the Holy Spirit acted in Grace and power, the enemy came in to disturb. It is still so. Whenever there is a door opened there are also many adversaries (1 Cor. xvi:9).

The flesh manifested itself in murmuring. The assembly took care of the poor; widows being specially helpless, were the objects of daily ministrations. The Jews themselves in connection with the synagogue had special funds for them. They must have also formed a recognized group in the early church (1 Tim. v:9, 10). The ministration is the distribution mentioned in Chapter iv:35, and as the multitude was very great, including, perhaps, hundreds of widows, this work was quite a task. Murmurings arose and these were born of jealousy, the result of unbelief. It is the first indication of weakness and failure. This reminds us of the murmurings of Israel as recorded in the book of Exodus. The same old thing, the changeless flesh, shows itself among the saved and united company of believers, indwelt by the Holy Spirit. The murmurings were on the side of the Grecians. Their complaint was against the Hebrews that the Grecian widows were being overlooked. The Grecians were not, as some teach, Gentiles, but they were Greek-speaking Jews, born in countries outside of Palestine, and therefore called Hellenists, or Grecians.

The murmuring is at once arrested. Seven men are chosen under the direction of the Holy Spirit. The Apostles declared "we will give ourselves continually to prayer, and to the ministry of the Word." The Holy Spirit thus separated the gifts called to minister in spiritual things from those in temporal matters. Note how prayer is put before the ministry of the Word. There can be no effectual ministry, no successful preaching and teaching of the Word, unless it is preceded by prayer.

The seven chosen ones are then named.

While we know little of these men and the service they rendered, with the exception of Stephen and Philip, it is an interesting fact that their names are all Greek. In this the grace of God is beautifully exhibited. The Grecians were the murmurers, and no doubt they were fewer in number than the Hebrews. A modern day church meeting would have proposed to elect a committee composed of equal numbers of the two parties. But not so here.

Grace and wisdom from above are manifested in this action. The entire seven were chosen from those who had complained. This was the blessed rebuke of Grace.

The seven were then set before the Apostles, and when they had prayed they laid their hands on them. As this "laying on of hands" is so much misunderstood, and has been made an act by which authority, power and blessing is claimed to be conferred, we must say a brief word on it.

It is always proper in reading and interpreting the Word of God, to see if not elsewhere in the Bible the terms or things to be interpreted are used, so that through them the right meaning can be ascertained. The laying on of hands is first mentioned in the Book of Leviticus. In the opening chapters of that book we read how the offerer was to lay his hand upon the head of the offering. Thus we read of the Peace offering: "He shall lay his hand upon the head of his offering" (Lev. iii:2). This meant the identification of the Israelite with the offering itself. And this is the meaning of the laying on of hands from the side of the Apostles. They identified themselves and the assembly with them in their work for which they had been chosen. It was a very simple and appropriate act to show their fellowship with them. All else which has been made of the laying on of hands is an invention. There is no Scripture for the present day usage in Christendom, that a man in order to preach the Gospel or teach the Word of God must be "ordained."

Stephen, full of faith and power, did great wonders and miracles among the people. Certain of the synagogue of the Libertines* and others disputed with Stephen. And they were not able to resist the wisdom and the spirit by which he spake. Stephen is accused of blasphemy. The charge is "blasphemy against Moses and against God." They succeeded in their satanic work by stirring up the people, the elders and the scribes. Three things are mentioned by them. He ceaseth not to speak words against this holy place, against the law, and that he should have said: "This Jesus of Nazareth shall destroy this place and shall change the customs which Moses delivered us." And then they looked upon him, and behold his face was like the face of an angel. All eyes were attracted to this wonderful sight. Steadfastly they looked upon a face of Glory; a face re-

*It is wrong to call these "Libertines" free thinkers. Jews had been taken to Rome as slaves. Their descendants who had been liberated were called Libertines, that is freedmen. They were known as such in Jerusalem and hence the name "synagogue of the Libertines."

flecting heaven's light, heaven's Glory; a face reflecting the Glory of Him into whose presence he soon would be called. And may not that young man named Saul also have been there and seen that face? And that dark countenance of that young Pharisee of Tarsus was soon to behold that same Glory-light, and then tell the world of the Gospel of the Glory and that "we all, with open face beholding as in a glass the glory of the Lord, are changed into the same image from glory unto glory."

CHAPTER VII.

1. The Address of Stephen (verses 1–53).
2. The Martyrdom of Stephen (verses 54–60).

This is the largest chapter in this book and concludes the first section. Stephen is the chosen instrument to deliver the final testimony to the nation. He was not permitted to finish it.

We notice at once a marked difference between the previous preaching by the Apostle Peter and the address of Stephen. The testimony of Peter was marked on the day of Pentecost and at the other occasions by great brevity. Stephen's address is the longest discourse reported in the New Testament. The name of Jesus is prominent in all the addresses of Peter. The fact that He was rejected by the people, crucified and that He rose from the dead, and the call to repentance, were the leading features of Peter's preaching. Stephen does not mention the Name of Jesus at all,* though he has the person of Christ and His rejection as the theme of his testimony. At the close of his address he speaks of the Just One of whom they had become betrayers and murderers.

Stephen had been accused of speaking against Moses and against God, also against the temple and the law. These accusations he is asked to answer. What he de-

*The name "Jesus" appears in the A. V. in verse 45; but it should be "Joshua" instead.

clared before the council shows plainly that the accusations are utterly false. His speech is, therefore, partly apologetic; but it is also teaching, in that it shows certain truths from the historic events he cites. And before he finishes his testimony the accused becomes the accuser of the nation; the one to be judged becomes the judge. Indeed his whole testimony as he rapidly speaks of past history in his great and divinely arranged retrospect, is a most powerful testimony to the nation as well as against the nation.

The great address falls into the following section: 1. Abraham's History (verses 2–8). 2. Joseph and his brethren (verses 9–16). 3. The Rejection of Moses. The rejected one became their Deliverer and Ruler (verses 17–38). 4. The Story of the nation's apostasy and shame (verses 39–50. Then Stephen ceased his historical retrospect, he addressed them directly. The accused witness becomes the mouthpiece of the Judge, who pronounces the sentence upon the nation. This is found in verses 51–53. His martyrdom followed.

Three things are mentioned of this first martyr. He was full of the Holy Spirit; he looked steadfastly into heaven, seeing the glory of God; he saw Jesus standing on the right hand of God.

This is the first manifestation of the glorified Christ, which we have on record. There are three of them only. He appeared here to Stephen. Then He appeared unto Saul, who consented unto Stephen's death. Saul beheld Him in that Glory, brighter than the noon-day sun, and heard His voice. The last time the glorified Christ manifested Himself was to John in the island of Patmos. These three appearings of the glorified Christ present to our view the three aspects of His Second Coming. First He comes to welcome His own into His presence. He will arise and come into the air to meet His beloved co-heirs there. This is represented by the first appearing to Stephen, standing to receive him. Then Israel will behold Him, they who pierced Him will see Him, like Saul of Tarsus beheld the

Lord. Then He will appear as John saw Him, the One who judges the earth in righteousness.

And now after this great and glorious vision, Stephen bears testimony to it. "Behold, I see the heavens opened, and the Son of Man standing on the right hand of God." He speaks of the Lord as "Son of Man." This is the only time outside of the Gospel records that we find this title of the Lord (aside from the old Testament reference in Hebrews ii).

They stoned him and Stephen, the mighty witness and mouthpiece of the Holy Spirit, fell asleep.

God's gracious offer and Christ had now been fully rejected by the nation. Stephen, who bore this last witness, is a striking evidence of the transforming power of Christ. How much like the Lord he was!

He was filled with the Spirit, full of faith and power, and like the Lord he did great wonders and miracles among the people. Like Christ, he was falsely accused of speaking against Moses, the law and the temple, and of being a blasphemer. They brought him before the same council and did what they did with the Lord, bringing false witnesses against him. He gave witness to the truth of the confession the Lord had given before the council, that He was to sit at the right hand of God. He beheld Him there. The Lord Jesus committed His spirit in the Father's hands, and Stephen prayed that the Lord Jesus receive his spirit; and like the Lord he prayed for the forgiveness of his enemies. May the same power transform us all into the same image.

Part II. The Witness to Samaria. Saul's Conversion and Peter's Witness in Caesarea.

Chapters VIII–XII.

CHAPTER VIII.

1. The first great persecution (verses 1–3).
2. The preaching of the scattered believers. Philip in Samaria (verses 4–8).
3. Events in Samaria (verses 9–24).
4. The Gospel in many villages of Samaria (verse 25).
5. Philip and the Eunuch (verses 26–40).

The final testimony to the rulers of the people had been given. It was rejected, and the Spirit filled messenger killed. The last offer had therefore been completely rejected. The Gospel is now to be sent to the Gentiles. The eighth chapter gives the record how Samaria heard the Gospel.

Saul, the young Pharisee, was consenting unto Stephen's death. Later he refers to the scene, which must have been impossible for him to erase from his memory. "When the blood of Stephen was shed, I was standing by and keeping the garments of them that slew him" (Acts xxxii:20). Concerning Saul the Lord said to Ananias, "I will shew him how great things he must suffer for my name's sake" (ix:16). What was done unto Stephen was done unto Saul. The Jews and Saul with them, as we believe, disputed and resisted Stephen in the synagogue. The Jews disputed with Paul, resisted him, and rejected his testimony. Stephen was accused of blasphemy; so was Paul (Acts xix:37). Stephen was accused of speaking against Moses, the holy place and the customs; so was Paul (Acts xxi:28; xxiv:6; xxv:8; xxviii:17). They rushed upon Stephen with one accord and seized him. The same happened to Paul (Acts xix:29). Stephen was dragged out of the city. So was Paul (Acts xiv:19). Stephen was tried before the Sanhedrim; so did Paul appear before the Sanhedrim. Stephen was stoned and Paul was stoned at Lystra. Stephen suffered martyrdom; so did Paul in Rome. And yet, with all the sufferings that Paul had to undergo, he rejoiced. His eyes rested constantly upon that glorious One, whom Stephen, filled with the Holy Spirit, beheld in Glory. Later we hear him crying out from the prison in Rome, "That I may know Him, and the power of His resurrection, and the fellowship of His sufferings, being made comformable unto His death" (Phil. iii:10).

The first great persecution then broke out against the church in Jerusalem. Saul was evidently the leader (Acts xxvi:10–11; 1 Cor. xv:9; Gal. i:13). But "the blood of the martyrs is the seed of the church." God permitted this persecution that His Word might now be scattered abroad by the suffering saints. Philip, the Grecian Jew, one of the chosen seven, not an Apostle, is mightily used in preaching the Gospel in Samaria. The first missionary move to extend the Gospel was, therefore, not brought about under apostolic leadership, nor by the decree of an apostolic council, but by the Lord Himself. He led Philip to Samaria, where He Himself had been, yea to the very city of Samaria, Sychar (John iv). Great results followed the preaching of the Gospel. Miracles took place. Unclean spirits were driven out, many taken with palsies, and those who were lame were healed, so that there was great joy in that city. Simon Magus was a sinister instrument of Satan. He bewitched the people of Samaria, claiming to be some great one.

The hour of deliverance came for the Samaritans when Philip preached the Word, concerning the Kingdom of God and the name of Jesus Christ. Signs and great miracles followed, and the Samaritans believed and were baptized. The miracles were done to show the power of God, to attest the preaching of the Gospel by Philip, and to expose the counterfeit powers of Simon. And he, like the sorcerers of Egypt, had to own that this was the power of God. He was amazed when he beheld the great miracles. But more than that, he also believed, was baptized, and then continued with Philip. But his faith was not through the Word of God. God's Word alone can produce faith in man, for faith cometh by hearing, and hearing by the Word of God. Simon was captivated by the miracles he had seen. Philip was deceived by him, but not Peter, who uncovered his wickedness.

That the Holy Spirit had not been given to the Samaritans and that He was received by them after Peter and John had come from Jerusalem and laid hands on them, has puzzled many earnest students of the Word. It has also led to erroneous teachings, as if the Holy Spirit must be received in a special manner after conversion.

The Samaritan believers had to be identified with those in Jerusalem, so much the more because there was a schism between Samaria and Jerusalem. Samaria had denied both the city of Jerusalem and the temple. This had to be ended and could no longer be tolerated. It was therefore divinely ordered that the gift of the Spirit in *their* case should be withheld till the two apostles came from Jerusalem. This meant an acknowledgment of Jerusalem; if the Holy Spirit had been imparted unto them at once it might have resulted in a continuance of the existing rivalry. And Peter is in the foreground and uses the keys of the kingdom of heaven here with the Samaritans as he did on the day of Pentecost with the Jews, and later with the Gentiles. Nowhere in the church epistles, in which the great salvation truths and blessings in Christ Jesus are revealed, is there a word said about receiving the Holy Spirit by the laying on of hands, or that one who has trusted in Christ and is born again should seek the gift of the Holy Spirit afterward.

The conversion of the Eunuch is full of blessed lessons. Philip was obedient to the call of the Lord and the Eunuch, the prominent Ethiopian, Queen Candace's treasurer, who had returned from Jerusalem, an unsatisfied seeker, believed on the Lord Jesus and went on his way rejoicing. Verse 37 is an interpolation and should be omitted. Philip was caught away and was found some twenty miles north of Gaza, at Azotus. From there he started out anew preaching the Gospel. In many cities his voice was heard. These coast cities were inhabited by many Gentiles and included larger places like Jamnia, Lydda, Joppa and Antipatris. The day of Christ will make known the labors and also the reward of this great Evangelist. Then he came to Caesarea. But did he stop with that? We do not know. Twenty years later we find him there and Paul was then his guest.

CHAPTER IX.

1. The vision of Glory on the road to Damascus (verses 1–9).
2. Instructions given to Ananias (verses 10–16).
3. Saul filled with the Spirit, is baptized and preaches that Jesus is the Son of God (verses 17–22).
4. Saul persecuted and back in Jerusalem (verses 23–30).
5. Further Acts of Peter.

The previous chapter must be looked upon in its main part as a parenthesis. The record now leads us back to the close of the seventh, and the person who was connected with the great tragedy enacted there is prominently brought now before us. The witnesses of the wicked deed had laid down their clothes at a young man's feet, whose name was Saul. This is the first time this remarkable man is mentioned. We also learned that he was consenting unto Stephen's death; he made havoc of the church and committed men and women to prison. While the scattered believers had carried the Gospel throughout Judea, Philip had gone down to Samaria and with great results preached the Gospel, and during the same time Peter and John preached in the Samarian villages, Saul carried on his work of persecution. This we learn from the opening verse of the present chapter. "And Saul, yet breathing out threatenings and slaughter against the disciples of the Lord, went unto the high priest." The conversion of this great persecutor and his call by the risen and glorified Lord to be the Apostle to the Gentiles is the event which is next described. It is the greatest event recorded in Acts next to the outpouring of the Holy Spirit on the day of Pentecost.

Saul was from Tarsus in Cilicia, where he had become acquainted with Greek life, literature, art and philosophy. The chief industry of Tarsus was tent making. This trade the young Saul learned. He had a married sister living in Jerusalem (Acts xxiii:16). He also was a Roman citizen.

Saul received his religious education in Jerusalem. We find this from his own words, "I am verily a man, a Jew, born in Tarsus, a city in Cilicia, yet brought up in this city (Jerusalem) at the feet of Gamaliel, and taught according to the perfect manner of the law of the fathers, and was zealous toward God, as ye are all this day" (Acts xxii:3).

That Saul was highly respected in Jerusalem and close to the leaders of the people, is seen by the letters entrusted to him and the commission to Damascus. He may have been even a member of the council, for "he voted." "When they (Christians) were put to death, I gave my voice (lit., my vote) against them" (Acts xxvi:10).

And now God's marvelous Grace and Power in salvation is to be manifested. Israel as a nation had rejected the offer and Stephen's death marked the end of that gracious offer. But God can manifest even greater riches of His Grace and display His great Love. Saul not alone belonged to the nation, which had rejected Christ, but shared in that rejection, but he was, so to speak, the heading up of all the hatred and malignity against the Christ of God. He personified the blindness, unbelief and hatred of the whole nation. He was indeed an enemy, the greatest enemy, the chief of sinners. Surely only Grace could save such a one, and Grace it is, which is now to be manifested in the conversion of Saul of Tarsus, the Grace which he was to know first by the vision of the glorified Christ, and which he, ever after, was to proclaim and make known to others.

The vision itself which burst upon Saul on the road to Damascus is one of the greatest in the whole Bible. It has baffled unbelief. Infidels of all descriptions, French rationalists like Renan, reformed rationalistic Jews, and the worst of all, the advocates of the destructive Bible Criticism, have tried to explain the occurrence in some natural way.

Renan said that it was an uneasy conscience with unstrung nerves, fatigue of the journey, eyes inflamed by the hot sun, a sudden stroke of fever, which produced the hallucination. And this nonsense is repeated to this day. Others of the critics have stated that it was a thunderstorm which overtook him, and that a flash of lightning blinded him. In that lightning flash he imagined that he saw Christ. Again, others have tried to explain his vision by some physical disease. Jews and others have declared that he suffered from Epilepsy, which the Greeks called "the holy disease." This disease, they say, put him into a state of ecstasy, which may have greatly impressed his Gentile hearers. In such an attack he imagined to have seen a vision and heard a voice. All these and other opinions are puerile inventions. The fact is, the conversion of Saul is one of the great miracles and evidences of Christianity.

The ninth chapter does not contain the full record of what happened on the road to Damascus. The Apostle Paul himself relates twice his own experience in chapter xxii:5–16 and in chapter xxvi:12–18. He also mentions his conversion briefly in 1 Corinth. xv:8; Gal. i:15–16 and 1 Tim. i:12–13. The three accounts of Saul's conversion are not without meaning. The one before us in the ninth chapter is the briefest, and is simply the historical account of the event as it had to be embodied in the Book of the Acts, as history. The account in the twenty-second chapter was given by Paul in the Hebrew tongue; it is the longest statement and was addressed to the Jews. The account in the twenty-sixth chapter was given in presence of the Roman governor Festus and the Jewish king Agrippa, therefore addressed to both Jews and Gentiles. But are there not discrepancies and disagreements in these three accounts? Such has been the claim from the side of men who reject the inspiration of the Bible. There are differences, but no disagreements. These differences in themselves are the evidences of inspiration. The differences, however, are simply in the manner in which the facts of the event are presented.

He saw then the glorified One and heard His voice. This great vision became the great turning point of his life. He received perfect knowledge and assurance, that the rejected Jesus of Nazareth is the Son of God. The great event is prophetic. It will be repeated on a larger scale when the Lord Jesus comes again and the remnant of Israel sees Him coming in the clouds of heaven.

The words which the Lord addressed to Saul:—"Saul, Saul, why persecutest thou Me?" contain the blessed Gospel he was soon to proclaim. He did not persecute Christ, but those who had believed on Him.

Every believing sinner is a member of the body of Christ. Christ in Glory, the Lord, who spoke to Saul in the way, is the Head of that body, the church. Christ is in each member of His body, His life is there; and every believer is in Christ. "Ye in Me and I in you." And this great hidden mystery flashes forth in this wonderful event for the first time "Saul, Saul, why persecutest thou *Me*." "I am Jesus whom thou persecutest." The poor, hated, despised Nazarenes, whom the mad, Jewish zealot Saul of Tarsus had driven out of Jerusalem, put into prison and delivered unto death, were one with the Lord in Glory. They were identified with Him and He with them. Their persecution meant His persecution, in their affliction He was afflicted. They were members of His body and that body was in existence.

Soon after we see the erstwhile persecutor preaching Jesus, that He is the Son of God. Persecution soon followed. He also spent a time in Arabia and then paid a visit to Jerusalem for fifteen days (Gal. i:17–24). Further Acts of Peter by divine power conclude this chapter.

CHAPTER X.

1. Cornelius of Caesarea and his Preparation (verses 1-8).
2. The Trance-vision of Peter (verses 9-16).
3. Peter with Cornelius at Caesarea (verses 17-33).
4. Peter Preaching to the Gentiles (verses 34-43).
5. The Interrupted Message (verses 44-48).

The ending of the preceding chapter tells us that Peter tarried in Joppa in the house of Simon the tanner. Was he breaking with his Jewish law and customs? Tanning as a trade was considered unclean by the Jews.

In Ephesians ii:11-18 we read of the Grace of God to the Gentiles.

Up to this time in the Book of Acts we have seen nothing of this gracious purpose, the blessed result of the finished work of Christ on the cross. Jerusalem heard the Gospel first. Once more the good news of the Kingdom was preached with a full offer of forgiveness to the Jews. God was willing to blot out their transgressions and to make good all He had promised to the nation. Many signs and miracles had been done in Jerusalem in demonstration of the resurrection from the dead of the Prince of Life, whom they had crucified. We have seen how the seventh chapter in this book marks the close of that special offer to Jerusalem. Immediately after the death of Stephen, the Gospel was carried into Judea and Samaria. In Samaria a people heard and accepted the glad tidings. They were a mixed race and practiced circumcision and obeyed parts of the law. In the ninth chapter the conversion of Paul is recorded and the Lord makes known that the persecutor of the church is to be the chosen vessel to bear His name before the Gentiles. Paul, however, was not chosen to open first the door to the Gentiles as such, but Peter, the Apostle of the circumcision. A new work is given him to do, which was indeed a strange work for a Jew. He was to go to the Gentiles, whom the Jews considered unclean. It was unlawful for a Jew to join himself to any Gentile; an insurmountable barrier divided them. For this reason the Jews considered the Gentiles as unclean, common, spoke of them as dogs, and had no intercourse with them. It is of interest to notice that Peter tarried in Joppa; from this old city he is to be sent forth to preach the Gospel to Cornelius and his household. Centuries ago another Jew had come to Joppa with a solemn message from his God, which he was commissioned to bear far hence to the Gentiles. Jonah, the prophet, took a ship from Joppa and refused obedience to the divine call.

But here is one who is obedient to the heavenly vision and who is to bring a higher message to the Gentiles, the good news of a free and full salvation. That Peter, the Apostle of the circumcision, was chosen for this great errand, was an important hint that the middle wall of partition had been broken down and that believing Jews and Gentiles were to form one new man.

Cornelius belonged to that class of Gentiles who, illumined by the Holy Spirit, had turned to God from idols, to serve the true and the living God. He was therefore a converted man, for God acknowledged him as such. Of salvation through the Lord Jesus Christ and the blessed assurance of that salvation he knew nothing. His prayers had been heard. The angel who appeared gave Cornelius the full directions where Peter was to be found. While the messengers were hastening to Joppa, Peter had his vision.

And what is the meaning of the vision? The vessel is the type of the church. The four corners represent the four corners of the earth. The clean animals it contained, the Jews; the unclean, the Gentiles. But all in that vessel are cleansed. The Grace of God in the Lord Jesus Christ has cleansed those who are in Christ. "But ye are washed, but ye are sanctified, but ye are justified in the name of the Lord Jesus, and by the Spirit of our God" (2 Cor. vi:11). Jew and Gentile believing, redeemed by blood, saved by Grace, washed and sanctified, are to be put into one body.

Then Peter reached Caesarea and preached to Cornelius and those who were gathered together. How different this message from those he delivered in Jerusalem. There are a few introductory remarks followed by a declaration of the facts concerning Jesus of Nazareth. Then he pressed the message home to their hearts. "To Him give all the Prophets witness that through His Name whosoever believeth on Him shall receive remission of sins." This was his last word to the assembled company. It is the first time we find the word "whosoever" in this book. He had nothing to say to this Gentile company about repentance and baptism. His message was interrupted. They believed and the Holy Spirit fell on them.

Something new had taken place. On Pentecost it meant water baptism as a condition of receiving the Holy Spirit (Acts ii:38) and the remission of sins; in Samaria the Apostles Peter and John, according to the wisdom of God, had to lay on hands, but here without water baptism and laying on of hands the Holy Spirit came upon the Gentiles. Nor was there any process of seeking, surrendering, examining themselves, giving up, praying for it, but by hearing of faith, in believing the message of the Gospel the Holy Spirit fell on them. And to show that every barrier between Jew and Gentile had been removed, that nothing inferior had been bestowed upon Gentiles, than that which came upon the believing Jews on the day of Pentecost, Cornelius, his kinsmen and friends spoke with tongues and magnified God. It was the conclusive evidence that Gentiles, uncircumcised and unbaptized, received the Holy Spirit like the Jews.

Water baptism follows. Up to this chapter water baptism preceded the gift of the Holy Spirit. This shows the place water baptism holds on the ground of grace. Water baptism has no place in the proclamation of the Gospel of Grace. It is not a means of grace, nor a sacrament. Peter, however, does not slight nor ignore baptism. "Can any man forbid water?" Then he commanded them to be baptized in the name of the Lord.

CHAPTER XI.

1. Peter's Defence in Jerusalem (verses 1–18).
2. The Beginning of the Church in Antioch (verses 19–21).
3. Barnabas sent to Antioch (verses 22–26).
4. The Prophecy of Agabus (verses 27–30).

Peter silenced the objections of his brethren in Jerusalem by a rehearsal of his experience. Verse 19 connects with Chapter viii:4. Antioch comes now into prominence as the great Gentile center of Christianity. A great number believed and turned unto the Lord. Then Barnabas was sent to Antioch to inspect the great work. They wanted to know in Jerusalem if the reports were true, and if true the assembly had to be recognized as such. This shows that the Oneness of the church, though not yet *fully* made known by revelation, was nevertheless realized through the Holy Spirit. And that a blessed relationship existed between the assembly in Jerusalem and the one in Antioch, is seen by Peter's visit in that city, when in the liberty wherewith Christ has made us free, he ate with these believing Gentiles and enjoyed fellowship with them (Gal. ii:11–12).

The movement also attracted the attention of the outsiders. They called them "Christians." The Jews, it is certain, did not give this name, but the Gentiles invented it. Antioch was famous for its readiness to jeer and call names; it was known by its witty epigrams. So they coined a new word, "*Christianoi*"—Christians. It is used exclusively by outsiders, as seen in the case of Agrippa, also see 1 Pet. iv:16. Jews and Gentiles alike were called by this name, "Christians," so that it bears testimony to the oneness of Jew and Gentile in Christ.

CHAPTER XII.

1. The great Persecution by Herod Agrippa I (verses 1–5).
2. The miraculous deliverance of Peter (verses 6–17).
3. The Presumption and Judgment of Herod (verses 18–23).
4. Barnabas and Saul returning to Jerusalem (verses 24–25).

With this chapter we reach the conclusion of the second part of this book. Jerusalem had heard the second offer concerning the Kingdom, and mercy was ready even for the murderers of the Prince of Life. But that offer was rejected. Stephen's testimony followed by his martyrdom marked the close of that second offer to the city where our Lord had been crucified. Then broke out a great persecution, and they were scattered abroad except the Apostles. From our last chapter we learned that others who were driven out of Jerusalem preached the Word in Phenice, Cyprus and Antioch. The twelfth chapter, with which this part of Acts closes, is an interesting one. It is not only interesting on account of the historical information it contains, but also because of its dispensational foreshadowing. Once more we are introduced to Jerusalem and see another great persecution. The wicked King is reigning over the city. James is killed with the sword, while Peter is imprisoned but wonderfully delivered; the evil King, who claimed divine power and worship, is suddenly smitten by the judgment of the Lord. Then the Word grew and multiplied, Barnabas and Saul returned from Jerusalem to Antioch, from where the great missionary operations were soon to be conducted. The events in Jerusalem, James' martyrdom under King Herod, Peter's imprisonment and deliverance, as well as the fate of the persecuting King, foreshadow the events with which this present age will close. After the true church is taken from the earth, that is when 1 Thess. iv:16–17 is fulfilled, the great tribulation will take place. While great tribulation and judgment will come upon the whole world, *the* great tribulation will come upon the Jewish people who have returned in part to their own land. In the midst of the masses of unbelieving Jews, there will be found a remnant of God-fearing Jews, who are converted and bear testimony to the truth. A wicked King, the man of sin, the false Messiah, will then be in power in Jerusalem. Part of that Jewish remnant will suffer martyrdom; these are represented by James, whom Herod, the type of the Antichrist, slew. Another part will be delivered as Peter was delivered. Herod's presumption and fate clearly points to that of the Antichrist (2 Thess. ii:3–8). All this may well be kept in mind in the study of this chapter in detail.

Interesting is the account of the prayer meeting held in behalf of Peter. When God had answered their prayers they were reluctant to believe it. Not one of the company believed that Peter had been released. Rhoda was the one who believed that it was Peter. And this is undoubtedly the reason why her name is mentioned in this book. The poor maid, perhaps a slave girl, pleased God because she had faith. While there was great earnestness in that prayer meeting, when the prayer was answered, unbelief manifested itself.

Part III. The Witness to the Gentiles. The Apostle to the Gentiles; his Ministry and Captivity.

Chapters XIII–XXVIII.

CHAPTER XIII.

1. The Divine Choice. Barnabas and Saul separated unto the work (verses 1–3).
2. The Beginning of the Journey and the events in Cyprus (verses 4–12).
3. The Gospel in Galatia. Paul's Address (verses 13–41).
4. The Gospel rejected by the Jews (verses 42–52).

The thirteenth chapter is the beginning of the third part of this book. The second great center of Christianity comes to the front. It is no longer Jerusalem, but the city of Antioch. The gospel which had been preached in Jerusalem, in Judea and Samaria, which Cornelius and his house had heard and accepted, is now in a special manner to go far hence to the Gentiles. The city in which the first great Gentile church had been established is the starting point. Peter, so prominent in the first twelve chapters of our book, is no longer the leading actor. He is mentioned only once in this second part of the Book of Acts. In the fifteenth chapter, in connection with the council in Jerusalem, his voice is heard once more. The special work in connection with the kingdom of heaven, in opening the door to the Jews and Gentiles (Acts ii and chapter x) had been accomplished by him. Now he disappears from our view, though he continued to exercise his apostleship in connection with the circumcision (Galatians ii:7). Paul, the great Apostle of the Gentiles, instead appears upon the scene, and his wonderful activity is described in the remaining part of the book. The opposition and blindness of the Jews in a continued rejection of the gospel becomes fully evident throughout this section, and the book itself closes with the testimony against them: "Be it known therefore unto you, that the salvation of God is sent unto the Gentiles, and that they will hear it" (Acts xxviii:28). Besides this we shall find in these chapters the acts of the Holy Spirit in the call and sending forth of the chosen instruments in the way He guided them, how He filled them, opened doors, and manifested His gracious power in the salvation of sinners.

The beginning of the great movement to send now the Gospel far hence to the Gentiles was inaugurated by the Holy Spirit. The assembled prophets and teachers ministered to the Lord in praise and prayer, when the Holy Spirit's voice was heard demanding the separation of Barnabas and Saul unto a work He had called them. The personality of the Holy Spirit is here fully demonstrated. They were thus sent forth not by the church, nor by a missionary society or committee, but by the Holy Spirit.

Accompanied by John Mark as a helper they sailed to Cyprus. Here at Paphos they found a Jew, a sorcerer and false prophet by name of Bar-Jesus (Son Jesus). Such evil persons, special instruments of Satan, appear repeatedly in this book, and generally when the Gospel was carried into some new regions. In Samaria it was Simon Magus; in Macedonia the damsel with the familiar spirit, and here this demon-possessed Jew. He was an enemy of all righteousness. He tried to keep the Word from the Roman Sergius Paulus. Thus the Jews tried to keep the Gospel from reaching the Gentiles. The judgment which fell upon this wicked Jew is typical of the judicial blindness which has come upon the Jews. But as this sorcerer who opposed the Gospel was not to see the sun for a season, even so, the blindness of the Jews is not permanent.

For the first time, and that in connection with this incident, the name of Paul is mentioned. Some have suggested that he took the name in honor of Sergius Paulus, but that is incorrect. Paul is a Roman name, and means "little." Later he writes of himself as "less than the least of all saints." He took the lowest place, and the name which signifies this comes now into prominence. Barnabas is taking the second place; not Barnabas and Saul, but Paul and Barnabas is now the order.

John Mark left them when they had come to Perga in Pamphylia. It was on account of the work (chapter xv:38). It was a failure and for a time he was unprofitable. See 2 Tim. iv:11 where we read of his restoration. He is the one who wrote the Gospel of the obedient servant, the Gospel of Mark.

In verses 16–41 Paul's great address in Antioch of Pisidia is reported. Then the Jews rejected the Gospel, and when they preached to the Gentiles they contradicted and blasphemed.

CHAPTER XIV.

1. The work in Iconium and the persecution of the Apostles (verses 1–6).
2. In Derbe and Lystra; the Impotent Man healed (verses 7–18).
3. The Stoning of Paul and further ministries (verses 19–24).
4. The Return to Antioch (verses 25–28).

Iconium was a Phrygian town, bordering on Lycaonia. Here again the unbelieving Jews stirred up the Gentiles. They abode there a long time, and in spite of opposition and persecution they spoke with much boldness the Word of God. Signs and wonders were also done by their hands. When their lives were threatened by the unbelieving Jews and Gentiles, they fled to Lystra and Derbe.

Derbe was the home of a pious Jewess by name of Eunice. She had married a Greek, who had died. Her son was Timotheus and she lived with her mother Lois (Acts xvi:1–3; 2 Tim. i:5). In Lystra another lame man is healed by the power of God. The ignorant heathen, seeing the miracle, thought the two apostles were gods and attempted to worship them. They abhorred their proceedings and refused the honor of men.

The enemy lurked behind this, no doubt, but the grace of God gave to the apostles the power to act as they did. How much of such idolizing is going on in modern days; how men, professedly the servants of the Lord, seek and love the honor and praise of men, is too evident to be mentioned.

Seeking honor from men and having delight in the applause of the "religious world" is a deadly thing, for it dishonors Christ, to whom all honor and glory is due. And how much of all this there is in the present day! It is but the result of not giving the Lord Jesus Christ the pre-eminence.

Jews then appeared coming from Iconium and Antioch and stirred up the people against them. The mass of people who were ready to worship Barnabas and Paul changed quickly and stoned Paul. Most likely the fury turned against him because he had been instrumental in healing the crippled man. As the stones fell upon him, must he not have remembered Stephen? And may he not have prayed as Stephen did? And after they thought him dead, they dragged his body out of the city. But the Lord, who had announced such suffering for him, had watched over his servant. He was in His own hands, as every child of God is in His care. The enemy who stood behind the furious mob, as he stood behind the attempt to sacrifice unto them, would have killed Paul. But he could not touch Paul's life, as he was not permitted to touch the life of another servant of God, Job (Job ii:6). His sudden recovery was supernatural. He refers in 2 Cor. xi:25 to this stoning, "Once I was stoned." Another reference to Lystra we find in his second Epistle to Timothy: "Persecutions, afflictions, which came unto me at Antioch, at Iconium, at Lystra, what persecutions I endured; but out of them all *the Lord delivered me*" (2 Tim. iii:11). Blessed be His name, He is the same Lord still and will deliver them that trust in Him.

Then after additional testimony in Lystra and a visit to Iconium and Antioch in Pisidia, to build up the disciples and to strengthen them, they terminate this first great journey by returning to the place from which they had started.

CHAPTER XV.

1. The false teachers from Judea. Paul and Barnabas sent to Jerusalem (verses 1–5).
2. The Council in Jerusalem (verses 6–21).
3. The Result made known (verses 22–29).
4. The Consolation brought to Antioch (verses 30–35).
5. Paul and Barnabas separate (verses 36–41).

A very critical time had now arrived for the church. An important question had to be settled. That Gentiles can be saved and salvation must be extended to the Gentiles had been fully demonstrated. The Apostle of the circumcision, Peter, had been used to preach the Gospel to a company of God-fearing Gentiles. Evangelists had gone to Antioch and the great Gentile center had there been founded. Paul and Barnabas had completed their great missionary journey and numerous assemblies of Gentiles, saved by Grace, were formed. The question of the salvation of Gentiles could no longer be raised. But we remember from the eleventh chapter of this book, that when Peter returned to Jerusalem, they that were of the circumcision contended with him. They objected to Peter going to men uncircumcised and eating with them. But those of the circumcision had not been fully satisfied with the status of the believing Gentiles. What about circumcision in their case? Should they not also keep the Law? In other words, the question of the relation of the believing Gentile to the Law and to circumcision had to be determined.

These teachers which taught that Gentiles, in order to be saved, had to be circumcised after the manner of Moses, disturbed greatly the church in Antioch. Paul and Barnabas with others were therfeore delegated to go with this question to Jerusalem. Galatians ii:1–10 must be carefully read for interesting and additional information. The question was settled in favor of the Gospel Paul had preached. James declared: "Wherefore my sentence is, that we trouble not them, which from among the Gentiles are turned to God." They were to abstain from pollution of idols, from fornication, from things strangled and from blood. Of great importance are the words which James uttered by inspiration at this occasion. It was the first church-council, and here the Holy Spirit revealed God's gracious purposes concerning the age that is and the age to come.

Note in verses 14–18 the four important steps: 1. God visits the Gentiles, to take out of them a people for His Name. This is the purpose of the present age. The called people constitute the church, the body of Christ. 2. After this I will return. This means the second Coming of Christ. When the Church is completed and all the members added to that body, Christ comes again, first, as subsequently revealed, for His saints and then with them. 3. The Restoration of Israel follows after His Return. The Tabernacle of David will be built again and will be set up. 4. Then all the Gentiles will seek after the Lord. This is the world-conversion. How strange that this divinely revealed program should be entirely ignored by all church-councils at the present time.

Then after the results of the council and the decision concerning the Gentiles had been made known by a letter, Antioch received consolation.

The beginning of the second missionary journey of Paul is described in the closing paragraph of this chapter. We read nothing of prayer or waiting on God for guidance. Paul said to Barnabas, "Let us go again." He wanted to go over the same territory. This was not the plan of the Spirit. Failure follows on account of self-will and self-choosing. Paul and Barnabas separate on account of John Mark. Barnabas took Mark and Paul chose Silas.

CHAPTER XVI.

1. In Derbe and Lystra again. Timotheus (verses 1–5).
2. The Preaching forbidden in Asia (verses 6–8).
3. The Vision of the Man from Macedonia (verses 9–12).
4. The Gospel in Europe (verses 13–40).

Read in connection with the first verses of this chapter 1 Tim. i:18, iv:14; 2 Tim. i:5–6, iii:15. The circumcision of Timothy, the offspring of a mixed marriage, was not demanded by the law. Paul in circumcising Timothy manifested his liberty; he acted graciously, not wishing to put a stumbling block in the way of the Jews (see 1 Cor. ix:20).

They travel on through Phrygia and Galatia but were forbidden to preach in Asia. This was at that time a large province in Asia Minor with many flourishing cities. It was not God's purpose to have work done at that time. They followed divine guidance obediently. Later Paul spent three years in Ephesus, the capital of that province, and all Asia heard the Word. They also wanted to visit Bithynia, but were not allowed to do so. Bithynia heard the Word at another time perhaps through Peter (1 Peter i:1–2). All this shows clearly how the Holy Spirit is an infallible guide in Christian service. He must point out the way and the places as well as the time when and where the Word is to be spoken. Then follows the vision of the Man from Macedonia. This Macedonian cry is answered at once. From the tenth verse we learn that Luke, the author of this record, joined the party. This is seen by the changed pronoun from "they" to "we." Then they reached Philippi. On the small river Gangites the first opportunity to minister is given. We wonder if Paul looked for the man he had seen in his vision. There was no man present. A company of women had gathered in the place "where prayer was wont to be made." Lydia of Thyatira is the first convert of Europe. She was a true worshipper of God like Cornelius. And it was the Lord who opened her heart. Satan's opposition is seen once more in the demon-possessed damsel. Satan is a cunning being full of wisdom. He tried through this damsel to establish a friendly relation with the servants of the Lord. But the Gospel does not need such support. After her conversion Satan changed his tactics. They were beaten with many stripes and cast into prison, their feet held in the stocks. What followed is familiar to all. God had worked in mighty power delivering His servants and saving the jailer and his household.

CHAPTER XVII.

1. The Gospel in Thessalonica (verses 1–9).
2. The Gospel in Berea (verses 10–14).
3. Paul in Athens (verses 15–34).

Three cities in which the Gospel is next preached are before us in this chapter. But there is a marked difference between these three places. In Thessalonica there was much hostility, the result of the success of the Gospel. In Berea a more noble class of Jews were found. Their nobility consisted in submission to the Scriptures, the oracles of God, and in a ready mind. There was a still greater blessing among the Jews and the Gentiles. In Athens the Apostle Paul met idolatry, indifference and ridicule.

An interesting fact is learned concerning the activity of the apostle in Thessalonica from the two Epistles, which he addressed some time after to the Thessalonians. These were the first Epistles Paul wrote. From these we learn that the Apostle not only preached the Gospel, but also taught the Thessalonian believers prophetic Truths and emphasized the Second Coming of Christ and the events connected with it. In the Second Epistle he reminds them of his oral teaching (2 Thess. ii:5).

The address Paul gave in Athens has three sections: 1. The Introduction (verses 22–23) in which he refers to the altar with the strange inscription "to the unknown God." Then he uttered the words "Him I declare unto you." 2 Who the unknown God is (verses 24–29). He is a personal God who made the world and all that is in it. He answered the Epicurean and Stoic schools of philosophy. Materialism and Pantheism were thus swept aside. 3. He closes with the message from God (verses 30–31).

He aims at their conscience to awaken them to the sense of need to turn away from idols to the true God. God sends to all one message, be they Jew or Gentiles, Greeks or Barbarians, to repent. And then he states the reason. A day is appointed in which He will judge the world in righteousness. The one through whom God will judge is a Man ordained by Him; then follows the declaration of the resurrection of this Man. The day of judgment here does not mean a universal judgment (a term not known in Scripture) nor the great white throne judgment. The judgment here does not concern the dead at all, but it is the judgment of the habitable world. It is the judgment which will take place when the Man whom God raised from the dead, our Lord Jesus Christ, comes the second time. His resurrection is the assurance of it.

CHAPTER XVIII.

1. In Corinth with Aquila and Priscilla. His testimony and separation from the Jews (verses 1–8).
2. Encouragement from the Lord in a vision (verses 9–11).
3. Paul and Gallio (verses 12–17).
4. From Corinth to Ephesus and Antioch. The second journey ended (verses 18–22).
5. Establishing disciples in Galatia and Phrygia (verse 23).
6. Apollos, the Alexandrian (verses 24–28).

Aquila and Priscilla are mentioned here for the first time. This interesting couple had established themselves in Corinth, and what a joy it must have been to the Apostle when he was led to their home. How sweet their fellowship must have been as they toiled together in their trade as tent makers and spoke one to another about the Lord. From the same chapter we learn that after Paul's ministry had terminated they went to Ephesus (verse 19). From 1 Cor. xvi:19 we learn that they were still there when that epistle was written. But in writing to the Romans Paul says, "Greet Priscilla and Aquila, my helpers in Christ Jesus" (Rom. xvi:3), so that they had wandered back to Rome and were in happy fellowship with the Roman assembly. 2 Tim. iv:19 tells us that once more they were back in Ephesus where Timothy had his abode. "Salute Prisca (an abbreviation of Priscilla) and Aquila." They were indeed strangers and pilgrims, but blessed to know that their wanderings were directed by the Lord. Priscilla is mostly mentioned before Aquila, from which we may learn that she, like other notable women of apostolic days, "labored for the Gospel."

It seems that Paul followed the same method of work as he did in Thessalonica. First, he reasoned in the synagogue every Sabbath and persuaded the Jews and the Greeks (verse 4). This must have been altogether on Old Testament ground, showing the divine predictions concerning Christ. When Silas and Timotheus arrived, then he was greatly pressed in spirit and testified to the Jews more fully that Jesus is the Christ. That there was blessed fruit we learn from his epistles to the Corinthians. He himself baptized Crispus and Gaius and the household of Stephanas (1 Cor. i:14–16). And he was with them in weakness, and in fear, and in much trembling. His speech was far different from the one he had used in addressing the philosophers of Athens. "My speech was not with enticing words of man's wisdom, but in demonstration of the Spirit and of power" (1 Cor. ii:3–4). His presence was base unto them. "Who in presence am base among you" (2 Cor. x:1). His bodily presence, these Corinthians said, is weak, and his speech contemptible (2 Cor. x:10).

The Lord encouraged His servant in a vision. The Jews attempt to harm Paul through Gallio failed. Sosthenes the chief ruler received a beating instead of the apostle.

If the Sosthenes who is mentioned in the opening verse of the first Epistle of the Corinthians is the same, then he profited immensely by his experience. Paul addresses him as a brother. We believe he is the same person, for the Grace of God delights to take up such characters and show in them what Grace can do.

From Corinth he went to Ephesus, then to Jerusalem and back to Antioch. Thus ended the second missionary journey. After this he established the disciples in Galatia and Phrygia. An extremely beautiful incident closes this chapter. A new preacher appeared among the Jews in Ephesus, Apollos the Alexandrian. He is described as an eloquent man and mighty in the Scriptures. In Alexandria, Philo, the great Hellenistic Jewish Philosopher, had flourished.

He was born about 20 B. C. and died after the year 40 A. D. He introduced Platonism into Judaism. In all probability Apollos was one of his disciples, but he accepted that which Philo did not believe. He had come most likely in touch with disciples of John the Baptist, and had been baptized with John's baptism unto repentance. He knew that Jesus is the Messiah, knew the facts of His earthly life and the miracles He did. Of the meaning of His death and resurrection Apollos knew nothing, nor had he any knowledge of the Holy Spirit. The entire truth of the Gospel of Grace was unknown to Him. The text in the authorized version that he "taught diligently the things of the Lord" is incorrect. The correct translation is "he taught diligently the things concerning Jesus."

Aquila and Priscilla were then used to expound unto him the way of God more perfectly.

CHAPTER XIX.

1. The second visit of Paul to Ephesus. The twelve disciples of John (verses 1–7).
2. The Apostle's continued labors. The separation of the disciples. The Province Asia evangelized (verses 8–10).
3. The Power of God and the Power of Satan (verses 11–20).
4. Paul plans to go to Jersualem and to visit Rome (verses 21–22).
5. The opposition and riot at Ephesus (verses 23–41).

The disciples whom Paul found at Ephesus were disciples of John. The question the Apostle asked them has often been made the foundation of wrong teaching concerning the Holy Spirit. It is claimed that the Holy Spirit must be received in a special manner after conversion. The little word "since" in Paul's question must be changed into "when," for it is mistranslated. "Did ye receive the Holy Spirit when ye believed?"

Paul makes the gift of the Spirit a test of true discipleship. If they were true believers they received the Holy Spirit *when* they believed, that is when they accepted the Lord Jesus Christ as their Saviour. If they did not receive the Holy Spirit then it is an evidence that they did not believe. "Now if any man have not the Spirit of Christ, he is none of His" (Rom. viii:9).

They heard next the full truth of the Gospel and believed, therefore they received the gift of the Spirit. Ephesus was the stronghold of Satan. When the power of God was manifested in the special miracles of Paul and the demons were driven out, then Satan also began to work. A great victory over the power of darkness followed.

Then Paul purposed in the spirit (verse 21) to go to Jerusalem. This verse marks an important change, which introduces us to the last stage of the recorded acts of Paul in this historical account. *Rome* is the goal which looms up before him. "I must also see Rome." And he saw Rome, but not in the way as he purposed in his spirit, but as the prisoner of the Lord. His journey begins now towards that great city, and at the close of the book we find him there a prisoner. The story of his journey to Jerusalem, a journey in which he perseveres though repeatedly warned by the Spirit of God, his arrest in Jerusalem, his trials and addresses before the Jews, before Felix, Festus and King Agrippa, his voyage to Rome and shipwreck and arrival in Rome, are the contents of the remaining part of our book."

The question has often been raised how the purposing of Paul in the spirit to go again to Jerusalem is to be understood. Is the word "spirit" to be written with a capital "S" or not? In other words, did he purpose in the Spirit of God, after prolonged prayer, to go up to Jerusalem? Did the Holy Spirit guide him to take up to the city of his fathers the contributions from Achaia and Macedonia for the poor saints? (Romans xv:25–26). It could not have been the Spirit of God who prompted him to go once more to Jerusalem, for we find that during the journey the Holy Spirit warned him a number of times not to go to Jerusalem.

He was called to evangelize; to continue to preach the glorious Gospel, and it was a turning aside from the great ministry committed unto him. But behind his burning desire to go up to Jerusalem stood the mighty constraint of love for his own beloved brethren. How he did love them and how his heart, filled with the love of God, yearned over them! This love is so fully expressed in his epistle to the Romans. "I say the truth in Christ, I lie not, my conscience also bearing me witness in the Holy Spirit, that I have great heaviness and continual sorrow in my heart. For I could wish that myself were accursed (or separated) from Christ for my brethren, my kinsmen according to the flesh" (Rom. ix:1–2). "Brethren, my heart's desire and prayer to God for Israel is, that they might be saved" (Rom. x:1). This holy love and courage prompted him to say, when once more his brethren had besought him by the Spirit not to go up to Jerusalem, "What mean ye to weep and break my heart? for I am ready not to be bound only, but also to die at Jerusalem for the name of the Lord Jesus" (Acts xxi:13).

In the close of this chapter we read of the great opposition and riot in Ephesus and the Apostle's persecution.

CHAPTER XX.

1. Paul in Macedonia (verses 1–2).
2. His abode in Greece, the visit to Troas and what transpired there (verses 3–12).
3. The journey from Troas to Miletus (verses 13–16).
4. The farewell to the Ephesian Elders (verses 17–38).

The record before us is very brief. Some have thought the reason is the fact that the Apostle had turned aside from His given ministry, and therefore the Holy Spirit had nothing to report. We believe that this is correct. The object of the Spirit of God is now to lead us rapidly forward to the last visit of the Apostle to Jerusalem, therefore much is passed over in the untiring service and labors of the great Man of God. After the uproar was over in Ephesus Paul embraced the disciples and departed to go into Macedonia. It is the first farewell scene on this memorable journey. He must have visited Philippi, Thessalonica, Beroea and perhaps other cities. Besides giving them much exhortation, he received their fellowship for the poor saints in Jerusalem.

Then there is the record of a blessed scene on the first day of the week in Troas. They remembered the Lord in the breaking of bread (1 Cor. xi:23–26).

The company then took ship to sail to Assos, but Paul made the journey of over twenty miles on foot. He wanted to be alone like Elijah as well as others. What thoughts must have passed through his mind! What burdens must have been upon his heart! What anxieties in connection with that coming visit to Jerusalem!

From Miletus Paul sent to Ephesus and called the elders of the church. The remaining part of this chapter contains his great farewell address to the Ephesian elders and through them to the church located there. Two great speeches by the Apostle have so far been reported in this book. The first was addressed to the *Jews* in Antioch of Pisidia (Acts xiii:16–41). The second was addressed to the *Gentiles* in Athens (chapter xvii). The address here in our chapter is to the *church*. It is of very great and unusual interest and importance. He speaks of himself, his own integrity and recalls to them his ministry. He declares his own coming sufferings and his determination not to count his life dear, but to finish his course with joy. He warns the church concerning the future apostasy and the appearance in their midst of false teachers.

CHAPTER XXI.

1. The journey from Miletus to Tyre and Ptolemais (verses 1–7).
2. In Caesarea (verses 8–14).
3. The Apostle's Arrival in Jerusalem and his visit to the Temple (verses 15–26).
4. The Uproar in the Temple. Paul taken prisoner (verses 27–40).

Coos, Rhodes and Patara are mentioned. Then they sailed over to Phenicia and landed in Tyre. Here they found disciples.

And the Holy Spirit through these disciples warned the Apostle at once that he should not go to Jerusalem. This, indeed, was very solemn. If these disciples had spoken of themselves, if it said that they were in anxiety over Paul's journey to that city, one might say that they were simply speaking as men; but the record makes it clear that the *Holy Spirit* spoke through them. Could then the Apostle Paul have been under the guidance of that same Spirit in going to Jerusalem? As stated before, the great love for his brethren, his kinsmen, burned in his heart, and so great was his desire to be in Jerusalem that he ignored the voice of the Spirit.

In Caesarea they were the guests of Philip the evangelist. Here Agabus, who had given a prediction of a great dearth years ago (xi:27) comes once more upon the scene. When he had come he took Paul's girdle and with it bound his own hands and feet, and then he said: "Thus saith the Holy Spirit, So shall the Jews at Jerusalem bind the man that owneth this girdle, and shall deliver him into the hands of the Gentiles." Here then another warning was given. It was the last and by far the strongest. Did Agabus really speak by the Spirit? The literal fulfilment of his predictive action furnishes the answer. The whole company, both his fellow travelers and the believers in Caesarea, began to beseech him not to go up to Jerusalem.

Then they reached Jerusalem. On the next day the company paid a visit to James, in whose house all the elders had assembled for the purpose of meeting with Paul and his friends. And now once more the Apostle relates what no doubt was dearest to the hearts of James and the elders, what God had wrought through His God-given ministry among the Gentiles. It must have been a very lengthy account; for he rehearsed particularly, "or one by one," the things which had happened in His great activity. After Paul had spoken, "they glorified God."

All had progressed nicely up to this point. But now the great crisis is rapidly reached. The meeting had been called in the house of James, and only the elders had been invited for a very good reason. Reports had reached Jerusalem that Paul had taught the Jews among the Gentiles to forsake Moses, and even to deny children the covenant sign, circumcision. Most likely the Judaizing element in the assembly of Jerusalem, the men who were so successfully overcome by the bold arguments of the Apostle at the council in Jerusalem (Acts xv., Gal. ii), the men who so strenuously taught, that unless the Gentiles became circumcised, they could not be saved—these men were responsible for the rumors. What could be done to convince the multitude that all this was incorrect, that Paul after all was a good Jew?

The elders suggest to him that there were four men who had a vow on them. These he should take and purify himself with them as well as pay the charges. This action, they reasoned, would not only demonstrate that the reports were untrue, but that he, the Apostle of Gentiles, "walketh orderly and keepeth the law." To make this temptation stronger, they re-stated that which had been agreed concerning the status of the believing Gentiles, according to the decision of the church council years ago. All was a most subtle snare. He was by that action to show that, with all his preaching to the Gentiles, he was still a good Jew, faithful to all the traditions of the fathers, and attached to the temple.

And a strange sight it is to see the Apostle Paul back in the temple, going through these dead ceremonies, which had been ended by the death of the cross. A strange sight to see him, who disclaimed all earthly authority and taught deliverance from the law and a union with an unseen Christ, submitting once more to the elementary things, as he calls them in his Epistle to the Galatians, "the beggarly elements!" And has not the whole professing church fallen into the same snare?

His arrest followed and he is taken prisoner. A great tumult followed. They would have killed him if the chief captain had not rescued him. He then was bound with two chains. Agabus prophecy is fulfilled.

Paul gives the Roman officer his pedigree. "I am a man, a Jew of Tarsus," and then requests the privilege of addressing the furious mob. This was permitted, and taking a prominent place on the stairs, where he could be seen by all below, and when after beckoning to the people, silence had been secured, he addressed them in Hebrew. The break of the chapter at this point is unfortunate. The next chapter contains the first address of defence of the prisoner Paul.

CHAPTER XXII.

1. The Address of the Apostle (verses 1–21).
2. The Answer from the Mob, and Paul's Appeal to his Roman citizenship (verses 22–30).

What a scene it was! On the stairs, midway between the temple–court and the fortress, stood the Apostle in chains, his person showing the effects of the beating he had received. Around him were the well-armed Roman soldiers, and below the multitude, with up-turned faces, still wildly gesticulating and only becoming more silent when they heard the first words from Paul's lips in the Hebrew tongue.

He relates his great experience. They were impatient listeners; the storm broke with the word "Gentiles." Another great tumult resulted and the many voices demanded that such a fellow should not live. It was a scene of utmost confusion.

The chief captain seems to have been ignorant of the Aramaic dialect. He gave orders that Paul be now removed into the castle itself, and be examined by scourging so that he might find out why they cried so against him. He was led away, and everything made ready for the cruel treatment, when the prisoner spoke: "Is it lawful for you to scourge a man that is a Roman, and uncondemned?" The centurion reported this to the chiliarch, the chief officer, who at once appeared on the scene. When he discovered that Paul was indeed a Roman by birth, they left their hands off of his person, and even the chiliarch was afraid. It was a highly illegal act to bind a Roman.

Not a few had pointed to this as a prominent failure in the career of the Apostle. According to these critics he made a grave mistake when he pleaded his Roman citizenship; he should have been silent and taken the unjust and cruel treatment without a murmur. If some of these harsh critics of the beloved Apostle were placed in the same condition, what would they do? As one has truly said: "It is easy to be a martyr in theory, and such are seldom martyrs in practice." He had a perfect right to tell the ignorant officers of the law who he was, and thus prevent a flagrant and cruel transgression of the law. And yet his conduct in Philippi was far different. Why did he not announce his Roman citizenship there? The power of the Spirit rested then upon him; it is different here.

CHAPTER XXIII.

1. Paul before the Sanhedrim (verses 1–10).
2. The vision of the Lord (verse 11).
3. The Conspiracy against Paul (verses 12–22).
4. Paul taken to Caesarea (verses 23–30).

And now we find him addressing the Sanhedrim.

For the last time the Jewish council is mentioned in this book. Three times before the Sanhedrim had been called together in connection with those who believed in the Lord Jesus (ii:5, v:21 and vi:12–15). Looking straight at the council, Paul did not wait for the formalities connected with the proceedings, but addressed the gathered Sanhedrim as men and brethren. And strange are the words with which he opened his defence: "I have lived in all good conscience before God until this day." In this he made a public declaration of his righteousness, which reminds us of his confession as a Pharisee (Phil. iii:4–6). This self-justification shows that he was not acting under the leading of the Holy Spirit. This bold language resulted in stirring up the anger of the high priest Ananias, who commanded that the bystanders should smite the Apostle on the mouth. And Paul was not slow to reply with a harsh word, calling the high priest "a whited wall" and demanding of God to smite him. No doubt the high priest was indeed a "whited wall" and fully deserved the judgment from God. But did Paul in speaking thus show the meekness of Him, whose servant he was?

In a clever way he tries to bring in dissension by his statement of being a Pharisee and the son of a Pharisee. A big commotion followed. Some of the scribes belonging to the Pharisees cried loudly in defence of the prisoner—"We find no evil in this man; but if a spirit or an angel has spoken to him, let us not fight against God." The latter sentence was a faint echo of the advice given by Gamaliel. The scene which followed beggars description. The shouting must have been terrific and Paul was in danger of being pulled to pieces by the council mob. Lysias, the chief captain, was obliged to interfere. The soldiers, at his command, came down and rescued Paul and brought him into the castle. The cleverness of Paul had been the means of liberating him from the hands of the Sanhedrim.

The night following the Lord appeared unto him and comforted him. No doubt he had sought before His face in confession and self-judgment. He is in the Lord's hands. Forty men had made a conspiracy not to eat and to drink till they had killed him.

The prisoner of the Lord is now delivered into the hands of the Gentiles. A large force of soldiers accompanied Paul for his protection. The danger was great, hence the great precaution the chief officer, whose name is now mentioned, Claudius Lysias, had taken. Could we have read in Paul's own heart we would have seen there the peace of Christ; the words of His Lord still resounded in that faithful and devoted heart—"Be of good cheer."

The letter of Claudius Lysias to the governor Felix is interesting. It shows how Lysias claims the full credit of having rescued Paul, because he was a Roman. He declares him innocent, yet delivers him into the hands of the governor.

One would also like to know what had become of the forty conspirators. If they were true to their vow not to eat nor to drink till Paul had been killed, they must have starved to death, which, we are sure, did not happen. Caesarea is reached in safety and Paul is delivered into the hands of the governor, who promised him a hearing as soon as the accusers would arrive. Jerusalem now laid forever behind him. Rome was before him.

CHAPTER XXIV.

1. The indictment of Paul (verses 1–9).
2. The defence of the Apostle (verses 10–21).
3. How Felix disposed of the case (verses 22–23).
4. Paul addresses Felix (verses 24–27).

If the Jews, after Paul's removal from Jerusalem, had not pressed the case against him, he would have been liberated. As he had gone years ago to Damascus to persecute the Christians there, so now the Jews follow him to Cesarea to accuse him before the Roman governor. They evidently did not lose any time. Only a few days had elapsed when a strong deputation from Jerusalem appeared in Cesarea. The high priest filled with much hatred against Paul had taken it upon himself to come in person. This must have been an unusual occurrence for a person of Ananias' standing to leave Jerusalem.

They brought along a certain orator named Tertullus, who accused Paul in the presence of Felix. The words Tertullus used against the great man of God are extremely vile and manifest the hiss of the serpent. He calls him "a pestilent fellow," a person of whom society may well be rid of. The indictment contains three counts. First stands a political accusation. This, in presence of the high Roman officer, was of the greatest importance. Any conspiracy against the Roman government was a capital offence. The charge of sedition or treason was thus at once laid at the door of the Apostle. The second offence Tertullus brought against Paul was of a religious nature. As ringleader of the Nazarenes, presented by him as a sect of the Jews, he had abetted that which was against the peace of Judaism and introduced not alone a disturbing element, but had transgressed another Roman law, which forbade the introduction of an unrecognized religion. The third charge was the profanation of the temple. Paul answers the indictment in a masterly way. His address contains a denial of the first charge; a confession and admission concerning the second, and a complete vindication of the accusation of the temple profanation.

Felix knew the accusations were not true, but he refused decision. Paul should have been set at liberty. Felix defers it till Lysias the chief-captain came to Cesarea. But he never came, and Paul was kept a prisoner. Felix and his wife, Drusilla, the daughter of Herod Agrippa I, a wicked woman, heard Paul and Felix trembled. Later Felix left Paul behind a prisoner, when Porcius Festus became governor.

CHAPTER XXV.

1. Festus and the Jews. Paul appeals to Caesar (verses 1–12).
2. King Agrippa visits Festus (verses 13–22).
3. Paul brought before the King (verses 23–27).

The new governor, Festus, had arrived at Cesarea, and then went up to Jerusalem, the capital of the province. The Jews had not forgotten Paul, though they had not attempted another accusation before Felix, knowing that the case was hopeless. But they made at once an effort with the new governor. No sooner had this official made his appearance in Jerusalem, but the high priest and the chief of the Jews made a report about Paul. Most likely Festus had not even heard of Paul up to that time. What really took place in Jerusalem, Festus later relates to Agrippa. When Paul was presented to Agrippa, Festus introduced him by saying, "Ye see this man, about whom all the multitude of the Jews have dealt with me both at Jerusalem and also here, crying that he ought not to live any longer" (verse 24). A scene of tumult must have been enacted in Jerusalem when Festus showed himself. The mob clamored for the life of Paul. When they noticed the reluctance of the governor, they concocted another plan. They requested that Paul should be brought to Jerusalem. On the way there they intended to murder him.

But Festus was divinely guided in it all, and when he asked Paul if he would go to Jerusalem, Paul appealed to Caesar. This settled his journey to Rome.

King Agrippa and Bernice paid a visit to the new governor. The father of this king was known as Herod Agrippa, and died under awful circumstances (Chapter xii) in the year 44. When his father died Agrippa was in Rome. He was too young to receive the kingdom of his father Herod. Eight years later, Herod, King of Chalcis, the uncle of Agrippa, died. He had married Agrippa's sister Bernice, and Caesar gave Chalcis to Agrippa. Later Agrippa received the title as king. Agrippa I. had left three daughters besides this son—Bernice, Marianne and Drusilla, the wife of Felix. Bernice, who was the wife of her uncle, after his death joined her brother Agrippa in Rome. She married a Celician ruler, but deserted him and joined again her brother, in whose company she paid this visit to Cesarea. And Paul appeared before the King. A great audience had gathered and much pomp was displayed. Then the prisoner was brought in. What a contrast! Perhaps they looked upon him with pity as they saw the chain. But more pity must have filled the heart of the great servant of Christ as he saw the poor lost souls bedecked with the miserable tinsel of earth. Festus addressed the King and the whole company. He frankly states what troubled him and that he expects the King to furnish the material for the statements he had, as governor, to send to Rome.

CHAPTER XXVI.

1. The Address of the Apostle Paul (verses 2–23).
2. The Interruption by Festus and the Appeal to the King (verses 24–29).
3. The Verdict (verses 30–32).

The opening words of the Apostle are indeed gracious. Even as he stands in chains the great Apostle counts himself happy. His happiness consisted in the knowledge that he was now privileged to bear witness of His Lord and the Gospel committed to him before such an audience. What an opportunity it was to him, and how he rejoiced that he could speak of Him, whom he served. He also honored the King by a brief remark in which he expressed his delight in speaking before one who was so well acquainted with Jewish customs and questions. Then he restates his life as a Pharisee.

At once he touches upon the resurrection of the Lord Jesus Christ. Why should it be thought a thing incredible with you, that God should raise the dead? The whole history of Israel bears witness to the fact that God can bring life from the dead. The very origin of the nation demonstrates this, for Sarah's womb was a grave, and God brought life out of that grave. Many promises of the past vouched for God's power to raise the dead. The nation had this promise that spiritual and national death is to give way to spiritual and national life (Ezek. xxxvii:1–15; Hosea vi:1–3). The resurrection of the Lord Jesus Christ proved Him to be the Holy One and the Hope of Israel. In this sense Peter speaks of His resurrection. "Blessed be the God and Father of our Lord Jesus Christ, who according to His abundant mercy hath begotten us again to a living hope by the resurrection of Jesus Christ from the dead" (1 Pet. i:3). The grave of the Lord Jesus was for the disciples the grave of their national hope, but His resurrection from the dead the revival of that hope. Once more he also relates the sad story of how he persecuted the saints. Upon that dark background he can now flash forth again the story of his conversion.

Then the proper moment had arrived to state the Gospel message before this company. It is a terse statement of the message which the Lord had committed unto him. All the elements of the Gospel are contained in the eighteenth verse. There is first the condition of man by nature. Eyes, which are blind, in darkness, under the power of Satan. The eyes are to be opened and through the Gospel man is turned from darkness to light, from the power of Satan unto God. In Colossians i:12 the same is stated. Then the blessings of conversion. Forgiveness of sins and an inheritance. Faith is the means of all this; sanctification, that is separation, in conversion "by faith that is in me." One wonders if the Holy Spirit even then did not bless the message to some heart, and the Grace of God bestowed these blessings upon some believing sinners. It may have been so. The day will make it known.

Festus interrupted him, and when Paul addressed the King directly, he answered him by saying: "Almost persuadest thou me to become a Christian." The meaning is rather "by a little more persuasion you might make me a Christian." No doubt conviction had taken hold on him. In this half mocking way he answers the Apostle. How many after him have acted in the same way and rejected the Grace, which stood ready to save.

The verdict of a private consultation is "This Man doeth nothing worthy of death." Herod Agrippa said unto Festus "This man might have been set at liberty, if he had not appealed unto Caesar." If Paul had not made his appeal to Caesar he might have then been freed. We have seen before that his appeal to Rome was according to the will of the Lord. To Rome then he goes. All is ordered by a gracious Lord.

CHAPTER XXVII.

1. From Cesarea to Fair Havens (verses 1-8).
2. The Unheeded Warning. The Storm. Paul's Vision and Assurance of Safety (verses 9-26).
3. The Shipwreck (verses 27-44).

Much has been written on this chapter. The voyage of the Apostle Paul to Rome and the shipwreck is often explained as being typical of the stormy voyage of the professing church, her adversities and shipwreck.

However, such an application needs caution. It is easy to make fanciful and far-fetched allegorical applications.

Besides church history other lessons have been drawn from this narrative. A recent commentator claims that the key-note to the interpretation is given in verse 34 in the word *salvation*. "This and cognate words occur seven times in the chapter: *Hope to be saved; ye cannot be saved; to be completely saved.* While the contrary fate is no less richly depicted—*injury, loss, thorwing away, perish, kill* and *to be cast away.* The history, then, is a parable of the great salvation, by which man is brought through death to life." We shall not attempt to seek for an outline of church history in the events of this chapter. The central figure, the prisoner of the Lord, must occupy us more than anything else. It is said that in all the classical literature there is nothing found which gives so much information of the working of an ancient ship as this chapter does. Even the critics have acknowledged that this chapter "bears the most indisputable marks of authenticity." "Historical research and inscriptions have confirmed the facts given in this chapter, while the accuracy of Luke's nautical observations is shown by the great help he has given to our understanding of ancient seamanship. None have impunged the correctness of his phrases; on the contrary, from his description contained in a few sentences, the scene of the wreck has been identified."

The Apostle is courteously treated by the Centurian Julius. Paul may have been in a physically weakened condition. The Lord's gracious and loving care for His faithful servant shines out in this. How clearly the whole narrative shows that all is in His hands: Officers, winds and waves, all circumstances, are under His control. So far all seemed to go well; but contrary winds now trouble the voyagers. The ship is tossed to and fro. If we look upon the ship as a type of the professing church and the little company, headed by Paul, as the true church, then there is no difficulty in seeing the issue. Winds which drive hither and thither trouble those who hold the truth and live in fellowship with the Lord, while the professing church is cast about. Then Myra was reached. Here they took a ship of Alexandria. Danger then threatened.

Most likely a consultation of the commander of the ship and the owner, who was on board, and the centurion, was held, and Paul was present. He gives them a solemn warning and cautions them to beware. This shows his close fellowship with the Lord. In prayer, no doubt, he had laid the whole matter before the Lord and received the answer, which he communicates to the persons in authority. They looked upon it as a mere guess, and the centurion rather trusted in the judgment of the captain and the owner.

And here we can think of other warnings given through the great Apostle. Warnings concerning the spiritual dangers, the apostasy of the last days, the perilous times, warnings against the seducing spirits and doctrines of demons. The professing church has forgotten these divinely-given predictions. The world does not heed them. Like these mariners, who believed in their own wisdom and disregarded the warning given, Christendom has paid no attention to these warnings. For this reason the ship is drifting, cast about by every wind of doctrine and rapidly nearing the long predicted shipwreck. Then there came the terrific tempest. Sun and stars were hidden for many days.

When despair had reached its heights, Paul appears once more upon the scene. When all was hopeless the prisoner of the Lord spoke the words of hope and cheer. He reminds them first of their refusal and disobedience. What had came upon them was the result of having not heeded the warning. He then assures them that an angel of God had assured him once more that he would have to stand before Caesar; but God had given to him all that sail with him. Only the ship is to go down, the lives of all who sail with him will be preserved. "Wherefore, sirs, be of good cheer; for I believe God, that it shall be even so as it hath been spoken unto me." And now they were willing to listen to him. They had to acknowledge their disobedience and believe the message of cheer as it came from the divinely instructed messenger, assuring them of their ultimate salvation.

And so, at least, in part, drifting Christendom can listen to the Apostle Paul, and if the mistake, the wrong course, is acknowledged, the heavenly-sent message is accepted, salvation is assured.

How calm the Apostle and his companions must have been after this assurance of their safety. The dreadful winds might continue and the ship drift still further. They knew they were safe, for God had spoken. Different it was with the crew of the ship. In great distress they feared the coming disaster and cast out four anchors. The shipmen attempted flight by a clever scheme. Paul discovered their plan and said to the Centurion and soldiers, "Except these abide in the ship, ye (not *we*) cannot be saved." God had given him all who were in the ship. The work of the sailors was needed when the daybreak came. And the soldiers believed the word of Paul, for they cut the ropes, which set the boat adrift the sailors tried to use. Then Paul exhorted them to eat. Once more he assured them that not a hair should fall from the head of any one. Before the whole company, two hundred and seventy-six persons, Paul took bread and gave thanks to God. The Lord had exalted the prisoner, and he really stands out as the leader of the distressed company. They all became encouraged by the words and action. All has its lessons. However the meal has nothing to do with the Lord's Supper. It tells us typically how necessary it is that we must feed on the bread of life in the days of danger, the times when everything breaks up. "And so it came to pass, that they escaped all safe to land."

CHAPTER XXVIII.

1. In the Island of Melita (verses 1-10).
2. The arrival in Rome (verses 11–16).
3. Paul calling the chief of the Jews and his message (verses 17–29).

Melita, which means "honey," is the island of Malta. It was even then a prominent place for navigation where many vessels wintered. Luke calls the inhabitants Barbarians, a term used by the Greeks for all peoples who did not speak their language. The wrecked company was not plundered by the people of the island, but instead received much kindness and were made comfortable in the cold rain which fell.

It was God who moved the hearts of these islanders to show such hospitality to the shipwrecked company for the sake of His servants. Paul is active even then. The shipwreck and privations must have told on the great man of God physically, yet we see him going about gathering a bundle of sticks for the fire. This labor must have been difficult, since as a prisoner he wore a chain on his hands. A viper, which had been benumbed by the cold and revived by the heat of the fire, fastened on his hand. We doubt not it was a poisonous viper. This is denied by some critics on the plea that poisonous snakes are not found in the island of Malta. However, that is no proof that such did not exist at that time. The inhabitants of the island expected Paul to fall dead. If it had been a harmless snake, why such an expectation? God's power was manifested in his behalf. It was a fulfillment of the promise in Mark xvi:18 "they shall take up serpents and it shall not hurt them." The viper also reminds us of Satan and his fate. As Paul cast the viper into the fire, so Satan will be cast into the lake of fire. Then there was a manifestation of the gracious power of the Lord towards the inhabitants of the island.

And then they reached Rome at last. What joy must have filled his heart and the hearts of the believers in Rome! How often they must have read his words, in the beginning of his letter: "I long to see you, that I may impart unto you some spiritual gift, to the end ye may be established; that is, that I may be comforted together with you by the mutual faith both of you and me. Now, I would not have you ignorant, brethren, that ofttimes I proposed to come unto you (but was hindered hitherto), that I might have some fruit among you also, even as the rest of the Gentiles" (Rom. i:11–13). He had never been in Rome. The Roman assembly was not founded by Paul and certainly not by Peter. The origin of that church is obscure, and the Holy Spirit has not given us a history of the beginning of the church of Rome. And now he whom they all loved, whose face they longed to see, was actually on the way to visit Rome. But in a far different way did he come than he expected when he wrote his Epistle. He came as the prisoner of the Lord. What a meeting it must have been!

And now it is for the very last time in this book, "to the Jew first." The first service the great Apostle rendered in Rome was not in the assembly, but he called the chief of the Jews together. He knew no bitterness in his heart against the Jews. In writing the letter to the Romans he had written, "I say the truth in Christ, I lie not, my conscience also testifying with me in the Holy Spirit, that I have great heaviness and continual sorrow in my heart. For I could wish that myself were accursed from Christ for my brethren, my kinsmen according to the flesh" (Rom. ix:1–2). "Brethren, my heart's desire and prayer to God for them is, that they might be saved" (x:1). And now, after all the sad experience he had made, the treatment he had received from his kinsmen, after he had found out their malice and deep hatred, the same love burns in his heart and the same yearning for their salvation possesses him. In Rome he manifests first of all his loving interest in his Jewish brethren. To these leading Jews he testified once more that he was innocent of any wrong doing. Briefly, he rehearsed his whole case and why he had been compelled to appeal to Caesar. For this purpose—to talk to them about this matter—he had called them. Then most likely he must have lifted his hands, from which the prisoner's chain dangled, and said, "because for the hope of Israel I am bound with this chain." The Jews, however, wanted to hear more from his lips of—"what thou thinkest; for as concerning this sect, we know that everywhere it is spoken against." They knew he believed in Christ.

A great meeting took place a short time later. Many Jews assembled in Paul's lodging. The meeting lasted from morning till evening. Once more he testified the Kingdom of God to a large company of Jews. He also persuaded them concerning Jesus both out of the laws of Moses and out of the Prophets. What a wonderful message must have came from his lips as he unfolded the prophetic testimony concerning the Messiah in the power of the Spirit of God! But what was the result? Some believed and some believed not. They did not agree amongst themselves. The end of God's gracious way with the Jews is reached. We repeat, for the last time, it was to the Jew first. The final crisis is reached. Judgment must now be executed upon the nation and the blindness is now to come, which has lasted so long and will continue till the fullness of the Gentiles is come in (Rom. xi:26). Stephen, whose death young Saul had witnessed and approved (viii:1), had pronounced judgment upon the nation, in Jerusalem. God's mercy had still waited. Marvelous Grace, which took up the young Pharisee, Saul, and made him the Apostle to the Gentiles! Through him, the chosen instrument, the Lord still sought his beloved Israel, even after Jerusalem had so completely rejected the offered mercy. We have seen how the Apostle's intense love for his brethren had led him back to Jerusalem, though warned repeatedly by the Holy Spirit. And now he is used to give the very last message to the Jews and speak the final word of condemnation.

The salvation of God is now to go far hence to the Gentiles.

A prisoner in Rome and yet active. He preached the Kingdom of God (not of heaven, the Jewish, earthly aspect of it), and ever speaking of that worthy name, that blessed and adorable Person, the Lord Jesus Christ. The ending of the book is sad and it is joyous. Sad to see the great Apostle a prisoner, shut up in Rome with his God-given Gospel. Joyous because the last verse mentions the Lord Jesus Christ and an unhindered ministry of the Gospel. The Book begins with Jerusalem and ends with Rome. It is a prophecy of the course of the professing church. The book closes in an unfinished way, because the acts of

Christ, the Spirit of God, and Satan, recorded in this book, are not finished. We hear nothing more of Paul, though we know that from the prison the Holy Spirit of God sent forth through him the blessed Epistles, in which He has been pleased to give us the highest revelation. And how much more might be written on all this!